Also by Theodore Roszak

Theodore Roszak

America the Wise

The Longevity Revolution
and the True Wealth
of Nations

HOUGHTON MIFFLIN COMPANY

BOSTON · NEW YORK

1998

I am indebted to many people for the interviews and consultations that wrapped some flesh around the demographic bones of this study. They include Martin Schiffenbauer, Robert Schutz, Roxanne Lanier, Harold Gilliam, Tyrone Cashman, Sally Bingham, Rachel Remen, Connie Lynch, Lucy Scott, Sue Brand, Barbara Weiss, Irving Kermish, Betty Soldz, Kerstin Joslyn Schremp, and Robert Giusti. Judy Clarence's research help was especially appreciated. Above all, I must thank my wife, who came through her rite of passage with the courage and high spirits that touched these pages with conviction.

For information about permission to reproduce selections from this book, write to Permissions, Houghton Mifflin Company, 215 Park Avenue South, New York, New York 10003.

Libr ar yof Cong r essCat aloging-in-P ub lic ationDat a
Roszak, Theodore, date.
America the wise : the longevity revolution and the true wealth of nations.
p.   cm.
Includes bibliographical references and index.
ISBN 0-395-85699-X
1. Aging — Social aspects — United States. 2. Longevity — Social aspects— United States. 3. Baby boom generation — United States. 4. Old ages assistance — United States. 5. Social change — United States. 6. Caring.   I. Title.
HQ1064.U5R666   1998
305.26'0973 — dc21   98-21645 CIP

Printed in the United States of America

Book design by Robert Overholtzer

QUM 10 9 8 7 6 5 4 3 2 1

There is no wealth but life. Life, including all its powers of love, of joy, and of admiration. That country is richest which nourishes the greatest number of noble and happy human beings.

— JOHN RUSKIN

Contents

America the Wise

Introduction

The Longevity Revolution

THIS BOOK has been guided from the outset by a single image. Discovery. Again and again I have found myself dealing with the people I write about as if they were the inhabitants of an unexplored land whose manners, morals, and customs have yet to be recorded. And yet, far from being some exotic breed, the people who fill these pages are as near at hand as my closest friends, my neighbors, my colleagues. They are simply those who have traveled the late twentieth century with me. It is no surprise that we have grown older along the way, less still that age has changed us in many ways we must have expected. But there is something few of us anticipated as we were being swept along in the whirl of great events and personal concerns, a fact that makes our place in history unique.

We are the first generation of the senior dominance. The beneficiaries of a revolution in life-extending medicine and public health, we enter the second half of our lives possessed of more political influence, greater wealth, and more vitality than any older generation before us. The values we choose to live by cannot help but be a commanding influence in shaping the century to come.

Age so empowered is a new historical phase. To that degree, those of us whose role it is to define the cultural themes of that phase are a New People. The responsibility and the adventure of that role are only beginning to dawn upon us as we pause to take stock of ourselves now that parenting and career-building fade into the past. We know that we will survive longer than any older generation before us. More than merely surviving, we will find ourselves gifted with the wits, the political savvy, and the sheer weight of numbers to become a major force for change.

With us, history shifts its rhythm. It draws back from the frenzied pursuit of marketing novelties and technological turnover and assumes the measured pace of humane and sustainable values. We may live to see wisdom become a distinct political possibility, and compassion the reigning social ethic. Great changes, and yet they stem from nothing more remarkable than life running its full course, as it now can for so many millions more. Longevity, when it embraces so many, cannot help but be a great maker of history.

Some revolutions are fought in the streets with banners and manifestos. These may be short-lived and rarely work out as planned. Other revolutions, like the industrial revolution, which is still unfolding through its high-tech and genetic engineering phases, are protracted social transformations that spread out over decades. We may gain some sense of their true dimensions only with the benefit of hindsight. Longevity comes to us as still another kind of revolution. As far-reaching as industrialism, it has made its way forward more subtly over the past two centuries, rising out of scattered reforms in public health and steady progress in medical research. Though it is a gentle revolution, I believe it draws upon forces far greater than those that have driven any political or social movement of our time. Its power wells up from the basic needs of the planet, within which we are (though we tend to forget it) one species among many. If that is so, then the longevity revolution, as we will explore it in these pages, may one day be seen as an environmentally imperative stage in the history of our society.

Longevity held no interest for me until I realized I had a reasonably good chance at making it to old age. Like many others of my generation, having lived through an era dominated by an ebullient youth culture, I was inclined to wait as long as possible before I turned to the chapters on age that wait at the end of life. I had no reason to believe I would find much of interest there. Dogged for many years by serious illness, I was not even sure I would live long enough to reach that part of the story. Then, in the late 1980s, I underwent a grueling medical crisis that nearly cost me my life. When the ordeal was over, I discovered I was in better health than I had known in thirty years. Even more remarkable, something was missing that had been haunting me for decades: the grim certainty that I would die young. That had departed with the disease. One morning, much to my amazement, I awoke realizing that I might very well reach the age of sixty.

In the crisis I experienced, I was lucky enough to find my way to a medical counselor whose practice had broadened to include all those aspects of disease and surgical trauma that are left unattended by conventional medicine — the fear, the existential trembling, the blank despair. I recall being told, "People like you" — ambitious, competitive professional types — "don't stop until you get hit right between the eyes. That's what has happened. You've been hit in a way you can't ignore. Nothing else would do it. Now you know. You are very, very sick. You might die. So . . . what are you going to make of that?"

If the disease itself had not brought my life to an abrupt halt, those words would have done the job. I suddenly realized that this was another way to understand my situation. Instead of fleeing from it, which was useless, I might try taking hold of it and staring it in the face.

You might die. What are you going to make of that?

Poorly prepared as I was, I decided to make all I could of it. I laid aside my work, took a leave of absence from my job, emptied my schedule, learned a few basic meditation techniques, and began to attend to a great deal of unfinished business. I was astonished to discover that every aspect of my life changed in magnitude and urgency. Some insights were small, but important. I recalled a remark I had read: "Nobody on his death bed ever regretted that he had not spent more time at the office." How true, how *obviously* true. Why had I never realized that before?

I came to see that there was actually very little that I *had* to do, very little in all the world that depended on me and me alone. I could not think of anything on my usually busy agenda that could not be left to somebody else to do. I stopped playing the decision-maker who had to make everything work, stood back, and gazed at my life with as much objectivity — and mercy — as I could. It was a memorable episode.

I soon realized that I was passing through a sort of forced early retirement. I had heard that many people have no idea what to do with their retirement. I decided to use mine to get serious about life. Had I not been serious before this, during my first fifty years? No, I had simply been *busy*. I had been overscheduled, anxious, job-career-and-money worried. I had been attending conferences, giving lectures, writing articles, penciling in appointments, as if all these things mattered. In brief, I had been a passably normal adult . . . meaning I had been a troubled soul. If some of what I had spent my time doing was of value, I had nevertheless been doing much of it in the wrong spirit and so had diminished its significance. I had spent fifty years getting older, but not much wiser.

Eventually, the crisis passed, thanks to state-of-the-art surgery. That was another revelation. For the first time in my life, I found myself taking medicine seriously, as a matter of life and death. *My* life, *my* death. Surgeons and nurses had done what no priest or therapist had ever succeeded in doing. They had, without realizing it, forced me to find the meaning of my life.

The years rolled forward. I was a survivor. I would grow old. At this point, I cannot honestly say I am still vitally in touch with the crisis that brought me such penetrating insights. The fact that I had a job to go back to and a pending literary contract made it difficult to hold on to the moment of truth. That was also something I learned: if we look aside for a moment, the distractions of daily life close in upon us like the persistent growth of weeds in a garden. Vanity has its strategies. In the Middle Ages, teachers of the *ars moriendi* — the art of dying — would have called these the temptations of the world, the flesh, and the devil. I would not phrase it quite like that, but temptations they were nonetheless.

Then just a few years ago my wife went through an even riskier medical crisis that would surely have taken her life twenty years before. Thanks to another surgical miracle, she survived. In both our cases, I was struck not only by the daring and skill that had come to our rescue, but by how utterly casual the doctors were about these ingenious procedures. This was simply what they did all day every day for scores of patients. "Have you performed many of these surgeries?" I asked the surgeon. "Hundreds," he replied with a smile and a shrug. Yet these doctors were saving lives — my life and my wife's — that would have been lost not so long ago.

After my wife's operation, she and I joined a cardiac rehabilitation program in which, though now in our early sixties, we were among the youngest members. All around us were companions in their seventies and eighties who were actually *improving* their health. Some were in better shape than we were. As a group, we came from many backgrounds, but all of us were united by the same good feeling: being there, simply *being there* to enjoy one another's company. We sang "Happy Birthday" whenever anybody in the class grew a year older. We knew how much that meant. One more year that might not have happened.

This mixture of risk, awe, and gratitude started me thinking about the dramatic changes in life expectancy that have occurred in my time. Those thoughts grew more searching when, as of the mid-1990s, the media began issuing warnings about the disasters that longevity was threatening to visit upon our society in the years ahead. Social Security ... Medicare ... how could we possibly afford these fiscal horrors? The "horrors" that pundits seemed to have in view included my survival and my wife's. I winced to hear so many people, many of whom I knew to be smart and well-read, repeating the same words of doom. Up ahead in the twenty-first century, they saw all these *old people* devouring our national wealth — old people who, apparently, would never include *them*. I came upon newspaper editorials blaming our cowardly leaders for not *doing something* about this impending crisis. Next to the editorials there might be cartoons that showed a crocodile labeled "Entitlements" swallowing a poor little bird labeled "Balanced Budget." Balanced Budget was the victim. Entitlements was the villain.

The dissonance between these two things — long life and fiscal fear — was enormous. It stretched my mind to the point of pain. The conventional wisdom of the day seemed to be at war with life itself as it might now be enjoyed by millions.

Clearly, there was something wrong with seeing things that way — as if money mattered more than life. How had we become so confused about the most fundamental values? And how might we see the matter with greater clarity and humanity? Quite naturally, I viewed these questions with a historian's eye — and discovered I had a few insights to offer. After all, the people who were supposedly darkening the future were the same people I had once written about in their youth. I had called them then a "counter culture," young people who, in surprising numbers, had bravely questioned the authority of all received ideas. They had not vanished in a puff of smoke in 1975 — though there were certainly those on the political scene who had been pretending they had. But here they were, two or three decades further along, causing a different kind of cultural trouble by the very act of staying alive a good long time.

People who are surviving into what they now know will be a long old age have begun to come to grips with longevity as a personal challenge. They are seeking ways to make creative use of their time, to keep their minds sharp and well-informed, and, not least of all, to face the advance of death with courage. But as a society, we have not yet begun to grasp the implications of mass longevity. In the pages that follow, we will explore the many contours of this demographic frontier. Most significantly, we will trace the steady shift in our social values, so long dominated by the dynamism of the young and middle-aged, toward the needs of an older society.

The aging of the American public is not some stroke of unaccountable bad luck. Although nobody seemed to notice it until the day before yesterday, *all* industrial societies are aging with the momentum of a biological necessity. They *have* to age. That is the logic of progress. And that is the main thing we must understand about longevity. It is *inevitable and good.*

Both words are important. "Inevitable" is what you cannot sensibly fight *against.* "Good" is what you fight *for* in life. Put "inevitable" and "good" together, and you have a historical movement.

In the modern world, nothing inspires people to greater deeds than belonging to a movement, especially if they believe they are riding the wave of the future. For the past two centuries, revolutionary spirits have asserted their claim to the future loudly and violently, as if they were not all that certain about their destined success. In the twentieth century, we have seen some very ugly politics grow out of movements that insisted *their* nation, *their* race, *their* class, *their* economic system, owned the future. The movements have come . . . and gone, marching away into the past, often leaving a bloody trail behind them. We have learned to treat movements with skeptical caution.

But there is one movement that has owned the future all along. A quiet, gentle, life-enhancing movement called longevity. Few have recognized its cultural importance because its power springs from the simplest of the heart's desires, a prayer to which all but the most despairing have given voice.

Let me live another day.

That was the movement I joined on the day I escaped the disease that might have killed me at age thirty, or forty, or fifty. With millions of others, I find myself animated by this stubborn, insistent impulse that meets the doctor's skill with affirmation, guides medical science to its goal, and gives healing a meaning larger than survival.

As a historian, I tend to see human affairs as stories spread out across time, tales that take twists and turns, offer us heroes and villains, and include narrow escapes, heartbreaking losses, moments of triumph. All this is true of the longevity revolution. In my special field of industrial history, that revolution has been fighting its way forward against enormous odds for two centuries. Though the media may only recently have discovered it, longevity has long roots. They reach back to that early industrial world of "dark Satanic mills" where life was brutish and short and living one more day was more than many people dared to hope for. In a very real sense, we can only now read the *real* history of the industrial period, its essential but long-hidden direction.

The past two centuries have been a troubled era. No period in history has been more tormented than ours has been by the trials of modernization. We have looked evil in the face. Behind us lie the horrors of world war, racial strife, industrial upheaval, revolutionary violence, imperialist competition, and class warfare. We have lived through a time that added the terms "genocide," "balance of terror," "wage slavery," "death camps," "final solution," "ethnic cleansing," and "ecospasm" to our political vocabulary. And yet . . . more people are living longer. Who would have expected so bright a prospect to emerge from so dark a period? I cannot help but believe that those whose lives were cut cruelly short by war or persecution would expect us to make the most of this great victory over despair.

My viewpoint on the aging of industrial society, then, is simple but radical in its implications. Longevity is here, it is inevitable, it is good. Our task is to stop resisting the inevitable and to embrace the good.

The generation under discussion in these pages — the New People, as I call them — has known more than its share of controversy. Castigated in their youth as spoiled brats and rebels without a cause, they have grown up to be called other unflattering names: "grabby boomers," "state-of-the-art hypocrites," "the most selfish and irresponsible generation this country has ever produced." Perhaps those who make the accusations have some valid case in point. When we set out to judge something as large and amorphous as a generation, we are rather like the blind men who tried to describe an elephant. Each had a piece of the truth, but only a piece. They were each a little right and a lot wrong.

Like most historians, I assume that every generation is a mixed bag made up of people who are bravely improvising their lives by the passing hour, hoping to get as much of it as right as they can, often falling short of their own highest expectations. Upon closer scrutiny, every generation reveals vices among its virtues, virtues among its vices. If I did not think there was a wealth of idealism and a willing spirit in the people I write for and about, I would not have started this book in the first place. Rather than laying still another judgment upon them, I offer an appeal.

In the years ahead, an increasing number of us will be living decades longer than our parents or grandparents. Imagine, then, adding together all those *extra* years of life. Think of those years as a *resource* — a cultural and spiritual resource reclaimed from death in the same way the Dutch reclaim fertile land from the waste of the sea. During any one of those years, somebody who no longer has to worry about raising a family, pleasing a boss, or earning more money will have the chance to join with others in building a compassionate society where people can think deep thoughts, create beauty, study nature, teach the young, worship what they hold sacred, and care for one another. Once we realize that, we should have no difficulty understanding the most important fact about the longevity revolution. It has given this remarkable generation the chance to do great good against great odds.

1

Discovering a New People

I publish and set forth these conjectures of mine, which make hope in this matter reasonable, just as Columbus did before that wonderful voyage of his across the Atlantic, when he gave the reasons for his conviction that new lands and continents might be discovered, which reasons, though rejected at first, were afterwards made good by experience, and were the causes and beginnings of great events.

— FRANCIS BACON, *The New Organon*, 1620

A SINGLE FACT overshadows our entrance into the twenty-first century, a demographic statistic that is simply stated and undisputed. *More people are living longer.* Never before has so large a part of the population been older than sixty as we find today in the industrial societies. Never before has the ratio of age to youth been so high.

As modest as these observations may seem, they carry formidable cultural implications — and not only for those who are moving into their senior years. Like all major demographic changes, whether plagues or famines, baby booms or great migrations, longevity will shape the course of history for generations to come. Even now, it is radically altering political power and social relations.

We are becoming accustomed to seeing cheery or worrisome facets of our changing demographics featured in the news of the day, in reports on the health or the wealth, the foibles and fashions of the senior generation. Some are heartening, even amusing — like the grandmothers' basketball league in southern California whose members, all over seventy and many with hip replacements, remain spirited competitors. Others are filled with an ominous pathos — like the wistful effort by a Denver health center to deal with a disease of the elderly that may run up a bill for $1 trillion by the middle of the twenty-first century. There the staff has rigged up a mock Norman Rockwell Main Street where Alzheimer's patients, their minds already adrift in time, may roam freely among the familiar sights and sounds of their still-remembered youth: soda fountains, a Bijou movie house, Glenn Miller favorites on the jukebox.

But longevity is far more than a human interest item; it marks not only a massive change but a permanent one. The aging of industrial society is irreversible: now that this demographic current has started, the only direction in which it can run is toward greater senior numbers. Even if there should be other smaller baby booms or "echoes" along the way, the certain destiny of every future generation is to grow older than the one before until the old outnumber an ever diminishing younger population. The largest-growing sector of our population as of the early twenty-first century comprises those over eighty-five. By the middle of the twenty-first century, those who fail to reach that age, except by reason of accident, will fall into a new medical category: premature death.

This is how longevity appears stated as a bald census statistic. But now add some cultural contours to our new demographic landscape, and the century ahead takes on intriguing possibilities.

Never before have people over the age of sixty controlled so much wealth or exerted so much political influence. In contrast to times past, when the elderly were marginal and powerless, seniors have become a coveted voting bloc and a potentially lucrative market.

Never before have people approaching their senior years enjoyed the advantage of so much education and travel. Nor have they ever bulked so large in the popular culture of the nation. They are avidly pursued for university coursework and museum shows, they are the most reliable season-ticket audience for the opera and symphony, they are a highly prized market for book clubs and the lecture circuit. For the first time in modern history, the senior population is beginning to be treated as if its tastes and interests matter.

Never before has the population aged seventy, eighty, and even ninety included so many physically and mentally active people. Most obviously, this is because no older generation has ever had so much access to health care. But there is also the fact that no previous generation has been so health- and fitness-conscious; today's seniors are eager to participate in caring for their own health by exploring alternative medicines and making radical changes in their habits of living.

Never before has a senior generation possessed enough technical skill, professional training, and intellectual astuteness to consider staying on the job well beyond the legal retirement age. Nor have people over the age of sixty-five ever looked so much like a viable and sizable workforce, a workforce that may be better equipped to compete for jobs than the younger generation.

Never before have so many people entered their senior years by way of a medical crisis, a contemporary rite of passage that brings them face to face with their own mortality. The cultural and political importance of that increasingly commonplace experience should not be overlooked. Death, if one survives its first call, is a great awakener of conscience and a call to serious reflection. The folk wisdom of World War II had it that there were no atheists in foxholes. Similarly, few people come out of intensive care wards less philosophically inclined than before they went in. I have found in talking to people who have had such a brush with death what is clearly a sense of gratitude, as if the experience, terrifying as it was, had suddenly deepened their lives and given them a welcome occasion for radical reappraisal.

Finally, add one more factor to this generational profile, a defining feature of the eighty million Americans entering their senior years as a new century begins. Never before has an older generation been conversant with so many divergent ideas and dissenting values. These are, after all, the people who, in their teens and twenties, lived through a time of principled protest that seemed determined to subject every orthodoxy, every institution, every received idea in our society to critical inquiry. I have sometimes suspected that the effort by many pundits to rewrite or repress the history of that period stems from their fear that, in age as in youth, the baby boomers represent an unpredictable force for change.

Then as now, those of a more conservative temperament were understandably concerned that so irreverent an attack upon authority could erode civility and weaken conformity. They were at least half right. Youthful dissent often produces upheaval and disrespect. But the right wing of American politics may have worse to worry about in the years ahead. Insurgency among elders may prove to be far more unsettling than rebellion among the young. In a society where numbers and power are destined to gravitate steadily in the direction of age, one cannot write off the views and values of the senior generation as mere youthful effervescence; nor can one simply wait for the insurgents to grow up and move along in life. The future belongs to maturity.

Then and Now

This last point is especially important for me. When I wrote *The Making of a Counter Culture* in 1969 (the subtitle was *Reflections on the Technocratic Society and Its Youthful Opposition*), I included this observation: "The ethos of disaffiliation is still in the process of broadening down through the adolescent years, picking up numbers as time goes on. . . . Generational conflict will not vanish when those who are now 20 reach 30, it may only reach its peak when those who are now 11 and 12 reach their late 20s."[1]

Given my age when I wrote the book, and given my place on the university campus, I could not imagine anybody radically changing the course of history except the young — unless it was the younger still. By "generational conflict" I meant the struggle of the then-young against the then-old in behalf of a more humane, more tolerant, more intellectually adventurous society. But in the years since then, I have come to see that the very notion of change permeating that study was a young man's way of seeing life. To believe that change comes from ideological fervor, that history is made by imposing bright, untested ideas on life, is a sad, though all too common, misunderstanding — whether the ideas are liberal, radical, or conservative. It takes some growing up and some growing old to learn that life-affirming and enduring change comes not from theories or principles ("headtripping," as we once called it) but from a wisdom of the heart — by which I mean truths people learn from a full and well-examined life.

So my prediction was wide of the mark, if for no other reason than that it paid too little attention to living history. Like many another social critic, I failed to see the obvious. Those who were in their teens and twenties in the 1960s were not destined to disappear when they ceased to be a "youthful opposition." If at some point they passed through a "big chill," there would be plenty of time for the chill to thaw. They would live on to become fifty and sixty and seventy, still there on the stage of history, battered perhaps by the years but better prepared to change the world than they were in their high school and college years. And given their need to defend and expand the nation's entitlements programs, they might feel an even more urgent need to transform their society than they had in their youth.

Meanwhile — and how ironically — the twelve-year-olds I had in mind when I wrote that passage were destined to have a very different course of life than I foresaw, one that made them more timid, more bewildered, more stymied, than I would have thought possible. The children of the baby boom generation reached their teens and twenties at the height of the Reagan presidency, during a conservative backlash of historic proportions. They came of age during a militant campaign to denigrate everything the protest movement of the 1960s and 1970s had championed. Throughout the 1980s, conservative think tanks vilified the counter culture of that day for challenging parental authority and, presumably, for all that followed from that challenge: movements for racial equality and social justice, women's and gay liberation, the ideal of participative democracy, a heightened environmental consciousness. Almost as if the social upheaval of the 1960s had fatigued America to the bone, protest went into hibernation to be replaced by what one historian has called a "daydream decade, when wish fulfillment became national policy."[2]

I now believe that a far more promising future — at least from my dissenting viewpoint on urban industrial society — depends not upon the youth of the nation but upon the initiative of those who are reaching their fifties and sixties as of the beginning of the twenty-first century. Not only is the older population of our day larger in numbers, but it constitutes *a different kind* of older population. Nothing we assumed about age in the past will fit these people. That is why we seem to be having some difficulty finding an appropriate name for them. Those who take up the subject of the baby boomers (or even of seniors already retired as of the 1990s) seem reluctant to call them "old," much less "elderly." As for the cute "gold," "gray," and "silver" euphemisms that were coined for our grandparents, all these have become cloying enough to set one's teeth on edge. Labels like these, freighted with an outmoded sense of fatigue and dependency, are terms we once used for a population that clung to the shadowed margins of life, *there* but not importantly there.

One need only make a firsthand survey of the over-fifty population we find around us — including yourself if you are in that category — to see the striking difference between past-old and future-old. How many are stereotypic cranks and codgers whom life has passed by? What one more and more commonly finds are hungry minds, physical vitality, keen perception, lively tastes, political know-how, even ambition: people who fully expect to get a lot older before they admit to being *old*, people not to be dismissed or treated with condescension.

These are the New People, a population different enough from any previous generation of seniors to deserve the name. And yet, as the name implies, they are a people in search of an identity.

Of course, they are not superhuman; time still inevitably takes its toll on mind and body, but at an increasingly later age. Though some among them may be delivered by their genes into the cruel ravages of dementia, not many will become doddering, senile incompetents. Like so many other social roles — male, female, black, Hispanic, Native American, gay — "old" is being radically redefined in our time by people themselves. Age is becoming varied to the point of unpredictability, and so it is becoming interesting to study. And even more interesting to experience.

The Senior Spectrum: From Fifty to One Hundred

As longevity assumes the dimensions of a second lifetime, we must be precise about the demographic definition of the New People. The terms "seniors," "elders," "retired" — all of which I use in these pages as the context dictates — run the risk of blurring more than they clarify. Just as we have learned, in dealing with youth, to distinguish childhood from adolescence, and adolescence from young adulthood, so we must begin making more refined distinctions about the senior years, distinctions that have less to do with calendar age and physical condition and more to do with sociology or culture. The greatest mistake one can make about age is to see it as a fixed social identity rather than as a spectrum encompassing a wide range of diversity and creative improvisation.

In the years ahead, as longevity embraces a larger and larger population, we will need a *cultural demographics* that draws upon aspects of mind and value even more than on physical condition. Age needs to be surrounded by history. We will want to know what people have lived through and what vision of life they carry with them into an ever extending seniority. For example, the entire population we will be studying here might, by way of a rough historical classification, be thought of as World War I seniors, World War II seniors, and Vietnam War seniors. In each case, the upheaval of war was the defining moment of their generation. But the wars were very different wars, and the experience they provided dictated very different values.

Within this historical-biographical continuum, the New People are one of three senior "cohorts" — as demographers call them — that differ significantly yet share a common fiscal interest and potentially a common electoral force. At times I will distinguish them as the *senior old*, the *middle old*, and the *New People*. Each of these groups is a cross-section of the society at large; nothing I say here about age is meant to discount the role that class, race, ethnicity, and religion play in defining and dividing people. But age is an increasingly important social identity, one that may become a stronger bond between people in the years ahead as they have more time to be old together.

THE SENIOR OLD

Now in their eighties, nineties, and over one hundred, the senior old are also known as the "oldest old," the term coined by the American Association for the Advancement of Science in 1984. The distinction had an admitted political purpose. It was meant to call attention to the fact that gerontologists regarded this generation as a special demographic category with needs and problems all its own that were not to be confused physiologically or sociologically with those of the younger old, especially where questions of intergenerational equity were concerned.[3] These people, whose lives have spanned much of the century, arrived at old age before any of the social-psychological changes we review in this book took place. Their childhood was lived in the aftermath of the first war to be called a "world war." They remember the great boom of the 1920s and the crash that followed. They were young adults when the phrase "Age of Anxiety" was coined; they became parents in time to send their children into another and bloodier world war. The oldest among them can remember when Social Security was created as a favor to the elderly; they may not be entirely certain that they are really "entitled" to such entitlements. Many among the senior old accepted the status of "old" in the 1960s and 1970s, when the elderly were expected to retire from life in every sense of the word. When Robert Butler made his classic study of them in 1975, he began by calling "old age," as they knew it, a "tragedy." He titled his book *Why Survive?* and did not come up with an encouraging answer.

Brave survivors though they are, many of the senior old have spent their final years haunted by the stereotype of senility. Often lacking the benefits of adequate health care, they may be finishing out their lives as the most restricted of our nursing home population. In that respect, they have been used ideologically to raise the daunting prospect that our society will be overwhelmed by a growing population of chronically ill, hopelessly demented basket cases. As Robert Binstock observes, the oldest old could become a means of scapegoating the entire aging generation for the rising cost of health care. "It is more than possible that the subgroup of persons aged 85 and over will become subject to stereotyping on the basis of multiple old-age categories. 'The oldest old,' in contrast with 'the aging,' could well become a common label for extreme conditions of frailty, disease, disability, and social dependency among the elderly."[4] It will be a major point of this book that the medical history and comparative political timidity of the senior old belong to the past. The senior old are "old" in a sense that is vanishing from society. Their place is already being taken by a different breed.

Decades separate centenarians from baby boomers, yet there is a curious bond across those years. People half the age of centenarians have begun to see their future in these aging faces. As we seek to unlock the secrets of longevity, the 100-plus population is receiving more professional attention than ever before, as if they have important secrets to teach us. Far from being the social curiosities they once were, the very old are, in effect, modeling an old age the rest of us can more and more realistically expect to reach. We take courage from all we learn about their often remarkable capacities, but we also have more to fear in what we see of their inevitable decline. Scholars and medical researchers around the world now study the oldest old to find out how they got to be 100, how they see the world, what their powers and limits may be. All this has become a matter of great fascination to a public reading paperbacks with titles like *DARE to Be 100, Stop Aging Now!, You're Not Old Until You're 90, How to Live to 100.*[5] One hundred is coming to be seen as a feasible life expectancy — but (so we hope) with a far higher standard of vitality and self-respect.

THE MIDDLE OLD

The middle old are well along in the project of changing the body and the soul of aging. Not only do they have more years ahead of them than any previous generation, but they *know* they have those years and are out to make the most of them. At senior centers where I lecture, in my history courses at the university, I continue to be impressed by the number of retirees I meet who display none of the mental or emotional hallmarks of age until they are well into their eighties. Thanks to the organizational and lobbying efforts of groups like the National Council of Senior Citizens, the Gray Panthers, and the American Association of

Retired Persons (AARP), and to the publications and programs that have grown up around those groups, the middle old, now in their sixties and seventies, realize vividly that they are part of a significant demographic transition.

The middle old include among their number the better-off, more active retirees of the post–World War II boom who have become a substantial market for upscale vacations, spas, aerobics classes, university extension courses, investment seminars, growth center programs, and retirement communities. Inevitably, the wealth controlled by the middle old, whether in the form of personal savings or their claim to entitlements, has drawn some treacherous attention. The financial community has tried to persuade the richest among them to abandon Social Security and Medicare in favor of privatized medical insurance and a stock market portfolio. So far, the middle old have proven to be wary, heeding the warnings of mainstream seniors' organizations like the AARP that depositing the Social Security nest egg in a precarious national 401(k) plan would, at best, benefit only the well-to-do few who have money enough to risk and perhaps more experience as investors. Indeed, the real purpose behind the effort by budget-minded conservatives to entrust Social Security to Wall Street may be to divide the senior generation by driving a wedge between the more affluent and those of modest means, so that the latter can be cut back to the minimum. There may be an unforeseen outcome to this strategy. It may unite the entire older generation against the entitlements critics. Nothing builds solidarity among people as effectively as a shared sense of danger and injustice.

Our first full-fledged "entitlements generation," the middle old have been politically targeted from more than one direction. Conservative critics have called them "greedy geezers," apparently for having saved enough of their own money to retire in comfort. More liberal political activists have castigated the middle old in states like Florida, California, and Arizona for voting to defeat bond issues and social programs that would benefit children and adolescents. As these critics see it, the entire older population — senior old, middle old, and new old — is pursuing an "anti-youth agenda" in favor of "Aid to Dependent Seniors."[6] Minority group leaders have charged that the nonwhite poor, concentrated in an "immigrant belt" that includes California, New York, Texas, and Illinois, are especially burdened by the costs of "publicly subsidized welfare" for seniors. In the coming century, they foresee "the prospect of young minority workers supporting the mostly white elderly." One demographer goes so far as to predict a "coming war" over entitlements dollars between states dominated by the "old white" and the "young diverse."[7]

Among the senior groups most often singled out for voting its selfish interest on issues like school bonds is the Silver Haired Legislature, a Florida lobby that has been described as a "political powerhouse."[8] Yet as of the 1990s, there is no good evidence that senior Americans have as yet gelled into any kind of a predictable voting bloc. "Diversity among older persons," one observer concludes, "may be at least as great with respect to political attitudes and behavior as it is in relation to economic, social, and other characteristics."[9] The American Association of Retired Persons, usually thought of as the authoritative voice of senior America, frequently reveals significant internal divisions and has been charged with being considerably more liberal than seniors who come out of the business community.[10] All of which is not to say that such a bloc could not form in the years ahead and become as powerful as organized labor once was. All the more reason to recognize the burden of conscience that lies on the middle old. If they continue to be portrayed as the grasping beneficiaries of a "racial generation gap," they will surely see their entitlements and those of future seniors come under ever more severe attack. As I suggest in later chapters, the worst course senior politics could take, both ethically and economically, would be to limit itself to a narrow, entitlements-based agenda that assumes there is not enough wealth in the nation to provide generously for young and old alike.

Until the baby boom generation moves into retirement, the public image and moral character of senior America rests heavily on the shoulders of the middle old. Some students of senior sociology have already called for retired Americans to face up to that responsibility. For example, Gerald Larue, who has created the field of "geroethics," argues poignantly for an "ethical elderhood."

> Like all ethical elders, I am naturally concerned with events, policies, and programs that affect the well-being and health of those in my own bailiwick. But that is not enough. That worldview is too small, too limited. We elders have moved beyond the world we inherited 65 and more years ago and have been instrumental in developing global awareness. . . . Our concerns for one another must be familial, bridging racial, ethnic, territorial, and all other gaps that today separate us.[11]

I would expect views like this to become more prominent as the middle old give way to the New People, whose political strength should make them far more secure about their own interests.

THE NEW PEOPLE

Baby boomers now entering their fifties are most clearly characterized by not feeling old at all, and, often enough, not looking it or acting it. "Funny, We Don't Feel Old," proclaims a band of Americans aged fifty to seventy pictured on the front cover of the *New York Times Magazine*. Their stories are personal accounts of undiminished ambition and bustling activity, a style called "productive aging" that we will want to investigate in later chapters. The image is becoming more and more familiar. Whether with enthusiasm or trepidation, everyone agrees that the New People will be a senior generation of great consequence.

For some, the nearly eighty million Americans born between 1946 and 1964 are the source of fiscal nightmares. But a simple head count with a price tag attached is hardly sufficient to tell the story. These are the children of a deeply transformative episode in American culture. They were as marked by the "Great Affluence" of the 1940s, 1950s, and 1960s as their parents had been by the Great Depression of the 1930s. What they learned about abundance and scarcity, wants and needs, from that remarkable episode in our history will be an indispensable part of the debate over entitlements. There is already a lively awareness among the New People that their independence in retirement is closely connected to their *interdependence* with the rest of the community. Older women among the New People, destined to be their generation's majority gender, have already grasped their role as "agents for change" in American life. They have wisely come to see ageism within the same spectrum of prejudice as sexism and racism.[12]

When, in 1972, Maggie Kuhn, a gentle but tough older woman from a YWCA and Quaker background, found herself unhappy with the existing style of senior politics, it was a good omen of things to come. Then in her mid-sixties, she decided to rally her peers to play a nobler role in the boisterous politics of her time.

> We wanted to go beyond the national groups for "senior citizens" that had already been established, the highly successful American Association of Retired Persons and the National Council of Senior Citizens. These organizations, we felt, didn't encourage older peo-

ple to take control of their lives or to concern themselves with large
social issues. Fighting for services and privileges for their members,
many organizations for the old fell into the special interest pit, as if
the old were saying to the young, "We worked damned hard and
we're going to get ours."

Her vision was more daring. "The old, having the benefit of life experience, the time to get things done, and the least to lose by sticking their
necks out, were in a perfect position to serve as advocates for the larger
public good."[13] The organization she founded somewhat fancifully took
the name Gray Panthers. A small, feisty group that welcomes intergenerational membership, the Gray Panthers have outlasted the Black Panthers and continue to pursue justice for elders with an eye to the community at large. If I were asked to guess what direction the New People
will take when they become the next senior generation, I suspect it will
be toward something rather like Maggie Kuhn's vision. That vision suits
the peculiar political experience of the New People. In their time, they
helped create the ideal of participative democracy and the politics of
advocacy, opting for a style much like that of the Gray Panthers. Maggie
Kuhn's way points toward adventure, and choosing adventure is the one
best way to stave off what age has meant at its most melancholy, namely,
that one stops growing and gives up on the future.

Much more than social action lies ahead for the New People. Especially as a senior generation in search of life's higher values begins to
discuss our national wealth, we may see our politics grow more searching than anyone could imagine when entrepreneurial values ruled the
world. It promises to be a distinguishing quality of the longevity revolution that great questions of fate and purpose, once confined to the
province of philosophy, will force themselves upon our awareness and
into the political realm.

The Demographic Frontier

This book is a reconnaissance expedition. It works from the assumption
that the New People are pioneering a demographic frontier where every
aspect of our culture — politics, the arts, work, love, family, education,
the media, the marketplace — will experience great change. That vista
stretches before us like a promised land of great philosophical possibilities. Yet, at this point, the way into that vast, unknown terrain is through
the narrow door of a single heated social issue. Entitlements. Under-

standably, what has first come to our attention about the longevity revolution is the senior generation's growing need for secure subsistence and costly medical care. As that need begins to slow the thrust toward ever greater industrial expansion, far-reaching political choices are being forced upon us. In the years ahead, those choices will no longer be made, as in the past, *for* seniors but *by* and *with* seniors, and most decisively by the New People, the most adventurous, assertive, astute senior generation we have known. In time, they will colonize the demographic frontier as a whole, making their needs ever more central. Surviving longer than seniors before them, they will eventually become the oldest old — but in unprecedented numbers, leaving behind them a new, activist identity for seniors who follow.

This is what makes the entitlements issue a key ideological battleground. As a matter of bread-and-butter daily necessity, the forty million Americans now living on entitlements are the largest component of the welfare state. They will soon be joined by another eighty million Americans as the baby boom ages into retirement. It is as if life itself in this era of longevity were recruiting tens of millions for a political orientation that undermines conservative opposition to big government. Hence the shrill urgency surrounding discussions of entitlements. In 1997 the conservative Paul Tsongas Project held a national public forum dedicated to "Generational Responsibility: The Future of Social Security and Medicare." It called for swift action "before the baby boom becomes the senior boom." That is the "window of opportunity." Apparently the hope is that citizens in their forties and fifties will prove unable to imagine living to retirement age and will conveniently rush to act against their own interests.

Senior citizens are odd political animals. As the stereotype would have it, they become more hidebound and cautious as they grow older. Thus, they are usually thought of as natural allies of the conservative right: property-conscious, backward-looking, and fearful of change. Yet no group is more dependent upon the big federal programs that conservatives are out to dismantle. If it were not for the entitlements programs, antigovernment conservatives might have little trouble riding roughshod over every social program in the federal budget. If expensive government programs are what conservatives have in mind when they revile the evils of liberalism, then, existentially speaking, the senior citizens of this country are the most deeply entrenched liberals on the political landscape. As every politician who stumps America's retirement communities discovers, seniors are apt to be tough-minded about the stake they hold in the nation's wealth. They are not easy to slap down. What have they got to lose that can be legally taken away from them? "Retirement," as the Gray Panthers say, "is like being rich. Nobody can fire you."

More than any mere fiscal consideration, that fact explains the panic that now dominates the entitlements debate. The strident concern that conservative critics display is much more than budgetary. What they fear is the growing power of the one group in our population that is best placed to question market values and competitive individualism. Not only are these numbers large and growing, but they are predominantly female — the constituency least likely to support individualistic and macho social values. As one gerontologist put it to me, "The future belongs to estrogen. That's what the conservatives are afraid of, especially when it comes at them in the form of millions of assertive older women who vote."

There may be something about the senior population that business and political leaders fear even more. *Wisdom*, the hard-won result of experience and reflection. Business elites who are working so feverishly to transform the planet into a hard-charging global economy demand an unquestioning obedience to the laws of the marketplace. To that end, they are committed to the manipulation of taste and the engineering of consensus. The last thing they want is a searching discussion of the meaning of life, its highest values and ethical responsibilities. In effect, they cannot afford wisdom. But questions that lead to wisdom are what fill the minds of people as they grow older.

In this there is a deep contradiction. The New People are with us in such numbers because of industrial progress; they are among the major beneficiaries of modern technology and medical science. Yet the values that come naturally with longevity are not the values that made that progress possible in the first place. In many ways, the values of the New People may become exactly the opposite. Their beliefs may lead them to a penetrating critique of modernity.

One can see this contradiction in very human and graphic terms in any airport. Air travel is one of the hallmarks of modernity. Every airport in every major city is a thronging hive of busy people on their way to do something important that requires rush and bustle — even if it is meant to be a vacation. On all sides one sees intense executive types, their heads filled with money and worry, studying their watches and muttering into cellular phones as they career through the crowds to catch a connecting flight or find their waiting limo. The air is filled with announcements of departures for Tokyo, Cairo, Brussels . . . and there, more and more often, one sees the elderly being slowly guided through the crowd in wheelchairs or electric carts, holding up the line, blocking the corridor, getting in the way. Airports were not built for them. That is why the airlines must hire more and more people to escort them to their seats, handle their tickets and luggage, or simply wheel them out of the way, a costly new service that will have to expand — for the old do indeed travel. They are customers no airline wishes to turn away. And yet . . . what a trouble they are!

I confess that I have begun to take a certain perverse satisfaction in seeing these prime beneficiaries of progress "getting in the way." I watch the irritated expressions on the faces of those who must stand and wait. I think, "If you're lucky enough, one day you will be that elderly passenger, still traveling the world at the age of seventy or eighty and slowing that world down. But by then there may be more of you than of aggravated young onlookers. When that time comes, expect the elevators and escalators to run slower, the traffic lights to change at a more leisurely speed, the freeways to lose their fast lane. And if you find that irritating, write it off as sound medical advice. You might be paying a psychiatrist $200 an hour to tell you to slow down and lower the stress in your life."

That the elderly should drop away and dissent from the dynamic, world-beating ambitions of the young is not remarkable. But never before have elders possessed the social weight to make their values count in matters of policy and the distribution of wealth.

"The Causes and Beginnings of Great Events"

Over the course of the last century, ever since futuristic thinkers began brainstorming "things to come," we have had many prophetic scenarios laid before us. Almost all of them have been obsessed with technology, committed to the idea that industrial development will continue onward and upward without limit. Futurologists continue to conjure up visions of space colonies and the exploration of galaxies far, far away. Nobody who has looked into the future foresaw a world dominated — some would say burdened — by the needs and values of *old* people. Nothing would have seemed more unlikely and less welcome.

Industrial society, even under the leadership of politicians and entrepreneurs bent with years, has always been in spirit a society of youth, never of age, a society obsessed with the latest, the newest, the daringly innovative. Old men may retain power in that society, but they dare not act their age, lest they seem too old to govern. Age, it has been assumed, belongs to the past; it reeks of decrepitude, despair, mortality, and is therefore given little voice in deciding the future. Nobody ever expected much of the old; they have rarely expected much of themselves. Now they will be with us in increasing numbers; their needs will claim an ever higher priority.

Someday our era, the era of the New People, will belong to the past. We will have undergone a fateful transition. Historians will then look back and say: this is where longevity began to make all the difference, this is where industrial society turned a corner and at last had the chance to catch its breath and reflect upon its greater human purpose. How will they record that transition?

Will it be seen despairingly as the time when our society defaulted on a promise to its senior population that it could not find the wit or the will to afford? Will it be the onset of a slump that blighted our brightest hopes? Will it be remembered as a war of the generations that pitted old against young and finally impoverished both? Or will the arrival of the New People be remembered as the opening of a true postindustrial era in which the compulsive drive to get and spend lost its appeal? At this point, there is no certainty about how the matter will go. Our current crop of political leaders surely shows no certain grasp of the situation. In the summer of 1997, at the G7 summit of industrial nations, the growing population of retired workers was unanimously identified as a major crisis in the making, one that threatened bankruptcy. Drastic changes would have to be made — though nobody knew quite what. It occurred to no one that the number of healthy, secure senior citizens a society supports might be designated as *the new criterion of economic success.*

We will, in later chapters, turn to the economic aspects of longevity, seeking to show that there are many ways to handle the costs. But it makes all the difference in the world how we regard that cost. Context is everything. Imagine that we find ourselves transported back to the time of Christopher Columbus. The great explorer returns to announce what he has found beyond the edge of the sea. But, amazing to say, the decision-makers and opinion-leaders of his day take no interest. Instead, they drown him out in an angry dispute over docking fees in the port of Lisbon! "Too expensive!" they cry. "No more voyages like this! We cannot afford them!" Had that happened, might we not expect that someone would have spoken up in exasperation, rather like this: "Here now, gentlemen! You are missing the point. There is a new world beyond the seas. That is the future. Remarkable things lie before you."

The image I use here, the voyage of discovery, holds a special place in the intellectual history of the modern world. It is the metaphor Francis Bacon invoked four centuries ago when he undertook to revolutionize Western thought. There are seas of the mind, he announced, that promise more riches than all the oceans that have yet been sailed. Among the intellectual discoveries he anticipated was the science that has given us longevity as its greatest benefit. In his time, Bacon believed the worst barrier to progress was despair, so he presented his work as a "gospel of hope" in which readers would find "the causes and beginnings of great events."

This book has much the same purpose. A new world is opening before us — not across the seas, not in outer space, not in cyberspace, but in time. *Living* time. Longevity is our voyage of discovery. As we will see in later pages, that voyage is affordable by any rational accounting — so easily affordable, indeed, that money is the least interesting issue to address. Far more fascinating are the powers of the mind, the resources of the spirit, that wait to be explored.

2

The Third Millennium Blues

HAD YOU OPENED any newspaper in the United States at the beginning of the twentieth century, you would almost certainly have come upon a dire warning. It might have read something like this: "What possible defense has the white man against awakening and oncoming Asia? Asiatics swarm by millions. They must not be allowed to overturn our civilization, nor be permitted to turn us into Asiatics by ruinous economic competition."[1]

Politicians took up the theme; churches and social groups spoke out on the issue. Across the nation, the public was convinced that Western society would soon be overwhelmed by the hungry hordes of Asia. The issue combined fear with righteous indignation and added up to a good hate — always a guaranteed political success.

It was called the Yellow Peril.

The Gray Peril

Now, at the dawn of the twenty-first century, Americans are once again hearing dark predictions of economic doom. But this time the threat arises much closer to home. It stems from the Gray Peril: the forty to fifty million retirees who are drawing their entitlements under Social Security and Medicare, and whose ranks will soon be augmented by eighty million baby boomers. Just as a century ago the teeming masses of Asia were usually drawn in political cartoons as scrawny, slant-eyed vermin swarming across the Pacific to devour our national wealth, so now we have similarly menacing caricatures of the Gray Peril. Newspaper editorial pages show us potbellied, bewrinkled oldsters living it up on the golf course, presumably on their children's money. Or they are shown lounging atop a mountain of cash, feasting on the wealth of the nation. "The widespread failure to die in a timely fashion," as Richard Leone sardonically puts it, "has inspired countless predictions of political chaos and economic ruin in the industrialized countries."[2]

It is particularly unsettling to realize that the image of the senior as greedy geezer first emerged in the March 28, 1988, issue of the *New Republic*, once a reasonably liberal publication. It appeared as part of a diatribe by Henry Fairlie against retired Americans: castigated as a selfish burden to the nation, seniors were depicted on the cover as an army of odious old parasites armed with golf clubs. Since then, that image has become the centerpiece of a conservative crusade. Peter Peterson, head of the Concord Coalition, an anti-entitlements think tank, has been among the most influential of these defenders of fiscal integrity, heading what may be one of the most effective lobbying efforts since Prohibition. Anybody who believes the senior vote can have its way in American politics would do well to study what Peterson has been able to accomplish with a few well-placed millions from the brokerage community. Author of a book-length jeremiad on entitlements called *Will America Grow up Before It Grows Old?*, Peterson has been campaigning on this front since the 1980s. In May 1996, he published a dire warning in the *Atlantic*. His argument was many-sided: senior entitlements are unsustainable, undeserved, unprincipled, and unfair. But more striking than any statistic he offered were the illustrations chosen for the article. They are little short of the kind of nasty propaganda imagery Dr. Goebbels might have employed in the 1930s to dramatize "the Jewish Menace." Seniors appear like an alien species of obnoxious, geriatric layabouts thronging the sunny shores of Florida, crowding their children out of the country, stealing the food from their mouths, and devouring the national treasury. One especially vicious cartoon depicts a cadaverous old guy in a hospital bed on IV tubes; the substance being transfused lavishly into his arm is . . . money. If anything, such an image tells us that for some critics money is the equivalent of our life's blood.

The language evoked by the Gray Peril can be as frenzied as the pictures. The old are becoming too numerous, they insist on living too long, but worst of all, they are just plain *bad*, a failed generation of weak, self-indulgent parasites. Peterson, for example, not only condemns entitlements as "a fiscal meltdown" but castigates the entire baby boom generation for its "unseemly" and "ruinously dysfunctional" way of life. He believes "we now face public budgets strained to the breaking point by demographic aging which will crowd out all forms of capital accumulation, private and public, material and human." As if he could imagine no worse fate for the nation, he asks how we would like to be living in "a nation of Floridas," amid a "gray wave of senior citizens that fills the state's streets, beaches, parks, hotels, shopping malls, hospitals, Social Security offices, and senior centers."

The anti-immigration propagandists of the nineteenth century might have raised the same question about all those repugnant yellow people. "How would you like to live in a nation of Shanghais?"

In the case of the Yellow Peril, the usual proposal was to lock the vermin out or send them back where they came from. The dreaded "gray wave" offers no such options. Still, one shudders to imagine what Peterson has in mind for our senior population. He is among those who have most forcefully proposed the rationing of health care. By this he means finding some way to deny dying seniors the expensive medical care that might keep them going another few weeks, months, or years at the public expense. Given the insensitivity of Peterson's critique, this looks more like a "final solution" than a cost-benefit analysis.

Resisting Longevity

Here, then, is a remarkable campaign that would have people believe that balancing the budget is more important than providing medical care for their parents — or, at some point in the future, for themselves. It is as if we were being asked to send up a perverse prayer: *If only the 1990s looked more like the 1890s!* Yet in astonishing numbers, opinion-leaders have compliantly accepted the anti-entitlements argument at face value. Perhaps that is because the anti-entitlements movement has offered the media the one thing they cannot resist: a good scare. Tell the world that the sky is falling, and what might otherwise be an utterly boring parade of actuarial numbers and fiscal priorities suddenly becomes top-of-the-hour news — even though the entitlements "crisis" is still twenty to thirty years away. What other issue in our lives is viewed on such a timeline?

The rhetoric employed by the media in handling entitlements betrays a determined effort to dramatize to the hilt. Articles in leading publications find the future of entitlements "mind-boggling" and warn that we are sitting on a "demographic time bomb" *(Wall Street Journal)*. Or entitlements are "a giant sponge soaking up so large a share of the

THE THIRD MILLENNIUM BLUES

federal budget that little will be left for anything else" *(New York Times)*. Sporting a big "Uh-Oh!" on its cover, the *New Republic* announces, "Social Security is on the skids." *Time* magazine warns that we are facing an "entitlements monster that will consume the budget if left unchecked." Anticipating the 1997 State of the Union speech, a *Time* magazine editorial writer presses President Clinton to cut back on senior benefits, titling its challenge "No Guts, No Glory."

Largely on the basis of polemical materials artfully assembled and vigorously disseminated by conservative groups like the Concord Coalition and the Cato Institute, entitlements doomsayers have made themselves the most vociferous and widely quoted viewpoint in the United States on the future of Social Security and Medicare. At least their own polling data suggest that large portions of the public have been convinced that only drastic measures — like the rapid privatization of Social Security — can save the nation from bankruptcy.[3] The issue has driven otherwise humane and liberal thinkers to intemperate extremes. Lester Thurow, for example, has called the elderly a "revolutionary class," but not in any good sense of the word. He charges that retired Americans are "bringing down the social welfare state, destroying government finances, altering the distribution of purchasing power, and threatening the investments that all societies need to make to have a successful future." Predicting that, "in the years ahead, class warfare is apt to be redefined as the young against the old," he darkly hints that the grandmothers and grandfathers of America may accomplish what no foreign foe or totalitarian movement has succeeded in doing. They will kill the democratic way of life. Democracy, he believes, "is going to meet the ultimate test in the elderly. If democratic governments cannot cut benefits that go to the majority of their voters, then they have no long-term future."[4] This comes close to saying that the only way we can save the nation is by disenfranchising the retired.

The Social Security Administration has replied to these fiscal horror stories by pointing out what should be obvious: any program tied to demographic change will have to be fine-tuned from time to time, as indeed Social Security has been on several occasions in the past. Robert Ball, the nation's foremost authority on the subject, has flatly stated that "there is no financial crisis in Social Security."[5] He and others have explained that over the next several years a relatively modest set of adjustments, which might include a gradual rise in the Social Security tax, will keep the system solvent well into the twenty-first century. The

Social Security Administration estimates that it can now meet all its commitments until the year 2029. If we were to do nothing between now and 2029 but wait for the system to "go broke," as its critics predict, Social Security would still be able to pay three-quarters of the pensions it owes. But why would we simply wait and do nothing? When Social Security has required adjustments in the past, we have made them. And we will make them again. Thus, if between now and 2029, we gradually raise the FICA payroll tax by a total of 2.19 percent (half to be paid by employees, half by employers) the system will remain solvent at the present level until 2070. The tax increase might be even less if Social Security takes over the pensions of several million state and local employees who are not now covered or if capital gains were to be included under the Social Security tax, which now falls only on payroll earnings. That is the real dimension of the so-called crisis.

Critics are not persuaded. In late 1997, Alan Greenspan, head of the Federal Reserve Board, went on record supporting the need to restructure the entitlements. Deciding beforehand that a tax increase was unthinkable and brushing aside other modest adjustments, he too proclaimed the program to be "unsustainable" and recommended stringent cuts plus rapid privatization. Other critics, playing upon public ignorance, invoke a scenario that might have been written for *The X-Files*. They insist that the system is *already* bankrupt; the government has been covering up the truth for half a century. Open up the Social Security trust fund and look inside. What will you find? Nothing but U.S. treasury bonds, worthless pieces of paper in the opinion of anti-entitlement critics. Peter Peterson goes so far as to charge that the Social Security system is a fraudulent operation, little short of a "Ponzi scheme."[6]

True, there is no big pot of money somewhere in Washington containing everybody's pension funds marked by name. Nobody ever said there would be. No insurance anywhere in the world works on such a basis. Insurance is always made up of a certain amount of money on hand surrounded and buttressed by a fiduciary responsibility, meaning a promise to live up to one's obligations — as Social Security has since it began. The system expresses our sense of national community. It is based on something more valuable than money in the bank: *conscience*, the ethical consensus among Americans as to how our national wealth shall be used. There are many elements of government that have forfeited their claim to the public trust. The military, CIA, FBI, IRS,

Federal Reserve Board — all these have blundered or lied or allied themselves to special interests. The Social Security Administration is not among them. Indeed, when it comes to handling money, its record is the best we can find in the land. Nothing very exciting or newsworthy happens at Social Security. Nobody has ever had to track down an administrator for embezzlement. In contrast, what is the public record of the financial community? Stories of major bankers, brokers, and fund managers being sued, prosecuted, or imprisoned for blatantly chiseling the public are the news of the day. Who are these people to offer themselves as a more reliable choice than Social Security?

Originally created to alleviate, if not end, old-age poverty, Social Security is an ongoing contract between the generations based upon the full faith and credit of the world's richest nation. It is grounded in our trust in ourselves. As Justice Benjamin Cardozo put it in 1937 in delivering the Supreme Court's decision in favor of the Social Security Act, "The hope behind this statute is to save men and women from the rigors of the poor house as well as from the haunting fear that such a lot awaits them when journey's end is near." If we leave out the moral force behind that commitment, we have lost the entire meaning of the program and have become ethically poorer.

The Dismal Science of Generational Accounting

In a 1995 critique of entitlements, James P. Smith of the RAND Corporation, fretting that Social Security and Medicare are "draining the capacity and incentive of workers to save for their own retirement," insists that "loud alarm bells are ringing for the nation's future."[7] Whenever those bells start ringing, one can be certain the generational accountants have had a hand in setting off the alarm. The creation of the economists Laurence Kotlikoff of Boston University, Alan Auerbach of the University of California, Berkeley, and Jagadeesh Gokhale of the Cleveland Federal Reserve Bank, generational accounting is the brains trust behind the conservative attack upon entitlements. A single-issue school of economics, its sole interest is the nation's senior dependency load — the distribution of wealth between retired Americans and their working children.

Kotlikoff and his colleagues seek to estimate, in present-value terms, how much people born in any given year will pay the government over their lifetimes and how much they can expect to get back in entitlements.[8] Of central importance to their analysis is the ratio between net lifetime payments into and out of Social Security and Medicare. This yields a percentage that can be projected across future generations. Thus, Americans born in 1930 have paid 30 percent of their income for what they have eventually received in return from entitlement benefits. Those born in 1950 will have paid 33 percent. But if current policies continue, Kotlikoff estimates that the children of the post–baby boom generation will have to lay out a flattening 84 percent of their lifetime earnings. "What that's telling you," he warns, "is that current fiscal policy is unsustainable and generationally unconscionable. We need to pay more and spend less today so our kids won't be taxed to death." Otherwise, the result will be a "fiscal train wreck."[9]

Kotlikoff's numbers have been sharply questioned. As Dean Baker of the Economic Policy Institute points out, the generational accountants make many unjustified assumptions about the future cost of medical care. For one thing, they assume a rate of continuing inflation that would make *any* form of health insurance, whether public or private, unaffordable.[10] For another, Kotlikoff quite misleadingly conflates the cost of Social Security with the cost of Medicare, even though these are separate programs funded in different ways, presenting different problems, and having different prospects. Social Security has no problems in its future that cannot be fixed by modest and gradual adjustments. Medicare's far greater problems have to do with costs — including waste, overcharging, and fraud — that plague the entire for-profit health care industry. Wrapping these two programs together as "entitlements" creates the impression that avaricious senior citizens are "getting" all the money in the package. Thus, speaking grimly of entitlements, the economist Paul Krugman argues that "the United States and other western governments have become engines for transferring income from workers to retirees."[11]

But Medicare reimbursements are not "income" for retirees. The money never passes into their hands. Like all health insurance reimbursements, Medicare is paid directly to doctors, hospitals, nursing homes, insurance companies, and pharmaceutical houses. Most of these, as medical corporations of some kind, are run for profit; their shares can be found in the portfolios of the investing public. If Medicare is an income transfer engine, it is a pump that sucks taxes out of all of us and delivers them to some of the wealthiest people in America. If anybody is paying golfing fees out of Medicare, it is apt to be the CEOs of the nation's prospering health maintenance organizations.

In Kotlikoff's eyes, none of the entitlements reforms currently under discussion comes close to doing the job that needs to be done. He contends that even the most rigorous proposals for balancing the budget in the early twenty-first century will cost the next generation a crushing 70 percent of their income. And even then, he observes, those who are drawing on the Social Security trust fund, according to the Congressional Research Service, will, on the average, use up everything they contributed within the first ten years of retirement, including the employer contribution. After that, they are living off a subsidy from current workers.

Of course, the "subsidy" that generational accountants are talking about is rather like the subsidy those same retirees, as parents, once gave their children when they fed them, clothed them, put a cozy suburban roof over their heads, built schools, playgrounds, and universities for them, hired teachers to educate them and doctors to medicate them. The tie that binds the generations cannot be reduced to a neat fiscal formula. The discussion of entitlements is complicated by a biological fact that does not yield to a purely economic analysis. It is called "family." The people who are giving and taking, earning and spending, are relatives. And as nature would have it, with the passage of time the babies grow up, get old, and retire. Despite all the groaning and gnashing of teeth we hear from the generational accountants, it pays to remember that nothing worse is happening here than that life is going on. The demographic configuration changes, but the underlying obligation of kin to kin continues.

The World Is Getting Older

Our aging population is not due to some peculiarly bad social planning on the part of the United States. It results from the logic of progress in the modern world. Barring another Black Plague that carries off more of the old than the young, every industrial nation is destined to become something like "a nation of Floridas." If that looks like a threatening prospect, then all the other First World societies have a bleaker future than we do.

By the year 2020, seniors over sixty will account for 25 percent of our population; in Germany and Japan, that figure will reach 30 percent. Japan now leads in longevity statistics: Japanese women have a life expectancy of eighty-three; in the country at large, the average age is forty. As of the 1990s, over 40 percent of all French women and

30 percent of all American women are on their way to living past eighty-five. By the time Chinese teenagers of the 1990s reach middle age, their country will have one citizen over sixty-five for every child below fourteen. The future can be made to appear especially catastrophic if we express what any of the developed nations owe their retired citizens as "an unfunded pension liability," that is, the amount of their gross domestic product that will have to be set aside to pay for pensions. The Canadians, for example, would have to set aside an impossible 250 percent of GDP.[12]

But why stop calculating at 2020 . . . or 2050? Time marches on. If we extend the numbers a few decades further in any industrial society one cares to name, there are likely to be more retirees than workers. It would seem that the young, steadily diminishing as they are in relative numbers, are destined for lifelong serfdom. At least that would be the case if we looked at the future through the lens of generational accounting. But statistics, when they leave out the human and historical context, can be profoundly misleading.

Consider a favorite statistical horror of the generational accountants: how many taxpaying workers will there have to be in the future to pay for the growing needs of the elderly? The numbers can seem staggering, especially if Medicare is lumped together with Social Security. To cover the cost of Medicare alone presently requires the taxes of 3.9 workers for every senior citizen. There will be only 3.1 workers to carry the tax load by 2015, only 2.5 by 2025, and by 2050 the figure will fall to 2.[13] The result sounds as outrageous as it is forbidding.

But this ratio, so often quoted, is simply not a relevant statistic. For if we reconfigure the numbers a bit, we arrive at an important insight. Think back again to the 1940s and 1950s. In that period, when most families were living off a single paycheck, wage-earners in every household were supporting three, four, or five dependents. That is what it meant to have a *baby boom*. Had Kotlikoff been on the scene when that boom was under way, he would no doubt have been warning us that the nation would soon be fiscally smothered in diapers or drowned in baby formula. And yet the baby boom did happen and it did get paid for. In contrast to the postwar period, when families were so much larger, in generations to come the number of dependents below the age of fourteen will diminish. As that happens, the *total* dependency load — youth dependency taken together with retirees — carried by each working member of society will actually grow smaller. In any case, the ratio that matters when it comes to calculating any society's dependency load is that of *productive capacity* to dependents. And that continues to rise, thanks to our ever expanding industrial technology.[14]

Like so many fiscally conservative critics, Kotlikoff makes the mistake of assuming that, if we eliminate a government program, the people who need that program will vanish in a puff of smoke. But consider what our situation would be if we did abolish entitlements and let "our children," for whom the generational accountants purport to have such concern, keep all their hard-earned money as discretionary income. Entitlements would be gone, but the people who depend on those entitlements would still be there. And what would the position of the working population be? Presumably, each worker would still have at least one or two retirees to support: they would be called Mother and Father, with perhaps a few long-lived grandparents included in the load. Where else would those people turn once they had left the workforce? And now the cost of their dependency would include all the medical bills as well as the basic necessities. Seen from that angle, the entitlements look like rather a good deal. They are the arrangement we have made as a society for pooling a collective moral obligation and discharging it as practically, dependably, and fairly as possible.

No question but that we should seek in every way we can to avoid the waste of our medical resources. But where does that effort begin? Not with cutting back on Medicare coverage. We should, instead, start by cleaning up the incompetence and waste in the nation's health care system. Until we do that, we will not know with any accuracy how expensive senior medical care really is. Health professionals have already begun to recognize that fact. In December 1997, two thousand Massachusetts doctors and nurses went on record in the *Journal of the American Medical Association* condemning "the dark side of market-driven health care." They even staged a replay of the Boston Tea Party by dumping the reports of HMO corporations into Boston Harbor as they issued a "Call for Action" to curb the fleecing practices of for-profit medicine in the United States. One interesting criticism of the effort came from the California Nurses Association. It commented that nonprofit hospitals can be just as exorbitant and wasteful as the for-profits.[15]

In a fall 1997 report commissioned by the National Coalition on Health Care, the RAND Corporation estimated that American medicine will cost over $1 trillion annually by the beginning of the twenty-first century. That cost has been rising steadily at a rate vastly higher than inflation, in spite of the fact that more and more Americans are living without medical insurance and doing without care. The reason we are paying more for medical care, both in total and per capita, than any nation in the developed world has much to do with the high number of cases that are misdiagnosed or poorly treated — all of which goes on the national doctor's bill. In a system like this, no sensible reform starts by making economies on patients in the intensive care ward.

Worse still, at some point the cost of slipshod practice merges with fraud. Since the mid-1990s, a steady stream of reports from the media, the Justice Department, and the Congress have documented the amount of swindling that goes on under Medicare, as well as under private health insurance. The culprits have included Columbia/HCA, the largest for-profit health care conglomerate in the country. How much, then, of the $200 billion that Medicare spends annually as of the 1990s is being paid for good, necessary care, and how much for illegal billing and overpricing? Malcolm Sparrow of the Kennedy School of Government, who has made a careful study of Medicare fraud, believes that as much as 38 percent of billing in the system is dishonest — roughly $60 billion annually.[16] Estimates of fraudulent insurance billing in health care as a whole, private and public, run as high as $100 billion a year, far more than would be recovered by curtailing services or raising senior deductibles.[17] When the Congress behaves as if it dare not touch the "third rail" issue of Medicare, one wonders whether its reluctance has to do with its fear of senior voting power or with its desire to shield the questionable ethics of some very large campaign contributors from still more shocking disclosure.

Fiscal Child Abuse

Perhaps the cruelest tactic used by the anti-entitlements campaign has been that of pitting young against old in generational conflict. In a consummate bit of parental guilt-tripping, the generational accountants have associated senior entitlements with greed, selfishness, irresponsibility, and self-indulgence — traits that make good mothers and fathers wince. Third Millennium, an advocacy group for twenty- and thirty-somethings, condemns Social Security as "a generational scam, fiscally unsound and generationally inequitable." The system is "robbing our children in order to indulge ourselves in the luxuries of a time gone by." It is little short of "fiscal child abuse." What would Third Millennium do about these evils? The government, it insists, must stop "invoicing future generations for today's spending sprees." It should raise the retirement age to seventy, means-test for pensions and health care, and "stop paying the greens-fee for well-heeled retirees."[18]

How justified are these accusations? Have seniors been greedy in accepting entitlements and in letting them be augmented through cost-of-living increases? If so, in many cases the benefits of their "greed" are being shared with their children. Consider the number of under-thirties who, in today's fluctuating job market, have been living at home, relying on parental room and board. These days jobs come and go at the whim of the global marketplace, but family ties hold strong. As early as 1987, sociologists began to report the phenomenon of "boomerang kids," the increasing number of insecure or downwardly mobile children who were returning home to live with their parents for lack of enough income to afford homes of their own.[19]

Cross-generational support is not limited to housing. As of the mid-1990s, economists believe more than 20 percent of all wealth in the United States was being passed from parents to adult children by way of gifts, and this did not include the cost of university education.[20] Shared family wealth explains the continued high level of consumer spending among younger, less than affluent workers, as well as their otherwise puzzling acquiescence in declining wages and job security. Money from home has been providing much of the ballast in our storm-tossed economic life. It has offset the growing amount of part-time and temporary employment, independent contracting, and general job insecurity that now characterizes working life in America. As Frances Goldscheider observes, the decade of the 1990s "is really depression for young adults" — relieved for many only by the families they can fall back upon when the job market turns against them.[21]

The family bank account has become an important, if unofficial, element in the national safety net. A 1997 study of grandparenting in the United States concluded that grandparents were spending as much as $8 billion annually to help feed and clothe their grandchildren. The money they are spending within the family is sufficiently large to attract the attention of merchandisers, who see grandparental generosity as a lucrative market. Even more important is the free day care and baby-sitting they provide, a service that the Commonwealth Fund estimates may be worth as much as $29 billion a year.[22] If the economic disparity between America's postwar and fin-de-siècle generations has not been as glaring as it might be, it is because a great deal of wealth is being informally transferred between the generations.

In September 1995, *Newsweek* ran a feature entitled "MediScare." It presented a cover picture of a young man struggling to hold his ailing, wheelchair-bound mother above his worried head. "Young vs. Old," the caption read. "Who will carry the burden?" Poor fellow! But the picture might have been closer to the truth if it were turned upside down. It might just as well show aging parents keeping an underemployed son or jobless daughter afloat in the swirling waters of the global economy.

Such parental generosity may not continue indefinitely. While some envious young adults like the members of Third Millennium characterize the senior generation as a population of cruise-ship sybarites, the inexorable pressure of medical needs is steadily eroding senior wealth. It is true that, thanks to entitlements, the over-65 white population in America is living better than in any previous era.[23] And though they cannot eat or wear the homes they live in, some 600,000 elderly citizens own homes valued at more than $100,000.[24] If anybody is going to gain any cash benefit from the parental home, it will be the children who one day sell it off after their parents die or go into nursing care. Other than that, the bequests that elders can leave to their children began shrinking as of the early 1990s, a fact that is bound to exacerbate generational friction.

As they survive longer, seniors are outliving whatever resources they set aside. Above all, they continue to be plagued by medical expenses beyond those that Medicare covers, especially as for-profit health care trims and cuts its coverage. These days some seniors display sassy bumper stickers on their cars that proclaim, "I'm Spending My Children's Inheritance." And so they are. But on what? Entitlements critics, assuming an austere Calvinist air, condemn retirees for spending as much as they do on "consumption." They omit to mention that, as time goes on, what seniors are primarily consuming is medical care. While they may be spending more relative to the younger generation of the 1990s, what they lay out goes increasingly to doctors, hospitals, pharmacists, and nursing homes — hardly the most enjoyable kind of spending.

Financial pressures like these may lead to an ironic result. Entitlements critics purport to be seriously concerned for "our children," but they may be working against the interests of the younger generation. Suppose they were to succeed in cutting Social Security and Medicare back and thus lowering the living standard of retired Americans. It would then hardly be surprising if many seniors felt compelled to augment their income by bouncing back into the workforce, seeking at least part-time work. Given the fact that the next senior generation will be the healthiest, best educated, and most skilled in history, these rebounding retirees would be eminently employable. In fact, many firms might find them more job-worthy than younger workers, who want secure, high-paying positions. Some firms are already showing a preference for older workers, who, having no family life to distract them, can put in more hours and work odd schedules. An *ABC News* feature (February 10, 1998) reports that employees aged fifty-five to sixty-four are the fastest-growing segment of the American workforce.

Older workers who have been on the job continuously for twenty or thirty years at higher salary levels may look unaffordable to employers; they may even be squeezed out of jobs in their fifties. But those same forcibly retired workers who then reenter the workforce for supplementary income may willingly take jobs that offer no benefits because they already have their entitlements; nor would they be as concerned about job security or advancement, since they would be on the other side of their careers. They might even prefer to hire on as temps or independent contractors. Bear in mind, these would not be the middle-old members of the senior population we know today; these would be baby boomers, many of them proficient in high-tech skills and professionally trained. They would, in short, be cheap, flexible, skilled, experienced, responsible employees, willing to work without benefits and with a minimal concern for long-term prospects.

Is this not exactly the workforce that corporate America is looking for in this era of the global economy? If so, those workers are waiting in the wings eighty million strong. And every over-65 boomer who feels compelled to keep working will be taking a job away from the younger generation. That could become as great a threat to younger workers in the twenty-first century as the cheap labor of Mexico and Taiwan has become to blue-collar workers on the assembly lines. If a new employment pattern of this kind begins to take shape in the years ahead, we may find younger Americans wishing mightily that this was a "nation of Floridas" where they could pack all the troublesome seniors off to anyplace well out of the job market.

Valuing Life

Any social change that involves redistributing large sums of public money is bound to present a "problem" of some kind, whether we are discussing defense appropriations, welfare, education, or environmental protection. View that change on a seventy-year timeline, as the Social Security Administration is required by law to do, and the problem gets bigger — meaning more expensive. Imagine trying to estimate the cost of maintaining the nation's streets and highways over the next century. Some would say the bill looked "unaffordable."

Some problems may be insoluble disasters; others are matters of intelligent adjustment. The problems raised by longevity are of the latter kind; they present an occasion for rationally reordering priorities. That can be controversial. Every great public issue involves trade-offs, choices, and competing claims. That is what politics is all about. Thus, it is hardly beside the point that those campaigning against entitlements include financial interests that have a great deal to gain from the solution they propose: privatizing Social Security. That is also politics, and very profitable politics at that. In the course of the next generation, privatizing Social Security would entrust as much as $1 trillion in mandatory savings to brokers and mutual fund managers who would collect handsome fees for supervising personal security accounts. Not only would privatization involve a costly transitional phase that would have to be covered by taxpayers as a higher Social Security tax, but it would result in investment portfolios that lacked any protection against inflation, the always unpredictable fluctuations of the stock market, opportunistic churning, and plain bad management. For those who suffer such losses, there would, we are promised, be a shadow Social Security system called "the safety net" to catch them. For "safety net" read "bailout," to be paid for by the taxpaying public if brokers swindle their senior clients blind or if the market goes into a tailspin, as the Japanese stock market of the early 1990s did. Not since the great robber barons of the nineteenth century stepped forward to take over the building of the nation's railroads — on the basis of generous federal and state land grants and subsidies — has there been so self-serving a proposal.

Some brokers are shamelessly projecting "can't lose" earnings of 10 and 12 percent on personal security accounts. They hardly inspire confidence. Still, one might make a reasonable case for including private securities in the Social Security trust fund; many public pension funds allow for cautious, well-regulated investment and, like the California Public Employees Retirement System, are now among the biggest players in the stock market. Among the proposals produced by the 1997 United States Advisory Council on Social Security was one recommendation that all the equities be placed in the hands of the Social Security Administration itself, to be managed as cheaply and cautiously as possible. That is not a course that privatizers fancy; in the words of the *Wall Street Journal*, "this would put the economy into government ownership." It would amount to "socialism-by-acquisition."[25] On the other hand, how much confidence can one have in the extravagant promises that are being made by those in the private sector who want to get hold of Social Security funds and invest them with no supervision or few safeguards?

Ultimately the solution to the entitlements issue is not a matter of fiscal manipulation. It does not have to do with costs but with *values* — and not the value of money, but the value of life. When we deal in matters of life and death, it is crucial to know what counts as a cost and what counts as a benefit. Disease costs, death costs, broken bones, bad teeth, and environmental pollution cost — and not only in dollars. They cost in physical suffering and emotional anguish, sleepless nights and anxious hours. Health and long life are the benefits that offset those far more serious emotional costs.

Today if one asks about the state of the economy, the answer may be framed in any number of ways. One might choose productivity as the key criterion, or profit, or price stability. Whatever one chooses is an expression of value, not fact. Suppose, then, that we stopped thinking of longevity as a set of numbers in a debit column and came to regard it as a *benefit* — the main benefit for which we expend our wealth. To keep the economists happy, let us make the item rigorously quantitative. Add up the years by which we are extending life expectancy. Give the total an official name. Call it the NLE: national life expectancy. Include a quality-of-life adjustment based on money spent for doctors' visits, hospitalization, medication, and so forth. Include an index for the feeling of general physical well-being. After all, if we believe we can measure something called "consumer confidence," then why not the confidence people have in their health, so much more important than consumption? Let the NLE count for more in the index of leading economic indicators as a measure of the national wealth than the gross domestic product. As long as the NLE keeps rising, let us celebrate that as prosperity — at least as warmly as we celebrate the rising Dow-Jones average. Then let us use whatever metaphor for good fortune we choose — we have scaled the mountaintop, we have crossed the finish line, we have won the war, we have struck it rich, we have hit the jackpot — but accept longevity *as* success and offer it to all who step forward to take it. We might even reward companies that make some significant contribution to the NLE, such as cutting back on auto emissions or finding a better treatment for diabetes.

It would not be impossible to produce formulas like these. If there seems to be a certain flippancy to this proposal, it stems from my skepticism about the entrepreneurial vision of reality, within which, seemingly, nothing has value, not even life itself, unless it can be counted out in dollars and cents. Nevertheless, in the years ahead this is the sort of radical economic reappraisal we may have to make once we accept the fact that there is nothing we can do about longevity but accept it, enjoy it, and value it.

The Highest Stage of Industrial Development

At the beginning of the twentieth century, few people could have foreseen that in another generation the United States would become an automotive economy devoting most of its industrial power to building bigger, faster cars and ever more sprawling highway and freeway networks. It was less likely still that anybody could have predicted the high tech and aerospace that would dominate our economy in the latter half of the century. By now, we are used to seeing cars, computers, and space shuttles as the grand climax of industrial development. But that may be wrong. Ahead of us may lie a higher stage of industrialism in which health care and biotech will absorb the lion's share of our resources, capital, labor, and skill. Those who do see that possibility do not welcome the prospect. On the contrary, that is precisely what economists and political leaders have in view when they lament the rising national medical bill and warn that it may devour all other forms of growth and investment.

Because health care has always been associated with disease, the money we spend on healing ourselves is still seen as a drag on the economy. When, for example, economists register what health insurance adds to the price of American goods, they bemoan this cost as a regrettable expenditure that undercuts our competitiveness in world markets.

So employers hasten to replace expensive full-time employees with part-timers or independent contractors who work without benefits. Or they outsource the work to cheaper labor markets.

This is not good economics; it is simply shortsighted management. Even on strict economic terms, skimping on the nation's health makes no sense except to those who collect short-term profits on lower prices. What we spend in the United States on health care is *somebody else's* profit or paycheck: doctors, nurses, lab technicians, hospitals, laboratories, paramedics, pharmaceutical houses. Are these not also part of our business society? If they prosper, in what sense is the economy suffering? Is it not the case that capital and resources are simply shifting to another sector of the economy in the same way that, at some point in the past, money that formerly went to blacksmiths began to flow to car mechanics, or the money that was once paid out to telephone operators began to be spent on those who build, sell, and service direct dialing systems?

Currently, health care absorbs about 15 percent of GDP in the United States. Some people warn that this figure may soon grow to 20, 30, 40 percent. But suppose that happens. Is saving the life of a premature baby less valuable than tail fins or database software? Which is of greater value: adding another one hundred megahertz to a microprocessor or adding another ten years to the national life expectancy? On what basis do we answer such questions? There is surely no law of the marketplace that dictates that General Motors or Microsoft must make more money than Kaiser Permanente or Squib Labs.

In an incisive analysis of the coming health care economy, Charles Morris calls into question the "counting conventions" that bias our view of service industries and of health care in particular. "There is a brawny illusion about manufacturing and other goods-producing industries that makes them seem more 'real' than services. . . . When an older person gets a hip replacement or cataract surgery, . . . it does not appear so obviously on the radar screen as an increase in wealth." He is convinced that "the argument that a continued shift away from traditional heavy industry toward health care will somehow impoverish the country is a compound of nonsense."[26] It may be that the long-standing association of medical care with age contributes to this peculiar prejudice. A healthy economy is, supposedly, made up of healthy, preferably young people and their needs, not the needs of the old. But as far as raw statistics are concerned, the economy is neutral. These are simply different consumer groups spending their money on different goods. One group spends on designer jeans, the other spends much more on cataract surgery. As the New People shift more of our money toward their needs, we will come to recognize that a healing economy can be as prosperous as any other.

As a basis for our long-term industrial future, health care offers many advantages. It is intensely technological and so puts our best technical brains to work on obviously necessary tasks like saving lives. It is labor-intensive, hiring people at both the skilled and unskilled levels at jobs that cannot be exported. As for productivity, one might consider the "product" of cesarean surgery to be one human unit, but the very idea is absurd. At some point, plain common sense must intervene to tell us that health care makes a more defensible use of capital and resources than the high-definition (and high-expense) television we are under increasing pressure to fund.

Morris believes that by the middle of the twenty-first century we could be spending 30 percent of GDP on health care. When that time comes, we may very well see more of our scientific brainpower at work in biotech than in high tech. There may be more caregivers in our economy, tending to the needs of the sick and elderly, than aerospace engineers. Hospitals and hospices may be taking in more money than theme parks. We may then wake up to the fact that health and longevity are, at last, the highest stage of industrial development. Rather than regarding healing as a costly liability, we will accept what physicians and physical therapists, aerobics teachers and pharmaceutical researchers, dietitians and nurse-practitioners offer us as the supreme value in life. By the time the longevity revolution has run its course, we may look back upon all that came before, from heavy industry to high tech, as a dark age of deplorable waste when people did not know what really mattered.

3

Entitlements and the
Ethics of Affordability

I F WE WERE TO BELIEVE the conservative think tanks that are
providing so much ideological firepower to the campaign against
entitlements, we might almost assume that Social Security and
Medicare were foisted upon an unsuspecting nation in the dead of night
by a conspiratorial gerontocracy. The truth is quite the opposite. Until
the Great Depression, elderly Americans had little voice in our political
life; their power and organization did not compare to that of the business interests that bitterly opposed all publicly funded pension plans.
Even in the boom years of the 1920s, the American business community
openly celebrated the "fearsome prospect of old-age dependency" as a
character-building force. It saw social *insecurity* as the "chief discipline
in the interest of wholesome living." As one conservative economist of
the period insisted, "the ultimate test of the wisdom of the various forms
of public provision for destitute old age must be, not merely the comfort
and gratification of the individual concerned, but the influence on the
moral fiber of the community."[1] When at last the Roosevelt New Deal
introduced a pension program — a modest one in comparison to those
in most other industrial nations — FDR's right-wing critics hastened to
warn that Social Security was "begging the unfit to be more unfit." The
plan, they argued, removed "one of the points of pressure which has kept
many persons up to the strife and struggle of life."[2]

The Silent Victims of "Progress"

Whenever seniors hear themselves portrayed as an invincible vested
interest, they should look to their history for the truth of the matter.

Older Americans may not think of themselves as victims, but theirs is a long, sad tale of bleak mistreatment. For generations they have suffered wrongs inflicted on them often by their nearest and dearest. With the exception of some traditional societies where elders may be honored — if for no other reason than that there are so few of them around — not many societies have treated their seniors as more than troublesome dependents who are expected to stand aside and let life pass them by. That has certainly been the case in the modern Western world, where the old have been seen as the claim of the dreary past upon the busy forces of progress.

The new industrial economies of the nineteenth century took an especially savage toll among older workers. The men burned out early at the heavy and dangerous work they did in the factories and mines, on the railroads, and in the oil and timber fields. The women grew old before their time in the sweatshops and mills. Even if older workers kept their health and strength, industrial accidents, for which there was no compensation or adequate medical care, might take them off the job at any point. During the early generations of the industrial revolution, the aged, unless they belonged to the propertied classes, ordinarily ended their working life assimilated to the status of "the poor." Even if they had worked all their lives, they were expected to die as marginal paupers. By the end of the century, major employers like the railroads had adopted mandatory retirement policies for older workers, but with no pension attached. Today, when retirement has very nearly been elevated into a culture of its own (supposedly the ideal condition in which to end one's days), we forget that it was introduced by efficiency-minded businessmen who took no interest in the security or the survival of those they dropped from the payroll. One simply fired the old in favor of younger, more agile workers.[3] If the elderly wished to avoid the humiliation of public assistance, they had no place to turn for care after they left the payroll but to their children. They might be classed among the "impotent" or "deserving" poor, but they were still viewed as a burden. If they suffered, they suffered in silence.

Social Security came late to the United States, long after the welfare state was taken for granted in Europe. It was a step forward, but a small one. Yet twenty years after the first Social Security check was sent out in 1941, "old" almost invariably still implied "poor." In his classic study of American poverty, *The Other America*, Michael Harrington placed the elderly population of the United States near the bottom of the social order. He observed what was already becoming the great demographic irony of modern times. "Only a society of abundance could produce such a high proportion of old people. We can afford them, we can create them, because we are so rich. But . . . these human products of abundance [are] denied its fruits. We tolerate them as long as they are poor."

Harrington estimated that half the Americans over the age of sixty were living below "minimum standards of decency," somewhere near the level of America's inner-city minorities and rural slum-dwellers, with whom they overlapped as the poorest of the poor. Their poverty rate was three times higher than that of any other group in the nation. The main reason for their declining status was the obvious one: sickness. The rapidly rising cost of good medical care and adequate health insurance — if the elderly could find it at all — was impoverishing them. And lacking medical care, they were trapped in a "downward spiral." As Harrington put it, "we have . . . a storage bin philosophy in America. We 'maintain' the aged; we give them the gift of life, but we take away the possibility of dignity. Perhaps one of the most basic reasons why America has such problems with its elderly men and women is that America really doesn't care about them."[4]

Who's Entitled?

While Medicare was under consideration in 1963 as part of his Great Society, Lyndon Johnson convened a Presidential Council on Aging. Among its tasks was to draw up a profile of the typical sixty-five-year-old American. The council's picture was dismal in the extreme. "Americans of that age were typically unemployed and without adequate income, lacking a high school education, living off a Social Security check, but with no private pension and spending most of their income on housing."[5]

The American Association of Retired Persons and, even more so, the National Council of Senior Citizens, an adjunct of organized labor with two and a half million members, played a key role in passing the Older Americans Act of 1967, and an even more crucial role in supporting Medicare against the opposition of the American Medical Association. After the Townsend movement of the 1930s, this was the first significant show of senior political power in our history. At the time, the press was quick to note the growing senior electorate. Even conservative leaders of the time like Senator Barry Goldwater and Richard Nixon began to court the votes of older Americans.[6] But in truth, beyond their potential voting power, seniors were still not a powerful lobby that politicians needed to view with respect. Perhaps the best thing about the Great Society reforms was that they were grouped together with a more generous Social Security provision as "entitlements," a label that could be turned into a cause.

But again, the motivation behind the Great Society programs was as much to serve the interests of the younger as of the older generation. They were welcomed as a way to free footloose, upwardly mobile children from being tied down by the needs of their aging parents. The journalist Max Frankel, who was present when President Johnson signed Medicare into law, relates a telling anecdote. He recalls saying to the president, "My mother thanks you." To which Johnson replied, "No, it's *you* who should be thanking me."

Given the affluence of the time, the younger generation of that prospering period voted enthusiastically to pack their parents off in mobile homes or to retirement communities. One might almost argue that the principal financial beneficiary of Medicare was the medical industry, which has cashed in on the program ever since. How else could the elderly afford the wonders of life-extending medicine? Writing just a decade after Medicare was inaugurated, one scholar concluded that Medicare

> had been bitterly opposed by conservatives as a form of "socialized medicine." But the result has not been socialism at all — rather, a corrupt medical form of state capitalism, which has combined the vices of both ideological worlds without the virtues of either. The American health system has encouraged physicians to become medical entrepreneurs — except that it is the patient who assumes the risk and the physician who takes the profit. Proprietary hospitals and nursing homes have become business corporations more profitable than Exxon or United States Steel. Drug companies have driven up the prices of medicine by conspiracy and collusion. No other society in the world has tolerated a system of medical care which was so expensive and so corrupt.[7]

Entitlements entitled more than the elderly. Doctors felt entitled to be paid their fees; children felt entitled to have their own independent family lives and lucrative careers. It was not the ruthless use of political clout that gave senior Americans the chance to move into retirement

communities. Such benefits were rather the spin-off of a postwar affluence that was raising middle- and working-class expectations all
across the land. If many seniors then came to value the added independence they derived from Social Security and Medicare, that was a
happy side effect of programs intended to let the younger middle-class
generation get on with its own design for upscale living. What Social
Security and Medicare have done since the mid-1960s is to establish a
new standard of living in the United States — not simply for the elderly,
but for their children.

Despite Medicare and steady improvements in Social Security, poverty among seniors remained intractable through the supposedly spend-
thrift 1960s. Robert Butler, one of our leading gerontologists, still saw
old age in the United States as a "tragedy." Yes, people were living longer.
The world was in fact experiencing an "elderly population explosion."

> But is it all worth it? The truth is that we cannot promise a decent
> existence for those elderly now alive. We cannot house them, em-
> ploy them or even feed them adequately. . . . We talk earnestly
> about our "senior citizens," but we do not provide enough for them
> to eat. We become angry with them for being burdens, yet we take
> for granted the standard of living that their previous work has
> made possible for us. Neglect is the treatment of choice. . . . The
> old are in the way, an ironic example of public health progress and
> medical technology creating a huge group of people for whom
> survival is possible but satisfaction in living elusive.[8]

Bear in mind that the date for Butler's study was 1975 . . . not 1875. As
Butler sadly observes, "all too many old people have been brainwashed
and pacified into believing they are powerless." The New People will
have little better to look forward to if they do not make effective
organization their highest political priority.

Writing in the mid-1970s, Sharon Curtin echoed Butler's lament for
old age in America in poignantly personal terms.

> I am afraid to grow old — we're all afraid. In fact, the fear of grow-
> ing old is so great that every aged person is an insult and a threat to
> the society. They remind us of our own death — that our body
> won't always remain smooth and responsive, but will someday
> betray us by aging, wrinkling, faltering, failing. The ideal way to age
> would be to grow slowly invisible, gradually disappearing, without
> causing worry or discomfort to the young.

What was needed, she felt, was "a revolt of old people."

> Any real change will have to originate with the old themselves. I
> think it is time for old people to turn their energies toward discov-
> ering their common oppression, from thinking about safe, gracious
> living out in some planned community to a fight for self-respect
> and their right to a place in the larger community.[9]

When Curtin raised that appeal, she saw nothing on the scene that
remotely resembled a senior revolt. The American Association of Retired Persons was in its infancy as a political lobby; seniors were still
largely a marginalized constituency. As the new century begins, there
still is no senior revolt. On those occasions when they have flexed their
voting muscle through the AARP, seniors have done little more than
defend programs that guarantee them minimal independence. They
have neither gouged the public treasury nor held the nation for ransom.
By no stretch of the imagination can lobbying for catastrophic medical
insurance or defending a cost-of-living adjustment that permits a Social
Security recipient to buy a better grade of beef be characterized as
"self-enrichment." Since the days of the Townsend Plan, the goal of senior political action has been to maintain a decent minimum standard of
life without unduly burdening one's children. Those who raise ground-
less fears about the recent electoral power of senior Americans are
perpetrating an opportunistic deception. The clout of senior Americans
hardly compares with that of any major financial interest or industrial
lobby.

But all that may be about to change in ways no political philosopher
could have imagined. As the inherited ideologies of the past would have
it, revolutionary change arises from the dispossessed and wretched of
the Earth. The obvious candidates for that role have been workers and
ethnic minorities, but never the elders of the society. Perhaps that is
because so few people survived into old age in the nineteenth century,
and those who did arrived at that status depleted of resources and
strength. Since they were no longer in the workforce, they were regarded
as dependents of those who were. Their interests were those of the
families that fed and housed them. Or, if they possessed material wealth,
they were assimilated to the ruling class.

Now as the New People move into their retirement years, they have
the chance to expand their own political interests into a senior populism
committed to large-scale public programs and compassionate policies. If

their orientation is not "radical" in the traditional sense of the term, they may nonetheless prove to be a greater challenge to entrepreneurial values than any radical movement of the past. And they may do more. They may at last give political standing to those questions about the greater purposes of life that we have always relegated to the realm of personal philosophy. It is a matter of asking of our society as a whole what every man and woman finally comes to ask of himself or herself: what has it all been for, whether my own lifetime of toil or the nation's centuries of growth and development?

Lost in the Crowd

"It is like wartime," Miss Taylor remarked.
"What do you say?"
"Being over 70 is like being engaged in a war. All our friends are going or gone and we survive amongst the dead and dying as on a battlefield."
She is wandering in her mind and becoming morbid, thought Dame Lettie.

— MURIEL SPARK, *Memento Mori* (1959)

Those who see the elderly as selfish opportunists and view their programs as a crushing liability of the welfare state blind themselves to the true pathos that many Americans still find awaiting them in their senior years. Entitlements critics convey the misleading impression that Social Security represents a ticket to the golf course surrounding a Miami Beach condo. But they must know that is not so. The economist Paul Elkins comes closer to the truth when he observes that we live in a society where "old people die of hypothermia while the shops overflow with videos and computer games." He might have added that in the United States we now spend more than twice as much on gambling (in excess of $500 billion) as we do on Medicare each year.

Nobody lives high on a Social Security check if that is all they have to fall back on in retirement. One-quarter of working- and middle-class retirees receive nearly all of their monthly income — as of the 1990s, a maximum of $1,500, and an average of $750 — from Social Security. About one-seventh have no other income at all, and about one-tenth fall well below the official poverty line. For many, retirement puts an end to a decent paycheck but not to work. As of the early 1990s, five million Social Security recipients still held meagerly paid, part-time jobs such as crossing guard, stadium guard, parking lot attendant, or night watchman in order to make ends meet. For these Americans — and their numbers will grow steadily — Social Security is all the difference between the deck and the sea. The great majority of recipients have a poor to moderate living standard or are dependent on relatives to stay alive.

The United States has more indigent elders than any of the industrial nations: 12 percent of all Social Security recipients. They would have every right to demand more. If from time to time they get a break on a cost-of-living adjustment, that is hardly a criminal offense, especially after a lifetime in the workforce. Who ultimately gets their Social Security money anyway? Their landlord, the supermarket, the electric company, the druggist, and the pharmaceutical houses. Like all money given to the low-income strata, Social Security is a transfer payment on its way through the hands of the poor to merchants, investors, entrepreneurs, and doctors.

As for those who can afford a comfortable retirement on a sunny beach, they have saved up for that purpose; they are spending their own money. Should these well-off seniors be means-tested and given less? That may depend on where the line is drawn. A retirement income of $40,000–50,000 may seem like a lot at first glance. But what if some of that money is being siphoned off to job-worried children? And what if some of it is being used up by uncovered medical expenses? As long as Medicare and Medicaid are under threat of drastic revisions, many seemingly well-off retirees may be putting money aside for future medical emergencies, especially nursing home care, to spare their children the expense. Ever since Social Security was put on the books by the New Deal, conservative elements have claimed that the program diminishes people's incentive to save during their working years. Yet seniors who did save for their retirement are now being used to paint a picture of all elders as parasitic freeloaders. Facing a critique like this is a no-win situation.

Images of greedy seniors are worse than insulting; they mask the true suffering that can still be found among the elderly. A 1995 report in the *Washington Post* offers us a bleak picture of what it means for the poorest to grow old in America. "They were the urban anonymous, living in the odd isolation of large apartment complexes or the modest homes they had clung to after the death of a spouse. Whatever the stories of their lives — their families, friends, and jobs, their triumphs and disappointments — when they died no one apparently knew or cared."

The report is about the victims of the great Chicago heat wave of 1995. The total number of those struck down during that terrible summer was 591, the vast majority of them elderly. Most had somebody to bury them, but there were some forty, with an average age of sixty-seven, whose bodies went unclaimed. The report continues, "The heat wave struck hardest at the elderly who may have outlived family and friends and so were left to spend their final days alone, unknown or unnoticed even by their closest neighbors."

"Lost in the crowd" — that was how the fate of these seniors was described by the local clergyman who has been coming to Homewood Cemetery each month to offer a brief burial ceremony for the city's abandoned dead.

Even when it comes to the supposedly ruinous cost of Medicare, we should bear in mind how modest a contribution it still makes to the lives of many of its recipients. The poor who go on Medicare (those who earn below $15,000) have far and away the greatest number of serious illnesses. They bring to Medicare a lifetime of the poor health practices endemic among those at the poverty line: bad diet, smoking, unattended chronic problems for which they could not afford to seek treatment. A 1997 survey estimates that three-quarters of the Medicare population earns below $25,000 a year. But the recipients in that category use over 80 percent of the costs, in contrast to the needs of the better-off. Those who earn above $50,000 in their senior years make minimal demands on the system.[10]

If the overwrought rhetoric of the generational accountants prevails in setting our nation's budgetary priorities, we are certain to be reading more stories like the Chicago heat wave in the years ahead: pitiful reports of forgotten senior citizens who have fallen into various black social holes. Even the most rugged individualist should find it difficult to write off the senior poor as chronically indigent failures. These are yesterday's working and middle classes, our parents and grandparents who built the economy we have inherited. Any savings they may have failed to lay aside for their retirement were most likely spent straightening teeth and providing a college education for today's taxpayers. Beyond that, they spent because they were good Americans — meaning good consumers. How harshly are they to be blamed for doing what the entire economic system of the nation — the merchants, the advertisers, the banks, the credit card companies — wanted them to do? If savings is what the business community can honestly say it expects from the public, would it consider banning advertising from television or illegalizing credit cards? Surely not. Demanding thrift in this wonderful land of brands is a counsel of perfection.

The Dark Side

As for those seniors who must accept whatever low-cost institutional care public authorities or private sources make available, they may be in for a risky time. "Elder abuse" is now a well-defined legal and sociological category. The harsh cuts in social services undertaken in the 1980s — part of President Reagan's militant campaign to "get the government off our backs" — led to widespread austerity in nursing homes. Complaints by the frail elderly were many times met by punishment, intimidation, and violence — often enough indeed to produce scandals that reached the front pages. The problem is not limited to professional caregivers; adult offspring, who may be too burdened to handle the responsibility, may also resort to physical and emotional abuse.[11]

Or more surreptitiously, elder abuse may disguise itself as standard medical care. My grandmother, who reached the age of 104, finished her life on a steady regimen of Halcyon, a tranquilizer that was once routinely used to relax and soothe the elderly. She began to turn seriously paranoid, fearing her own children, behavior easily identified as senility. She finally refused to eat, one of the most common ways for the depressed and desperate elderly to die. The death certificates for such cases usually give heart failure as the cause. Only after her death did the truth about Halcyon break into the news. The drug, it was discovered, produces severe emotional dislocation, primarily paranoia. Except for such intervals of unaccountable fear and suspicion in her last days, my grandmother, feeble as she was in many ways, was mentally alert to the end of her life. The conventional medical treatment she received stemmed from her busy doctor's conviction that the best he could do for her was to dope her up. After all, she was such an old lady!

There is another, more sobering statistic that reveals the true facts of aging for many Americans. The Centers for Disease Control and Prevention report that as of the 1990s elderly Americans have been running the highest suicide rate in the nation.[12] "They see it as a solution to their problems," reports one counselor who deals in depression among the elderly. The statistics bear a striking correlation to the enveloping political climate. When Dr. Townsend launched his campaign for old-age pensions during the Great Depression, one of his most urgent goals was to address the suicides that were becoming commonplace among elders who did not wish to burden their hard-pressed children.[13] Then, between 1940 and 1980, the period that gave older workers wartime jobs and later saw the creation of the entitlements programs, suicide among seniors declined sharply. But from the advent of Reaganomics in 1980 through the early 1990s, suicides among those over sixty-five rose by nearly 10 percent to become the highest rate for any age group. Among the most heartbreaking stories of our time is that of the elderly couple who have run out of friends, relatives, and resources and who finish their lives in a double suicide.

In dealing with the lives of the elderly, we are up against an intractable existential dilemma. The young may simply lack the capacity to imagine the trepidation with which less than wealthy seniors face their final decades. Youth carries with it certain commonplace advantages: the ability to scuffle and change jobs amid bewildering economic fluctuations, to wait out the crises in one's life and go on to better days. That is exactly what age takes away. After a certain point, elders cannot get back into the workforce and find some way to supplement declining or lost income. Older workers, especially older men in lines of work that require agility and muscle, may find themselves under pressure to move out of their jobs in their late fifties — before they are injured and apply for extensive medical care and disability awards. Once they slow down, even if it is because the job hurts, they rapidly lose their value in the workplace.

When we hear proposals for raising the retirement age, we should ask whether that reform would apply to miners, truckers, outdoor construction and steel workers. How much heavy lifting do we want to expect from men and women over sixty? For that matter, how many seventy-year-old pilots, air traffic controllers, or brain surgeons do we want to keep on the job simply because they cannot afford to retire? They may persevere at their work, but in some of these occupations it may be best for the public safety to allow earlier rather than later retirement.

Even if older workers hold up well for a good many years after sixty, they must always fear physical incapacity and with it the dependency that takes away all hope of "getting back on your feet." Think how it must feel, then, if the message seniors more and more frequently hear in the media is that they are an intolerable budgetary burden. Not all of them will find the courage to grow feisty and fight back. Even those who do may be sadly deceived in their efforts. Thanks to the fiscal panic that entitlements critics have helped to spread, playing upon the anxiety of the elderly is becoming a growth industry in the United States. Older Americans, living in isolation and on meager means, become easy targets for direct mail and telephone solicitors who inundate them with urgent announcements that their Social Security and Medicare benefits are about to vanish. One typical letter, marked "personal" and mailed in an official-looking express envelope, declares, "The liberal monster is primed to rip your Social Security to shreds. Enclosed is the one document that can protect your benefits." But that document has to be accompanied by a $75 contribution. There are nearly indigent seniors who have donated hundreds of dollars to fright-mail scams like this. Some say they lie awake at night dreading the loss of the only source of income they have.[14]

In the discussion of longevity, we may have to probe depths of fear and demoralization that the young cannot even imagine. The time may come when even the luckiest among us will have to look into those depths. In that moment, will our fellow citizens have something better to offer us than a desolate hour in the middle of the night, a cheap pistol, a bottle of barbiturates?

Just as there are issues that do not gracefully translate across the barriers of gender, race, and class, so too there are matters that do not easily cross the barrier of age. The world as one sees it looking back from age seventy or eighty is radically different from that same world seen looking forward from twenty. Family, work, wealth, security, love, faith, and hope are all transformed in the lens of age. We have not even begun to talk frankly about the great issues of this approaching cultural reappraisal, nor will we as long as issues of money dominate the demographic facts of life. A society that tilts as sharply toward the senior years as ours now does clearly needs to find a new measure of social progress that includes longevity itself among its highest values. Otherwise, we may be left to conclude that the gift of long life is more a curse than a blessing. Despair may then become the most lethal disease among the elderly, and the one for which the doctors can find no cure.

The Ragged Fringe

In the course of this study, we will come upon several daring visions of our longevous future. They can be found at all levels of our culture, from specialists in the field to popular science magazines. The head of the American Academy of Anti-Aging Medicine announces that by the mid twenty-first century "physical immortality will be a reality." A popular magazine that reports on life-extension research and medications carries on its banner the slogan "Living Longer, Extending Life Span, Reaching for Immortality."

Yet it may be the case that, in gaining the ground we have already won for life extension, we have used up most of the progress we can expect to make. Improved hygienic conditions, public health measures like vaccines, heroic forms of surgery, better diet, lifestyle changes, and environmental care may eventually leave us at the intractable boundaries of the physical organism. One medical historian has proposed an "insult accumulation theory," which holds that aging must of necessity contribute to the increasing morbidity rate. His gloomy conclusion is that older people carry a load of scars and blows into their later years; the traumas add up; the result is disease of some kind striking at a weakened organism.[15] Many microbiologists believe that as the cells of the body grow older, their vulnerability to disease increases. Medical science may ultimately run out of measures to postpone that result.

Whether at the age of 30 (as in Paleolithic times) or 130, eventually the inherent frailty of the flesh enters its claim. Even if we could all one day expect to become centenarians, somewhere not far beyond there may lie a physical barrier that we will never cross. This has led Anthony Smith to a gloomy conclusion. "Put at its crudest, the advances in medicine are enabling more and more of us to achieve senility."[16] Dr. Allan Roses, a specialist at Duke University in the genetics of late-onset diseases, takes the same position. He believes that even if we eliminate all other causes of death, those who might then reach an age of about 140 will finally succumb to Alzheimer's disease. Our best hope in his eyes is that the disease can be delayed for more and more people until they pass the age of 100. But after that, he believes, "we are all moving toward Alzheimer's Disease, but at different rates and ages."[17]

That is where the dilemma of the ragged fringe begins.

By "ragged fringe" I mean the inevitable vulnerability of the physical organism, the point at which we must find the wisdom that Sigmund Freud once called "acquiescence in fate."

We tend to see every advance in medical progress as a clear victory over death, as if we were driving back an enemy who will one day be defeated and sue for surrender. But the military metaphor misleads. Death is not a foe over whom we will ever gain a final victory. Every elderly person who does not simply drop dead after years of perfect health must at last slip away into some protracted state of physical decline, possibly requiring more and more care as life draws to its end. Death's strategy in the face of each new medical victory, if we must speak in these terms, is that of strategic retreat — until at last we, the "victors," are worn down and must give up.

This grim fact does not preclude continuing good news on the aging front. For example, the National Long Term Care Survey, a 1996 federal study of some twenty thousand seniors over the age of sixty-five, concludes that a growing number of the elderly are now able to care for themselves. Incapacitating illness among the Medicare population has been dropping 1 to 2 percent each year since the survey started in 1982. Chronic diseases like high blood pressure, arthritis, and emphysema among those who reach sixty-five are steadily declining. One demographer estimates that these improvements alone, mainly due to better public health, nutrition, and hygiene, have saved Medicare $200 billion between 1962 and the mid-1990s.[18]

Similarly, disabilities among the aged are being postponed more and more effectively. Estrogen supplements keep women in far better condition longer. Even the nursing home population has benefited from high-resistance strength training that doubles the power of quadriceps and makes those once bound to wheelchairs ambulatory.[19] The New England Centenarian Study at the Harvard Medical School has discovered that seniors who reach their nineties tend to be healthier than those in their eighties and seventies. Move ten years further along, and some 20 percent of surviving centenarians may still be alert and competent — some even holding intellectually demanding jobs.

All to the good. But at *some* point, durability and good luck give out. Our life span outruns the health span. Despite the resiliency of many in the ninety-plus population, half of those who reach that age can be found in nursing homes in deteriorating physical and mental condition. And what else would we expect? Keeping people in good shape into their seventies, eighties, and nineties only postpones the inevitable for another decade or two. Few would question the value of those extra years. But somewhere not far beyond them waits expensive surgery and medication, the intensive care unit, and nursing care — and with them rising medical bills. Thus, the more people who reach a healthy seventy or eighty or ninety years, the more people there will be moving into the ragged fringe. From each individual's viewpoint, an additional decade, even one more year, of active life is a blessing. But from society's viewpoint, it does not matter how long physical decline and incapacity are delayed; sooner or later, they appear and the costs mount.

There are gerontologists who have taken a strong position on this matter. Leonard Hayflick, for example, is "apprehensive about extending average life expectancy beyond age one hundred once the leading killers are resolved, because the result would be disease-free but nonetheless functionally weaker, still inexorably aging people. . . . Old people will simply become older, condemned to the vicissitudes of a continuing aging process. And that outcome, I believe, is undesirable for most people."[20] Hayflick argues that we should round off longevity research when it has eliminated the current major killers — heart disease and cancer — and settle for a life span of about 120.

He may be right. The extra years that medical science adds beyond ninety or one hundred may not be worth living — as judged rationally and in the abstract. But that is rarely how this most vital of life-and-death decisions is made. Unless people are in great pain, they may cling to life out of fear or longing. Or they may build up false expectations about the years ahead as less than rational forces come to play an inordinate role in the coming elder culture.

In this sense, medical science is the victim of its own claims and successes. It has achieved so much that it is easy to believe its triumphs may continue forever. The very fact that new things keep coming to light — new techniques, new medications — encourages us to hang on longer. There will always be researchers who promise miracles: skin that will not wrinkle, eyes that will not dim, limbs that will not lose the vigor of youth. Estrogen is doing wonders both physical and mental for older women and may one day also be prescribed for men, who have already been promised drugs that will overcome baldness and impotence. Cosmetic surgeons are busily finding ways to put a good face on old age. The media will play a key role in this, presenting uplifting reports of energetic seniors still climbing mountains or winning dance contests. Such stories encourage the belief that one's own senior years may yet benefit from unexpected discoveries.

At a certain point, matters of medicine overlap with matters of commerce. Business interests are bound to work up an ever greater investment in merchandising hope. Retirement community entrepreneurs have an obvious reason to paint rosy pictures of their clients sporting on the green; cruise-ship and vacation firms are already populating their commercials with carefree seniors dancing the night away. Pharmaceutical companies are certain to fill television and senior magazines with more and more tantalizing advertisements for pills and tonics guaranteed to revive the failing body. "It's a great time to be silver," announces a vitamin supplement firm, featuring a vignette of happy, active elders. As the senior market grows, others will find ways to exploit such wishful fantasies. The New People may soon find themselves surrounded with treacherous illusions of eternal youth. Keeping the discussion of longevity real is going to be a struggle.

I count myself among those who doubt the value of adding a few more months of enfeebled life when the measures become heroic and exorbitant. Suppose we could choose in advance which procedures are worth their long-range cost; suppose we could agree what "worth" means in this context. Perhaps then we could close down certain lines of research before we had committed both our hopes and resources to them.

But that calculation is quite unrealistic. At first sight, everything that extends life looks desirable. That is what the physicians behind the advance draw upon in winning public approval and financial support for their research. People do not leap into the ragged fringe; they edge into it step by step as they accept each new medical marvel. The bait is hope. It is only when they are already on the fringe that they and their doctors may learn that the life they have gained brings with it intolerable pain or disability and the need for more medical care than anybody anticipated. Until our culture provides some very different way of understanding death than as a defeat, what can we expect but that seniors and their families will gamble on survival?

And what will we do if the ragged fringe should one day be filled with severely incapacitated nursing home inmates and Alzheimer's victims who are somebody's loved ones? The answer is obvious: *we will care for them.* It will cost, and we will pay the cost. We will accept it as our peculiar modern plight in the same way that our ancestors accepted plagues and famines. The struggle to keep the ragged fringe as distant and as narrow as possible will surely continue, but medical science may one day have to tell us that "living long and dying fast" is the best we can hope for. In that cruel interval between the "long" and the "fast," the New People will be called to nobility. They will have to pioneer policies of altruism that have no precedent in human history. They will have to see the care we afford the old and the ill as a prime measure of our social character.

Memento Mori

In analyzing the cost of entitlements, one must make no rosy assumptions. Aging will not bankrupt us, but nonetheless the industrial societies of the world have been swept into a permanent and expensive demographic shift. We must accept as given that longevity requires a substantial reallocation of the national wealth. As of the 1990s, the total cost of medical care in the United States was over $800 billion (11 percent of GDP). One estimate predicts that it will mount to $2.2 trillion by 2010 (15 percent of GDP).[21] The expected rise is due not only to the aging of the nation but to the increase in such medically dependent populations as premature babies and AIDS patients. Is that too much? Or too little? The President's Council of Economic Advisers cannot decide the matter for us. There is no iron law of economics we can invoke. Only we ourselves, working by what our hearts and consciences tell us and on the advice of the best ethical counselors we can find, can give the answer. Unless we find ourselves in some future cold war that brings with it an arms race as costly as that of the 1950s, 1960s, and 1970s, the cost of an aging population may indeed rise until it outweighs all other budgetary responsibilities. But, as I suggest in later chapters, the total benefits of longevity — cultural, ethical, and even economic, the gains it brings us in wisdom, compassion, and spiritual fulfillment — may far outbalance that cost.

Once we accept that perspective on the matter, we can face up to the fact that even many of the short-term economies that are being proposed for Medicare will not save money over the long run, not if we keep the dilemma of the ragged fringe clearly in view. No matter how many rabbits we pull out of the budgetary hat, demographic reality begins with the recognition of the one overriding fact we have taken as the basis for this study: more (and more) people are living longer (and longer). Combine that fact with the simple truth that few people stay healthy to the day they die, or die quickly when they do reach old age, and it becomes clear that, even with rigorous cost containment, the cost of senior medical care is bound to rise steadily. That is inherent in modern medical technology.

For example, the gerontologist Bernard Starr has wisely recommended greater use of preventive medical counseling as part of Medicare. He suggests that counseling be connected with a mandatory schedule of monetary incentives and disincentives. In a *Barron's* magazine article titled "This Longevity Is Killing Us," Starr points out that, "despite our spending a greater percentage of gross domestic product on health care than any other country, a scant 3 percent of that spending goes for prevention." He advocates a number of reforms, among them: granting credits toward health services premiums for those who participate in fitness programs; requiring chronic smokers to do community service with patients dying from smoking-related emphysema; and assigning personal health-care counselors to the members of all health plans, including Medicare and Medicaid.[22]

All this is well worth doing from the individual's viewpoint. But factor in the true long-term costs. Testing and screening always produce a number of false warnings that require more expensive testing to check and confirm. On the other hand, if the tests are correct, they are apt to find problems early and result in higher costs at that point to treat patients who must finally develop other conditions that will eventually kill them when they are farther out on the ragged fringe. Extending life is a worthy goal, but it does not save money.

Nobody conceived of Social Security and Medicare as object lessons in the high price of progress, but that is what these programs are turning out to be. They are forcing us to ask an unprecedented question: what is life worth by the day, the week, the year? When we say that life is infinitely precious, do we really believe that? Working from hearsay, early anthropological studies reported that the Inuit once left their elderly to starve on an ice floe when food was short in the community. Would we institute measures like that in a society where the hospital may be located within sight of the theme park and the shopping mall?

The science fiction film *Logan's Run* tells of a society where everybody is deceived into committing suicide at the age of thirty. Those who agree to self-immolation are promised safe passage into a land of ease and plenty. It is the only way the society can maintain its high investment in entertaining diversions and sybaritic pleasures. In another anti-utopian saga, *Soylent Green,* the elderly are encouraged to volunteer for painless euthanasia. In a hopelessly overpopulated world, they are encouraged to die the way Socrates supposedly died, dozing off peacefully after drinking hemlock. They can even choose the music they wish to have played in the background.

Unless we are prepared to dispose of our elders in some similarly economical way, all our thinking about the costs of longevity has to begin with sober acceptance of the fact that we are dealing with a responsibility that is here to stay and is going to rise in cost as more people experience the benefits of modern medicine. No honest study of longevity can avoid that fact.

Memento mori. Think upon death. That phrase, once carved on the walls of every medieval church, now finds a place in public policy. It reminds us that affordability is an ethical, not an economic, category. All of us, but especially the young and healthy, have to ask about that final stage of life: *what do I want to find waiting for my parents, for my children, for me, when each of us gets there?* The sooner we face that question, the easier our transition will be into the compassionate community we must become.

4

The Ecology of Wisdom

IN THE YEAR 1798, Thomas Malthus published a slender book that was destined to have more influence than any work of its size in modern times. Little more than a few hundred pages in length, his *Essay on Population* was hailed at once as a brilliant, if sobering, contribution to economic theory. Read by the young Charles Darwin, the book would eventually launch the field of evolutionary biology. Moreover, as the first serious effort to connect a species to its environment in a dynamic and reciprocal way, it has come to be appreciated as a founding document in environmental science. Malthus worked out a simple but ingenious relationship between human beings and their food supply. His conclusion that fertility must always outstrip sustenance was, he believed, a "fixed law of nature." Thus, there will always be a "struggle of existence." Kindness, altruism, charity — all these are no more than "mere feathers that float on the surface."

"More People Are Living Longer . . . Good!"

We now know that Malthus, despite the impact he had on social philosophy, was wrong. In thinking about human beings the way one might more properly think about rodents, his theory overlooked a basic cultural factor: industrial societies become more cunning as they grow in numbers. The same scientific and technological genius that creates overpopulated industrial cities can be used to find solutions to overpopulation. As the last few centuries have shown, we have found myriad ways to increase food production and limit reproduction. But Malthus left out one more factor, perhaps the most crucial of all when it comes to our long-term demographic destiny. He never touched upon longevity as an environmentally imperative phase in the history of modern society. Less still was he aware of the revolutionary changes longevity brings with it in ethics and economics. Yet just as deserts spread where land is over-grazed and rain forests flourish in a tropic climate, so industrial societies must age and, as they age, profit by their experience. That is what makes the campaign against entitlements so ludicrously misguided: it fails to grasp the magnitude of the phenomenon it seeks to alter.

Something vast and irreversible is happening in the demographics of the modern world, a revolution that permanently affects our relations with the Earth as a whole. But in contrast to other developments like acid rain or global warming, which threaten to diminish the quality of life, longevity is — potentially — the best thing that has happened since the advent of industrial cities. With all the force of a "fixed law," it confronts us with an ultimate limit to growth. If we might fancifully imagine the biosphere thinking about the antics of its troublesome human children, the thought that may loom largest in its mind at the beginning of the twenty-first century is, "More people are living longer . . . good! About time they grew up." Not only was Malthus wrong about population, he was *radically* wrong. Unable to foresee the longev-ity revolution, he was ignorant of the single most important social factor in our future. There is no guarantee that the New People will achieve environmental enlightenment, but the aging opportunity is the next best thing: a pressing social transformation that makes enlightenment all but obligatory.

I recall the words of a Sierra Club activist as he despaired for the fate of the Earth beneath the punishing assaults of urban industrial society. He was convinced, as so many environmentalists have been, that popu-lation will grow, that consumption will increase, that resources will dwindle, that pollution will mount, that species will perish — all as the result of human greed to which he could see no limit. He was, in short, a Malthusian. "There is only one solution," he concluded with wishful resignation. "We have to import a new human species that has some sense of eternal values." The New People *are* that population — or as close to it as we are likely to come.

That, at least, is the possibility we will explore in this analysis of the longevity revolution as a global, environmental factor.

Cultural Demographics

In the early 1960s, when our society was more daringly youthful, an American president who seemed to embody the exuberance of the period rallied the nation to spend billions of dollars to land a man on the moon. Today it is likely that the same Americans who, in their youth, cheered John Kennedy for his bold decision are preoccupied with less spectacular goals than colonizing outer space. One would not be surprised to learn that they are far more worried about holding their jobs in an unsettled economy and paying off their overworked credit cards. Not much further down on their list of priorities might be a nagging anxiety about finding affordable medical insurance and providing for a secure retirement. Those who may be facing (as of the mid-1990s) upwards of $30,000 a year to pay nursing home costs for their aging parents may wonder, as they make each monthly payment, where their children will one day find the money to afford as much for them. Concerns like these are not limited to seniors; they implicate whole families and finally whole societies as matters of public policy.

Viewing the political and economic behavior of people in this way might be called *cultural demographics* — a head count that does not leave out the hearts and minds of the population. That is actually the way marketing analysts use the term "demographics" when they are sizing up a product. Raw numbers matter, but a refined evaluation of preferences, income, gender, ethnicity, and class is even more important. The intention is frankly commercial; it concentrates on obvious money questions. What will any particular public buy? How much will it buy? At what price? How can we get their attention and induce them to spend?

Environmentalists usually regard this approach to markets and audiences as the enemy's way of thinking. But there is something they might learn from the hucksters. It is as simple as recognizing that, in its relations with the natural environment, a human population cannot be dealt with in the same way as other species. Leave out tastes, values, ideals, sensibilities, and the numbers tell very little about the use that population will make of its space and resources — surely not enough to make sensible predictions or intelligent policy. How much pressure will a human population place upon its habitat? Is it not obvious that the answer has everything to do with whether the population in question is a community of medieval monks living a life of fasting and prayer or a suburban tract filled with swinging singles addicted to luxury cars and young marrieds who spend most of their leisure time at the mall?

Cultural demographics assumes that age is among the factors that most decisively shape people's collective environmental relations — even when the people themselves may have other things on their mind.

Thus, for cultural demographics it is a matter of importance that many members of the baby boom generation are beginning to register the fact that they have provided poorly for their retirement years. A 1997 survey by the AARP concluded that the vast majority of middle-aged Americans had given little realistic thought to the cost of a lengthy retirement; many were only just waking up to what awaits them. Wishfully, almost desperately, an increasing number were placing their faith in the stock market. In the view of one researcher on the project, the survey found more "false confidence" than sound planning.[1] Some retirement counselors are now warning Americans in their forties that they will have to accumulate over a million dollars to guarantee a comfortable retirement. Whatever the truth of such intimidating estimates, they make for cautious choices.

Those choices can begin to influence values as early as midlife — about the time people begin to fear that losing their job could spell disaster. The fear is well founded. If they find themselves in dire straits, what will they have to fall back on? Welfare has ceased to be an entitlement; it has been stripped to the bone, and the unemployed are now identified (in the eyes of conservative leaders) as little better than a public nuisance. To go for any length of time without a job, a retirement plan, or medical insurance is to be performing without a net. All these fears mount as one ages out of the workforce. At the age of sixty, one is too old to scramble, especially if there is nothing to scramble for but part-time jobs flipping hamburgers. Multiply personal hopes and fears like these by tens of millions and the result is a force that cannot help but change the economic agenda.

A workshop practice used by some environmental activists is to ask people to "think like a mountain." There is another more difficult exercise worth trying. *Think like a marketing analyst.*

In later chapters we will survey the way maturity alters habits of consumption. Suffice it to say here that the senior market, as advertisers currently see it, has rotten "demographics." True, the numbers and the dollars are there, but so too is a sales resistance that advertisers find formidable. It is hard to sell to grown-up people on the basis of hot copy and glossy imagery alone — and all the more so if that population has other things on its mind, like a heart condition, an ailing spouse, failing joints, the cost of supporting live-in children, or a far greater interest in courses at the university extension than in a dynamite new car. But for that very reason, the cultural demographics of seniors ought to look promising to environmentalists. The analysis of senior values may begin with simple statistics, but it will finally have to integrate the ideas and ideals that people take with them into their later years. Within such a perspective, matters that are often treated purely statistically can assume a very different force.

Death, for example. The death rate normally appears in demographic charts as a simple calculation: so many deaths per thousand. But in living experience, death is not a statistic; it is as profoundly personal as anything can be. How people deal with mortality as it closes in upon them has everything to do with their habits in life. Simpler creatures ask no questions of their ultimate fate. We do. For cultural demographics that is a significant point, because the answers we find prescribe meaning. And the meaning we find for our lives becomes a part of our greater ecology.

How to Count a Population

The arrival of the New People confronts us with a new population problem, one that belongs to the industrial societies rather than the Third World. Heretofore, the image that has come to mind when we think of "overpopulation" is the back alleys of Calcutta or Kinshasa, filled with starving, jobless people — hungry, powerless masses whom the rich have seen fit to treat as invisible. Population alarmists, viewing the plight of these impoverished societies, have urged aggressive population policies, but more than that, they have raised an impassioned moral appeal. In addition to achieving population control in the underdeveloped nations, they have called for consumption control in the affluent societies. They incorporate per capita resource use into their analysis, arguing that the citizens of First World nations consume far more than their share of energy and resources. In the words of Paul and Anne Ehrlich, "Americans are superconsumers and use rather inefficient technologies to service their consumption. . . . America's total environmental impact is roughly six times that of the 900 million people of India." In this sense, the Ehrlichs see the United States as the "most over-populated nation in the world."[2]

The images that population alarmists have of First World consumption are the gas-guzzling automobile and expensive beef — luxuries that can be easily targeted for ethical condemnation. Suppose, however, there were *another* population in the First World that was large and growing, but whose need was not for luxury goods. Suppose this was a dependent population that required a reasonable provision of food, clothing, shelter, and medical care. And what if that population, unlike the propertyless and disempowered millions of the Third World, possessed rights that could not be ignored? What if it had the power to elect governments and demand the necessities of life? That would give us a new politics of population, one that could arise only in the developed economies. That is exactly what we see happening in the First World today, where active millions are living out a second life that frequently stretches twenty and thirty years beyond retirement, and where millions more, who are highly dependent on costly medical services, now fill hospitals and nursing homes.

Clearly, we need a new demographic calculus. We must ask what the age range of the population is and what effective claim its older members have upon care and sustenance. Life expectancy and life span must be added in. And more than that. Along with those purely quantitative factors, we must take into account the changing quality of life that comes with an aging society. In the advanced industrial societies, the economic impact of all population statistics must now be calculated as life expectancy multiplied by the cost of the social services and medical care that are likely to be necessary at each age. In the United States, this would be the cost of entitlements plus other forms of senior care, including private family care that may remove a husband or wife from paid labor outside the home.

Thus, for example, when demographers predict that the population of the United States will stabilize at some 305 million by the year 2040, it is important to add that more than one-quarter of that number will be seniors over sixty and on their way out of the workforce — many into volunteer services, higher education, and political activism, and some into intensive, long-term nursing care. Among the latter will be a small nation of some 14 million Americans suffering from Alzheimer's disease. With less than half that number stricken by the disease today, the annual cost of advanced Alzheimer's care is $100 billion. One estimate places the cost of the Alzheimer's population in the year 2050 at $1 trillion.

The new demographic calculus should also include the future shape of the population: namely, that it will continue trending toward age and away from youth for the indefinite future. That fact — especially if we take into account the mature ethical values associated with age — has everything to do with social policy and fiscal planning. For example, cultural demographics includes the growing use that retired citizens are making of educational resources *and what they may be learning that makes a political difference.* The may, after all, be reading a great deal of environmental literature with a view to becoming good environmental citizens.

That is the hope of Rabbi Zalman Schachter-Shalomi in one of the most searching philosophical examinations of longevity. Based upon the workshop he has been leading in "spiritual eldering," Rabbi Schachter-Shalomi expects to see the coming older generation "foster a renewed relationship with our devastated planet Earth." He is convinced that elders have a stronger inborn sense of "organic connectivity to our environment." This is an expression of their "completing instinct," the dominant psychological reflex of our later years. "By exploring the spiritual dimension of life, [elders] encourage younger people not to equate standard of living with quality of living. As both older and younger people learn to find fulfillment in nonmaterial ways and consume less of the Earth's resources, they reduce the damage inflicted on the environment and become willing collaborators in healing the planet."[3]

Schachter-Shalomi has called for councils of senior ecowardens who will monitor the local environment and a national environmental senior corps through which elders can serve as consultants. Whether the New People will become environmentally enlightened in so conscious and active a way is impossible to say. But the "organic connectivity" Schachter-Shalomi has in mind might express itself more humbly in ways that are not obviously ecological. It may make itself felt as the increasing influence of mature taste and common sense, a force that can work in many subterranean ways to tame the worst excesses of the industrial marketplace.

The formulation that follows assumes nothing more than such a minimal change of behavior and values on the part of the world's aging populations. In a highly schematic way, it summarizes what we have said so far about the longevity revolution and then extends the analysis as an environmental impact statement that includes the cultural demographics of the New People. What we have here is a set of three interconnected loops that feed into one another as they move forward in time. If the pattern they describe holds true, then it may represent the most important insight into population dynamics since Thomas Malthus opened the field in the early days of the industrial revolution.

The First Loop: Greater Longevity, More Costly Entitlements

To begin with the obvious: thanks to progress in public health, nutrition, and modern medical science, we have found ways to extend life expectancy and possibly the life span. As the number of senior citizens in the population increases, the need for and the cost of medical care rises. Both the need and the cost act as incentives for research and investment, encouraging more medical progress. Research in longevity becomes an ever livelier field. Health care (insurance, pharmaceuticals, hospitals, nursing homes) becomes a new, extended stage in industrial economies, attracting steadily more capital, technical talent, and entrepreneurial skill. As new techniques are discovered and applied, more people benefit from the advances. Accordingly, the ratio of older to younger in the population increases.

Entrepreneurial values contribute to longevity in other ways, some of them highly ironic. These days enlightened employers, seeking to hold down the cost of medical insurance, take pains to look after the health of their workers. They offer heart-healthy foods in the company cafeteria, they encourage regular physical checkups, perhaps they open a gym on the premises to provide aerobic training. If the employer does not offer such care, insurers might, sending out literature or lecturers to pitch for better diets and exercise and to warn against smoking.

No doubt the result is real savings. But it is also longevity. The same healthy practices that save money on the payroll lead to a larger, more long-lived retirement population. So the cost of entitlements rises and with them the payroll taxes that employers must pay. At which point, the very companies that did so much to encourage good health may complain about the cost of Social Security. They may even contribute to one of the conservative think tanks that clamor for an end to entitlements. But if the cost of entitlements results in so great a fiscal burden, then employers would do better to discourage a healthy lifestyle. Why not serve lard sandwiches and french fries in the cafeteria and provide free cigarettes?

Unless we can imagine some reason why medical science and sound advice about health should be brought to a halt, it is difficult to see how longevity and entitlements can be kept from circling round and round and increasing with each cycle. Moreover, if we include in our calculations the effects of any single major biotechnology breakthrough in reversing the aging process, the circle might begin to accelerate, producing more older people who would extend their careers not only in literature, art, and finance but in medical science, thus multiplying the medical expertise of our society. With each turn of the circle, more experienced and qualified scientists would give us more research in longevity and, very likely, more significant results.

The Second Loop: The Growing Dominance of Senior Values

As the number of senior citizens grows, their collective voting power increases — at least in the democratic societies. Voting is, to be sure, a modest form of political action, but older citizens have ways to amplify their power at the ballot box. They have more money to contribute to political campaigns than younger voters and more time to make available in the political process. As the active years extend deeper into old age, we may expect to see more seniors working as campaign volunteers and lobbyists. We can also expect to see them running for office — and winning, especially if their rivals continue their granny-bashing ways. Accordingly, the influence of their needs and values upon the political agenda is bound to increase. While there is a wide range of opinion in the senior population, their values would clearly lead them to work toward expanding welfare state benefits and all goods and services related to those benefits.

At some point, diverting resources to the welfare state sector serves as a brake upon entrepreneurial dynamism and conventional economic growth. Something like this is already happening in Japan, whose population is aging faster than that of any other industrial society. As Japan registers the demand for the social services it must provide for its seniors, there is less capital to pump into the dynamic high-tech ventures that have kept the economy booming for so long. Because the Japanese are reluctant to run budgetary deficits, the dilemma shows up more dramatically with them, but it is only a matter of time before all of Japan's rivals face the same choices.[4] The entrepreneurial community may feel considerable ideological unease about the reordering of priorities that comes with an aging society. But ironically, it has only itself to blame for the result. As long as capital flows toward profitable returns in health care, pharmaceuticals, and biotechnology, smart investors are helping make us an older society.

In the ongoing debate over entitlements, liberals have charged conservatives with cutting back on senior entitlements in order to finance upper-income tax breaks. Conservatives, of course, hasten to deny the accusation, but were they more candid about the matter, they might frankly insist that holding down the taxes of the entrepreneurial class is a defensible concern. Unless the rich get richer, how is the wealth to trickle down? Economic growth, after all, requires investment and expansion. In Laurence Kotlikoff's view, "every dollar the Treasury has to borrow is a dollar denied to the private sector for investment. Over time, that diversion of resources will curb economic growth and leave America poorer."[5]

Conservatives might then warn that the capital we need to launch new industries is being used to keep the elderly ambulatory. Are hip replacements and cataract surgery worth what they are costing us? The high-tech future on which the investment community has its eyes fixed will at some point be gravely compromised if Medicare expenditures continue to grow. And what else can they do but grow?

The Third Loop: The Vanishing Young

As younger couples register the increasing cost of entitlements or are forced to assume responsibility for aging parents, they are apt at some point to respond by seeking to reduce domestic expenses. The cost of elder health care is not the only pressure on them; they also need to provide for their own medical needs and their children's. That will get more expensive regardless of any change in Medicare. By the late 1990s, it had become clear that managed care, once thought to guarantee cheaper medical services, had saved as much money as it could by imposing unaccustomed austerity on doctors and patients alike. The public's response to managed care, and especially that of retirees under Medicare, grows ever more critical. In response to public pressure, state after state has passed some form of a medical bill of rights that undermines frugality. Forced to spend more on their clients, health maintenance organizations (HMOs) see their profits fall and their stocks lose value. Their response is to raise premiums across the board for old and young alike, but the young, lacking Medicare, feel the pinch more acutely.

Such expenses may lead to smaller families in order to maintain a high-consumption standard of living. This effect is already visible in some societies. In Germany as of the early 1990s, the birth rate had become a matter of acute political concern. Births per family fell to .07, well below the replacement level of 2. As a result, Germany is among the few countries that have sought to turn back the demographic tide. The state of Brandenburg has undertaken to promote larger families by offering a cash subsidy for each new baby. The reward is in addition to other state benefits, including *Kindergeld*, substantial monthly payments to offset child-rearing expenses. Unless Germans can be bribed into higher rates of reproduction, by 2030 there will be nine German retirees "living off" every ten German workers.[6] In Czechoslovakia, where births have fallen well below the replacement rate, the government has run anti-contraception ads, advising couples to "stop taking care." Billboard ads show Johann Sebastian Bach as twenty naked clones.

At some point, young people in the industrial world may begin to resent being born into the senior dominance, but they also know that, without entitlements programs, they would become fully responsible for aged parents — a less financially advantageous choice. One result of this situation might be a high degree of demoralization among younger citizens. They may see less and less promise for their own lives in a society beholden to senior values. They may feel increasingly less inclined to participate in the political process or even to vote — a decision that lessens their power still more. Meanwhile, the consumer demand associated with younger people is apt to become less effective as the youth market diminishes. In general, the daring, energetic entrepreneurial values that might win their support may lose their influence.

While superior medical care is the most obvious force behind the shifting ratio of young-on-the-job to elders-in-retirement, other factors are at work. Some have an air of sociological inevitability about them. Families everywhere in the industrial nations are getting smaller. Couples are marrying later (if they marry at all), waiting longer to have babies (if they have babies at all), and then having fewer of them. That trend is intimately, perhaps inextricably, connected with aspects of the modern world that many identify as "progress" and "freedom." Women especially experience their changing status as liberating. It is an opportunity to spend more of their lives exploring careers, traveling, learning. So they wait longer to begin families, or perhaps never do. As medical science progresses, women need not feel desperate about delaying motherhood into their late middle age; they can afford to wait as long as age forty-five — or, in at least one highly publicized case, until sixty. It is even possible for younger women to store ova so that they can be fertilized at any point in their lives by the sperm of their choice. The biological clock has very nearly been put out of commission.

This changing pattern in reproduction began to appear in the United States in the 1970s. In that decade, the number of childless women in their twenties doubled, followed, in the next decade, by a tripling of births for women between ages thirty and thirty-five — the largest increased birth rate for any age group in the society. Most of the later mothers were working women who would have fewer babies, often no more than one. The change corresponded to a new vision of life. As one feminist psychotherapist observes, "Most of today's women are not interested in going from the classroom to the diaper pail without having some time to achieve a certain amount of self-knowledge. The phrase 'giving birth to myself before I give birth to a baby' is one that more and more women are using to describe their approach to having children."[7]

Singles and domestic partners living together out of wedlock may never produce families at all. Childlessness is becoming a far from unusual married condition, one that is less and less viewed as "unnatural." There are, in fact, support groups at work on the matter. They seek to change the image of those who are childless by choice so that they will pass as "normal." As the demographic analyst Joel Cohen observes, the industrial societies are all rapidly drifting toward a near stationary population based on long life and low fertility.[8]

As of the late twentieth century, about a dozen highly developed European nations had achieved the sort of population stability that environmentalists advocate. Lester Brown of the World Watch Institute neatly summarizes how this has come about.

> Declines in fertility flowed from economic gains and social improvements. As incomes rose and as employment opportunities for women expanded, couples chose to have fewer children. The improved availability of family planning services and the liberalization of abortion laws gave couples the means to achieve this. Population stabilization in these countries has been the result, therefore, of individual preferences, the product of converging economic, social, and demographic forces.[9]

Some analysts have flippantly, but perhaps accurately, characterized these preferences as a matter of parents having a refrigerator instead of having a baby. The assumption is that young working couples at some point choose to substitute consumer durables for extra children. Can the same transition to a stable population be expected in other countries? That is an open question until we know what demographic changes industrialization will bring about in major test cases like China, India, and Indonesia.

Another factor affecting family size may be the growing acceptance in industrial societies of homosexual households, single-parent households, and unmarried cohabitation. This is the "postmodern family condition," as the sociologist Judith Stacey has called it. Her studies assume that the classic Victorian family — the breadwinner father, the full-time mother at home with the children — is now a relic.[10] When that family prevailed, it was possible for women to specialize in pregnancy and homemaking — provided they did not die in childbirth along the way. And if they did, the husband could easily find another wife and carry on procreating. Hence, the prolific middle-class households of the nineteenth century. If that domestic arrangement were still with us, there would be no need to bemoan the declining ratio of young to old; we would have baby boom upon baby boom.

If that is indeed what conservatives want when they speak of "family values," then there is an ironic twist to the story of the waning classic family. Those on the political right may despair over the cost of entitlements and prefer to transfer that expense from the welfare state to families. But they have actually contributed to the very situation that makes that responsibility unaffordable for most people. The leaders of corporate America have behaved as one would expect them to behave. They have disempowered unions and depressed wages, placing American labor in competition with desperate workers in distant lands. That harsh reality has forced more and more women out of the home and into the workforce. Many of the new jobs celebrated on the financial pages are part-time, low-paid jobs for working mothers racing to stay ahead of the credit card. Even then, such costs as nursing home care for aged parents are well beyond the reach of a two-paycheck working-class family. If something has to give in the grip of the tightening household budget, it is apt to be the number of children couples choose to have.

It would, of course, be a mistake to assume that family planning is always a rational matter, but insofar as it is, life in the longevous society is apt to reinforce all these influences. As younger couples try to stay afloat in the sea of consumer choices, they are likely to register the increasing demand of entitlements upon their paychecks and respond to it by trying to reduce domestic expenses. As the working population is taxed more heavily to pay for senior programs, it will tend to cut back further on reproduction in order to maintain a standard of living that advertising insidiously insists we must have. These factors make each successive younger generation smaller relative to the older, and that, in turn, diminishes the ratio of young to old. The result is a demographic circle from which it is difficult to see any way out.

Or can we imagine rebellious young marrieds deciding to produce larger families, even though they will be forced to live poorer?

Some of Our Sperm Are Missing

We should not overlook the possibility that other, subtler biological factors are at work in the demographic downsizing of youth. Some population specialists believe that successful reproduction is growing a great deal riskier in the modern world, hence the increasing reliance on in vitro fertilization services. They report that the sperm count in the industrial societies is dropping off rapidly both in quantity and potency. Studies like those at the Reproductive Biology Unit in Edinburgh suggest that there has been as much as a 50 percent drop in the sperm generated by men born within the last fifty years.[11]

Why is this happening? One theory attributes the effect to "a cocktail of pollutants," sometimes called "endocrine disrupters," in the urban-industrial environment.[12] These chemicals, which have the ability to mimic female hormones, have estrogenic properties that can interfere with the development of the testes during gestation. Such "hormone imposters," as Theo Colborn calls them, derive from synthetic chemicals, mainly pesticides.[13] They may also be responsible for the increase in testicular cancer. Among the possible toxic culprits are PCBs and DDT, plus several chemicals widely used in ordinary detergent, floor polishes, plastic tubing, and food wrapping. If this is so, then a maturing industrial economy may "naturally" fluctuate toward lower reproductive rates as it increases the distribution of cheap, synthetic materials, many of which are valued for their "convenience" and seen as enhancing the standard of living.

There is one more form of population control that may appear in late industrial society. In the years ahead, the use of anti-aging medications is apt to increase greatly as word of miraculous possibilities spreads. But some researchers believe there is a trade-off between the sexual urge and longevity. Dosing on anti-aging hormones may diminish the sex drive and so the birth rate. Michael Rose, a researcher in aging at the University of California at Irvine, predicts that many of the hormones involved in mating will grow more quiescent in those who use life-extending medications. He says of our longevous future, "Randy teen-agers will be a thing of the past. . . . We'll lose the high-testosterone surge of insanity that so much American culture is based on."[14]

In such unforeseen ways, it becomes ever harder for industrial economies to keep their numbers growing, except perhaps by immigration. But in time even immigrant families adapt to the prevailing values of the urban industrial mainstream, and their demographics fall into the same pattern. The third generation of Hispanic migrants living in Los Angeles does not continue the lifestyle of a poor, newly arrived family of five or six from central Mexico. If prevailing, middle-class consumption standards are not enough to change old ways, then inadvertent hormone ingestion may do the job. There would seem to be an inherent restraint that connects affluence with diminishing fertility, as if the ecology of the planet uses our own synthetic chemicals against us, hitting us where it hurts.

Grandpa Vanderhof's House

It has always been the role of elders to raise the great questions of meaning and purpose that loom large as death approaches. As we grow older, we naturally become more inward and contemplative, wondering what it has all been for: the effort and the anxiety, the hard pursuit of success and acquisition. *You can't take it with you.* As familiar as the phrase may be, it is one of those clichés that we all come to accept as indisputably true.

In the famous American comedy of that title by Moss Hart and George S. Kaufman, the central figure is Martin Vanderhof, the *grandpater familias* of an odd New York household. Around him he has gathered a small utopian ménage of madcap artists, crackpot inventors, amateur scientists, and assorted layabouts and misfits. In the living room of Grandpa Vanderhof's community,

> meals are eaten, plays are written, snakes collected, ballet steps practiced, xylophones played, printing presses operated — if there were room enough there would probably be ice skating. In short,

the brood presided over by Martin Vanderhof goes about the business of living in the fullest sense of the word.

Grandpa Vanderhof, far from being a character role reserved for a crotchety old geezer, is a sophisticated and ingratiating philosopher. He is described as "a man who made his peace with the world long, long ago, and his whole attitude and manner are quietly persuasive of this." He is, in short, one of the few true elders to hold a place in modern literature.

At the climax of the play, Grandpa has reason to explain to Mr. Kirby, the harried, gratification-deferring businessman, what his bizarre household is all about.

> GRANDPA: You've got all the money you need. You can't take it with you.
> KIRBY: That's very easy for you to say, Mr. Vanderhof. But I have spent my entire life building up my business.
> GRANDPA: And what's it got you? Same kind of mail every morning, same kind of deals, same kind of meetings, same dinners at night, same indigestion. Where does the fun come in? Don't you think there ought to be something *more*, Mr. Kirby? You must have wanted more than that when you started out. We haven't got too much time, you know — any of us.
> KIRBY: What do you expect me to do? Live the way *you* do? Do nothing?
> GRANDPA: Well, I have a lot of fun. Time enough for everything — read, talk, visit the zoo now and then, practice my darts, even have time to notice when Spring comes around. . . . See?
> KIRBY: Yes I do see. And it's a very dangerous philosophy, Mr. Vanderhof. It's — it's un-American.

Un-American, perhaps, but profoundly, marvelously ecological. A modest, communal way of life filled with family, friendship, and the joy of the inspired moment — things of infinite worth, but no cash value. Later in the play, Grandpa prevails, and Mr. Kirby, admitting that he has been keeping a saxophone hidden away in his closet, decides to revise his way of life. A CEO who opts for fun . . . at that point we know we must be in the realm of pure fiction.

The demographic transition we are in may not at first glance seem to connect with familiar environmental issues like preserving wilderness or saving endangered species. It seems purely social and economic. That is exactly what is unique about the environmental significance of longevity: it wears a human face, the face of people who are near and dear to us and who are able to speak for their own interests. If the New People prove wise enough to adopt Grandpa Vanderhof's vision of the good life, they will begin at last to deflect our single-minded drive for growth, profit, and achievement.

When *You Can't Take It with You* was written in the depths of the Great Depression, people like Grandpa Vanderhof were marginal figures in our society, few in numbers and feeble in power. Even so, one could not imagine the part being played by anybody but an elder. The play voices an elder's vision of life even if, in that troubled time, few Americans were likely to subscribe to it for more than the two hours they were in the theater. Grandpa Vanderhof was sixty years ahead of his time. His dialogue with Mr. Kirby distilled the environmental impact of a longevity revolution nobody could then foresee.

5

The Compassionate Economy
Affluence and the Caregiver Ethic

Nothing makes economic sense unless its continuance for a long time can be projected without running into absurdities. There can be "growth" toward a limited objective, but there cannot be unlimited growth. Permanence is incompatible with a predatory attitude which rejoices in the fact that "what were luxuries for our fathers have become necessities for us." . . . The economics of permanence implies a profound reorientation of science and technology, which have to open their doors to wisdom and, in fact, have to incorporate wisdom into their very structure.

— E. F. SCHUMACHER, *Small Is Beautiful* (1973)

NO SOCIETY will have ever concentrated so much of its skill and energy in its unemployed population as the industrial economies of the twenty-first century. At some point after 2050, jobless adults in the world's industrial societies may outnumber the working population. This is especially apt to be so if we include the involuntarily retired — all those in their forties and fifties who have been technologically unemployed or downsized out of their jobs years before they wish to leave the payroll. There have already been highly controversial court decisions that grant employers the right to fire workers under fifty as a matter of economic necessity. Since older workers tend to earn more, companies that seek to clear them from the payroll can always contend that they have acted for financial reasons, not on the basis of ageism. That claim has been hotly disputed. The courts have decided one way and then the other. Litigation on behalf of older employees is bound to continue, if for no better reason than that lawyers stand to make a fortune on age discrimination suits.

Time on Their Hands

Whatever position the law may finally take, those who leave the work-force, whether voluntarily or not, will include an increasing number of healthy, active, highly skilled men and women. By the time they begin their retirement, they may even be the beneficiaries of breakthroughs in biotechnology that will have brought them a life expectancy that stretches beyond a hundred years. There they will be, retired by the millions, with nothing but time on their hands.

Leaving so much skill untapped is the one cost of retirement that nobody is likely to regard as affordable. Finding ways to recycle this enormous pool of senior energy — one commentator calls it "quite possibly this country's only increasing natural resource"[1] — is apt to become an industry in its own right and, in fact, is already under intense study by social scientists and policy-makers.[2] The job boom of the 1990s in the United States was largely related to the increased recruitment of retired workers, many of them at bargain basement wages.[3] As naturally as water flows downhill, we will soon find ourselves improvising a postindustrial economy in which increasing numbers of older Americans will work voluntarily as the spirit moves them, at occupations — perhaps vital occupations — that are nothing like employment as we have known it. They will have only the most tenuous connections with standard hiring, ordinary scheduling, or a conventional paycheck. Transferring over to so divergent a pattern of working life may take some painful adjustment, but in fact it should be seen as a sign of our economy's ever increasing productivity. Needing less labor to produce the necessities — and even the wasteful luxuries of daily life — we have more leisure than we have yet learned to handle gracefully.

Ironically, the elderly were among the first to experience these changing conditions of industrial life, though not in any way for which they could be grateful. They were the first to suffer the economic dislocation of labor-saving technology. The industrial economies have been steadily disemploying working men over the age of sixty-five since the early twentieth century. Their labor was no longer needed, neither on the land nor in the factories. Their place had been taken by new technological processes. In 1900, two out of three men over sixty-five were still on the payroll; by the final decade of the century, only one in five were still employed, and many of them were working only part-time. In the United States, where a tightfisted social Darwinist ethic governed the marketplace in the early twentieth century, the redundant old were not granted a comfortable retirement; they were simply scrapped and forgotten. Only since the 1930s have the unemployed elderly had the minimal support of Social Security to fall back on. Nevertheless, as one sociologist puts it, "the old are forerunners of a future leisured society."[4]

Affluence Revisited

Many are apt to see the fiscal issues raised by the approaching mass retirement of the baby boom generation as something new. But the entitlements controversy actually takes us back to a discussion that began in the 1940s. For a full generation following World War II, economists and politicians of every ideological stripe brainstormed schemes that would grant a basic subsistence to all citizens as a matter of right. In the 1960s major American publications ran editorials and articles on the "guaranteed annual income," as it was most frequently called, all of them addressing it as realistic, if not inevitable. Dwight McDonald, writing in the *New Yorker* in 1970, was typical in advocating "the principle that every citizen should be provided, at state expense, with a reasonable standard of living regardless of any other considerations. . . . The governmental obligation to provide, out of taxes, such a minimum living standard for all who need it should be taken as much for granted as free public schools have always been in our history."

Proposals like this were America's version of a worldwide moral transformation. It was called "the revolution of rising expectations," a spreading conviction that the human race was at last able to abolish the curse of scarcity. The substance of that hope was in fact our own country. We were the standard of affluence everywhere. People looked to us to see how the plenty might be shared. There were many variations on the theme. Liberals advocated an approach modeled on Social Security or other New Deal programs; conservatives preferred family allowances or, like the libertarian Milton Friedman, championed a negative income tax.[5] The latter was especially popular with opponents of big government; at one swoop it would eliminate the crazy quilt of expensive, overlapping state and federal programs — aid to dependent children (AFDC), farm price supports, welfare, public housing, Social Security — replacing them all with the Internal Revenue Service. The IRS would be empowered to send anyone whose income fell below a standard cost-of-living exemption a check to make up the difference.

In his bid for the presidency in 1964, Barry Goldwater, the founding father of America's radical right, embraced Friedman's negative income tax as part of his platform. Goldwater lost the election, but his rival Lyndon Johnson at once launched the War on Poverty, which became the official centerpiece for new ideas about sharing the wealth. In 1966 Johnson summoned the National Commission on Guaranteed Incomes. The commission began a two-year series of hearings that finished by recommending "the adoption of a new program of income supplementation for all Americans in need."[6] But by the time it reported back, Johnson's political future had been eclipsed by the Vietnam War.

The same year the National Commission began its hearings, the U.S. Chamber of Commerce, the leading voice of the American business community, convened a conference titled "The National Symposium on Guaranteed Income." The event assembled ranking economists of the day to discuss establishing a legal right to the necessities of life for all American citizens whether they held jobs or not. The conference agreed on no single program, but there was an overwhelming consensus that, whatever form it might take, the proposal was an idea whose time had come.[7]

The figure who did the most to publicize the fact of industrial abundance and explore its implications for economic theory was John Kenneth Galbraith. His 1958 book *The Affluent Society* named the period. Surveying the American scene from the vantage point of the great postwar boom, Galbraith wrote in amazement at the nation's productive potential. Here was wealth that might well spell the end of poverty. He was among the first in the intellectual-academic mainstream to recognize that America's expanding economy changed all the rules of the economic game. Hitherto, he observed, economic thought had been based on "poverty, inequality, and economic peril." That was the world of yesterday. "Poverty," Galbraith reminded his readers,

> was the all-pervasive fact of that world. Obviously it is not of ours. . . . So great has been the change that many of the desires of the individual are no longer even evident to him. They become so only as they are synthesized, elaborated, and nurtured by advertising and salesmanship. . . . Few people at the beginning of the nineteenth century needed an adman to tell them what they wanted.

If our lives in the affluent society were still haunted by insecurity, the problem was no longer scarcity but our inability to consume enough to keep our productive plant turning over and to keep people employed. The link between paychecks and production was now the key economic problem. In an age of abundance, people were still expected to work forty hours a week for wages, but on the production line their work only augmented the store of goods to the point that the system was constantly in danger of foundering in its own plenty. What was needed, Galbraith argued, was "a reasonably satisfactory substitute for production as a source of income. This and this alone would break the present nexus between production and income." Accordingly, Galbraith proposed a modest variation on the guaranteed annual income. When the economy slumped and people lost their jobs, let them be given an unemployment wage, which Galbraith called CGC: cyclically graduated compensation. CGC would increase in value as the number of unemployed increased and decrease as full employment was approached. In this way, the jobless would retain their self-respect and at the same time continue to discharge their necessary economic role as consumers.

Because he was seeking to rationalize a regime of continued high production, Galbraith envisioned a workforce that would fluctuate in and out of the job market. Thus, he missed a promising possibility: buying some people out of the workforce *permanently*. That is called "retirement." In his analysis, Galbraith did touch on Social Security as an aspect of public policy, but it never occurred to him to nominate *subsidized retirement* as a model for compensated joblessness. It is understandable why Galbraith should overlook so obvious a solution. The longevity revolution had not yet become visible; entitlements were not yet major policy. Even so, Robert Theobald, one of the principal theorists of the guaranteed annual income, saw what Galbraith did not. He observed that "basic economic security can be best regarded as an extension of the present Social Security system to a world in which job availability will steadily decline." But by the time he wrote, Theobald feared that "we shall fail to adopt those policies, such as the guaranteed annual income, which are essential in the new era we are entering."

What accounted for his pessimism? Like many others, Theobald saw forbidding signs of social disintegration on all sides. The "liberal dominance" of American politics was collapsing, and with it the belief that "existing structures could create the new programs required to deal with our new problem/possibilities." For that reason, "predictions about

steady improvements in man's condition . . . are both naive and dangerous. The only conceivable course for the immediate future is further
fragmentation and this will result in further conflict willy-nilly."

The year was 1970.

Entitlements for Everybody

Early in the decade that followed, the once lively national dialogue on
the guaranteed annual income was closed down so completely that it
requires an archaeological dig through the historical record to recover
any trace of it. One comes upon the books and articles that argue the
idea like once opulent cities buried under the wasteland of contemporary economic thought. Even reasonably well informed people know
nothing about the matter. It is as if we had lost all record of the great
voyages of discovery and people had gone back to believing that the
Earth was as flat as a pancake.

Why was the discussion so abruptly terminated? Not for any economic or technological reason. The problem of finding enough work to
go around continues to plague every industrial economy in the world.
By the 1970s new automated systems were coming on line that made
labor even less necessary. As that happened, technological unemployment was growing ever more entrenched, as it continues to be. In France
and Germany, the unemployed have become all but a permanent organized movement. The unskilled young as well as the retired old find no
place in the workforce. Entry-level jobs have been steadily vanishing
along with the assembly lines of the nation. We are, in short, becoming
a more productive, less labor-intensive economy than ever. Why then
did the guaranteed annual income drop from the national agenda? The
answer, as Theobald feared, was political. By 1970 the nation was in the
midst of social upheaval. The war in Vietnam had divided the country;
the spreading student protest was indicting the central institutions of
the nation; the countercultural assault upon parental values was at fever
pitch. With the social fabric coming undone, neither our political leaders nor corporate America were of a mind to dream utopian dreams.

By now it should be clear that proposals like those of Friedman and
Galbraith anticipated the debate over Social Security we find ourselves
in today. Entitlements are but a scaled-down replay of the guaranteed
annual income, this time limited to the elder population. Rather than
reinventing the wheel, then, those who wish to defend entitlements

would do better to reopen the discussion of affluence, and so return the dialogue to where it left off at midcentury.

The New People, children of the Great Affluence that flowed from World War II, were born into that dialogue. With a neat philosophical symmetry, it is now their demographic destiny to retire into it. But this time it will not be possible to put the question on hold as it was in the 1970s. There will be too many people involved and too many votes at stake. As they move into their later years, the New People will usher in the senior dominance of our society. What they make of that dominance cannot help but be a major force in our national life. Just as entrepreneurs, feverishly wheeling and dealing in the marketplace, have long determined the nature and quality of our lives by how they invest their money, soon the New People will shape our society just as decisively by how they invest their time, their wits, and their moral energy. They have the best model they could ask for before their eyes: the entitlements they have been given. Why should entitlements not spread through the society?

An Economy of Subliminal Abundance

Can we afford entitlements for everybody? We are not apt to answer yes until we regain the same vivid sense of our true affluence that prevailed through the postwar period. Our situation is once again as Galbraith saw it in his analysis of the American economy in the 1950s. He argued that the conventional wisdom of our leaders had not yet caught up with the reality of our industrial abundance. "Illusion," he warned, "is a comprehensive ill. The rich man who deludes himself into behaving like a mendicant may conserve his fortune although he will not be very happy."

Our political and business communities are still behaving like that "rich man," pretending that scarcity prevails. Economists grimly announce that we are in an "era of constrained fiscal resources," when in fact there is more affluence as well as more technological power available now than when Galbraith wrote. Over the last generation, our industrial power has been many times multiplied by the cybernated systems that have revolutionized every aspect of our lives. The media are filled with exuberant talk about high tech, but the abundance it brings with it has become subliminal.

"Subliminal" may seem like an odd term to use in this context. The word derives from psychology, not economics — specifically from the psychology of perception. It refers to a stimulus that fails to register on consciousness. What Galbraith referred to as "illusion" might better be seen as just such an odd quirk in the social psychology of industrial societies. People tend over time to lose sight of how affluent they are. They drift away from experiencing luxuries as luxuries and at last experience them as "necessities" to the point of feeling hard-pressed in the midst of plenty. Finally they conclude that we can neither accommodate the needs of the sick and disabled nor grant survival rights to the elderly. That quirk now allows conservative critics to argue that the nation cannot afford entitlements — or for that matter, anything that will have to be paid for by taxation. In the midst of overwhelming plenty, we persist in acting as if we were bankrupt.

How rich are we? Take one telling instance of subliminal abundance. The automobile. It is an example that has played a significant, even colorful, role in the lives of the New People; it should call to mind a number of fond, nostalgic episodes from their youth, such as the suburbanization of America that took place in the 1950s and 1960s, the drive-in movie theaters of that day, and any number of cheery television commercials for the great chromium behemoths that dominated the road. Once upon a time, through the first thirty years of the twentieth century, the automobile was an obvious luxury. Those days were long gone by the time the New People came of age. By then the car had evolved into a necessity that impinged upon jobs, shopping, and chores of all kinds. From there, the car rolled steadily forward to displace most cheaper, more practical forms of public transport, which were literally torn out of the social fabric at enormous expense during the Eisenhower 1950s as part of the new highway program.

Today a busy suburban mother does not think twice before driving some miles to the shopping center to buy a quart of milk; a father may use the car to drive still farther to buy a washer for a leaking faucet. Neither mother nor father has any other practical way to buy the milk or the washer. Nor have they any other way to get to their jobs to earn the money to buy the milk and the washer. As a result, they no longer see commuting as extravagant. A pattern of life has closed around the car that would require us to redesign the working life of the nation and dismantle whole metropolitan areas in order to diminish our dependency on the car. Yet, though we regard it as a necessity, the car is a dazzling manifestation of our social wealth. Simply look around you next time you are on any freeway; estimate what it costs to transport so many people, usually one person to each internal combustion engine. Calculate the cost of the cars, the fuel, the freeways, the city streets, the parking lots, the entire traffic control system, the insurance we must all pay, the medical care and litigation that follow accidents.

Jane Holtz Kay, a sharp critic of the American automobile economy, has sought to make just such an estimate. Along the way, she discovered that American taxpayers lay out hundreds of thousands of dollars for every mile of highway that must be repaved.[8] And that is only the beginning. As of the mid-1990s, her best approximation was that the car culture costs each of us $6,000 a year in direct expenses for owning, running, fueling, licensing, and insuring the vehicle. In addition, Kay has concluded that the "external" costs — the cost of parking facilities, traffic police, land use, and so on — range anywhere from $3,000 to $9,000 per citizen per year. At an even more subliminal level, Kay has further estimated that the price we pay each year for people stuck in traffic and off the job may total as much as $40 billion. But we have long since stopped tracking these costs, just as we overlook the installment debt that people are carrying on their cars, which amounts to nearly half of all consumer debt in the economy. At a modest estimate, we are spending well over $1 trillion a year on what Kay calls our "car culture," vastly more than the cost of welfare and senior entitlements combined.

The same commonsense analysis that we apply to cars could be carried out with respect to any number of necessities of life. Our supermarket pattern of buying food, the shopping mall pattern of buying clothes, the suburban pattern of housing, our way of dealing with refuse and sewage, our public health, our forms of entertainment and recreation . . . none of these is any longer carried out in a direct, local, and low-cost way; all have become complex and convoluted, with maximum overhead and echelons of highly salaried intervening personnel to administer, supervise, and transport. There are forms of affluence in our society so enormous that asking people to estimate their dimensions would be like asking a flea to measure the size of the elephant it rides on.

We live in a society so rich in time and money that entertainment has become an "industry," taking in more profit than the durable goods sector. Today CEOs who run theme parks and market computer games earn more money than the steel masters and railroad barons who built our industrial infrastructure. Even during recessions, the public has hundreds of billions of dollars to burn at gaming tables across the nation. The Pentagon, despite the end of the cold war, continues to spend hundreds of billions on weapons systems with no enemy in sight. In 1997 it requested more than $300 billion alone to "upgrade" war-planes over the next two years. The American consuming public in the 1990s paid out upwards of $50 billion annually in interest charges on its credit card debt — money that buys it precisely nothing. The abundance of the world's industrial systems rolls forward, but political philosophy and moral sensibility remain stalled in a market-based moral orthodoxy that insists people must still compete to hold their place in life.

It would be the supreme irony if the debate over entitlements were to open out into a renewed investigation of the guaranteed living standard, a public discussion that was broken off in the 1960s. The New People might then remember that entitlements are the single surviving remnant of affluence as we once knew it, a promise of security we thought might be universally shared.

Be Kind to Old Animals

The people we think of as "senior citizens" at the turn of the twenty-first century (the middle old and senior old, as we have defined them) are so new to the implications of longevity that few of them have seen the years ahead of them as an opportunity for anything as strenuous as reappraising affluence. Many of them have retired into an empty space filled with card games or love-boat cruises. That is retirement as we have known it; a withdrawal into inconsequentiality. There are commercial forces at work that would delight in keeping things just that trivial and profitable. But the current generation of seniors — especially those in the middle-old range who have put aside some money — is already growing restless with a life limited to the card table and the golf course. As a sign of significant change, a distinctive new occupation has already grown up around that restlessness. It is called "volunteer vacationing."

Volunteer work has long been seen as a province of the elderly, whether as museum docents or hospital candy stripers. But the volunteering involved in these vacations is of a wholly different order. Indeed, the term "vacation" obscures the reality. This is actually rigorous public service, but with a novel twist. These public servants pay to work. They often lay out a good deal of their own money to cover the cost of transport, lodging, food, and care. Environmental organizations like

Earthwatch and the National Audubon Society, as well as government agencies like the U.S. Forest Service or the Fish and Wildlife Service have been making the most extensive use of senior volunteers. They now organize vacations that allow participants to do significant conservation work: repairing public facilities in wilderness areas, building trails, taking censuses of wildlife, planting and restoring parks. Sometimes the effort includes assisting on digs to find and catalog fossil remains or preserve native habitats.

There are also inner-city vacations, like those of Habitat for Humanity, whose purpose is to build homes for the poor, and Third World vacations that demand substantial stamina. The American Hiking Society, for example, advertises vacations that involve "hard, manual labor in rugged, remote locations, many at high altitudes." Fortunately for older participants, the assignments are not restricted to heavy lifting. There are other opportunities for teachers, technicians, cooks, housekeepers, child-minders, and gofers. But whether the volunteers are providing brains or brawn, clearly the satisfaction in vacations like these is very different from that of strolling the Champs-Élysées.[9]

Sometimes the chores that turn up for retired Americans are strangely specialized. Around the country, there is a growing movement on the part of zoological societies to engage retired volunteers in a strange new occupation: the often very painstaking care of overaged animals. The assumption is that aging creatures share a cross-species bond of sympathy with one another. If that is so, and if these programs result in better care and longer life for the animals, they may actually yield important gerontological findings. There have never been many very old animals in the world. "Sans teeth, sans eyes, sans everything," rhinos, tigers, and elephants in the wild fall victim to rivals, hunters, or predators. But in captivity they linger on whether they like it or not, developing the common diseases of the old: arthritis, diabetes, osteoporosis, even dementia and suicidal depression. The U.S. government has now retired scores of aged and sickly chimpanzees that were raised for the NASA space program or for laboratory experiments. After spending years in cages, some of the chimps have developed serious psychoses. Placed in zoos, they too are falling under the care of elders, who are expected to be infinitely patient with them.

Lurking in the background of these programs is the quaint notion that the animals might teach their human caretakers something about aging gracefully. That is how a commentator in an *NBC News* feature on the subject put it. He was impressed with how "uncomplaining" the old beasts are, how dignified in their decline. Was I wrong in detecting a subtext, a message to the elderly asking them please to cost less and make less trouble?

There is just the slightest touch of pathos, and perhaps condescension, in programs like this — the suggestion is that old animals and old humans have outlived their usefulness except to one another. There is also something of the lore of "second childhood" involved. As infants, humans play with stuffed animals; in their old age, they get real animals to entertain them. One could imagine a film comedy: how Wally the warthog teaches the grumpy old codgers to mellow out and die with dignity. But if one can see beyond their comic aspect, these programs reveal a curious and growing sense that the old have special gifts of patience, dedication, and compassion — even toward other species.

The old animals program is a marginal effort, but along with volunteer vacations, it distantly anticipates the elder economy we are even now beginning to build. The old are being credited with — or is it assigned? — a willingness to take time and be kind in the service of their community. Encourage people to be like that, praise and reward them for it, and they may become that way in increasing numbers. Even the usual admiration for those who take up such work is revealing. It is almost as if the old are becoming a blank screen on which the society projects its moral idealism — at the same time carefully segregating them from the demands of "real life." This, we seem to be saying, is how all of us would be proud of using our time — if only we had the chance. The translation might be: if we were not trapped in this constant struggle for status, fame, success, and money, then we too might have the chance to be fully human. In the Middle Ages, people thought of the monks in much the same way. They exemplified the moral standard of the community: a life of contemplation, spiritual fulfillment, and charity that others insisted they could not afford to choose.

The Caring Imperative

The volunteer task everybody associates most readily with retirement is caregiving. Whether in hospitals, nursing homes, or private homes, seniors can be found taking care of all those who are forced into dependency, including one another. Among the AARP's most successful efforts is its Long-Term Care Volunteer Ombudsman Program, which works in nursing homes protecting the rights of the frail elderly. But in effect, many New People are already in training to take up society's caring imperative. They, especially the women, are being schooled in coping and kindness long before they themselves retire. When their retirement does arrive, many women of the baby boom generation will have emerged from one of the twenty-five million American homes that have been taking care of an elderly relative.[10]

The American Association of Retired Persons estimates that three-quarters of the people looking after a sick or disabled family member in those households are women; others place the figure at 90 percent. Women have become the default caregivers of our society; they have been thrown into that role and forced to make the best of it. Theirs has been called the "sandwiched" life. No sooner do they finish raising their children than their ailing parents move in for care.[11] As of the early 1990s, the average age of women taking care of their parents was fifty-seven; more than one-third were over sixty-five and were destined to spend more of their lives "parenting" their parents than they had spent caring for their children.

Imagine for a moment women in their fifties and sixties saddled with this role for most of the rest of their lives. When anti-entitlements critics step forward to speak for "our children," this is what makes their claim ring so hollow. Far from being helpless babes in arms, many of those "children" are themselves on the brink of retirement. And many more are already so burdened with home care that the last thing they want is to be "saved" from the "entitlements monster." As women demand help with this responsibility, our society will in a sense become more "feminized" in its values — though the real solution is to see acts of kindness as gender-neutral, as much the calling of men as of women. But that, in turn, calls for a reappraisal of gender roles, a project that I address in chapter 9 as among the highest priorities in a longevous society.

One characteristic of the New People has often been satirized. They "workshop" everything. That is, they get "into" things, turning every experience into a study, from death and taxes to straightening up their desks. Identify something as a "problem" and, as if by magic, "experts" emerge and courses are scheduled at the university extension. It was inevitable that as caregiving came to be an unofficial occupation expertise would grow up around it. The books, magazines, hotlines, websites, and counselors multiply by the year. The books bear names like *How*

Did I Become My Parent's Parent?, *Caring for the Parents Who Cared for You*, *Caring for Yourself While Caring for Your Aging Parents.*[12] As the titles suggest, much of the advice has that kind of frankness we have come to expect from a psychologically sophisticated — and saturated — society. It is directed as much to the needs of the giver as the receiver. This approach is both honest and practical. Nobody who has served in a worthy cause these days is unaware of burnout and the toll it takes. Burnout is the result of assuming any task without some psychological sensitivity to its burdens and liabilities. So the books advise caregivers to define the limits of what they can do, consider their own health, give themselves a break when they need it, let their frustrations hang out periodically, and seek assistance fast when they cannot cope.

Candor like this is a hopeful sign. What is bound to come of it is a prompt realization that the fiscally cheap solution of unloading elder care on families is not necessarily the best solution. It is saving money at the expense of middle-class and working-class families. Worse, it may be a way to destroy even the best-intentioned families by burdening them — especially the woman of the house — beyond endurance. The result of that will be not only poor care but resentment, hard feelings, strife, and abuse. As the elderly live longer, and as gerontological medical science advances, many of the problems of old age require more than amateurish, part-time attention. Caring for an ailing parent is no longer a brief stint; it may go on for ten or twenty grueling and expensive years.

The classic Victorian family dealt with aged parents by seating them by the fire, bringing them an occasional cup of tea, and waiting for them to die. The wait was usually not long. Maybe the love was there, but not the skill and patience that elder care now demands. Nobody in the past had to administer medication (injections, IV-feeding, dialysis), take blood, stool, and urine samples, give physical therapy, prepare special foods, offer aerobic exercise, groom, dress, and bathe a fragile body, tolerate dementia, and deal with depression — one's own as well as the parent's. And beyond all this there is the vexation that comes with paying bills and collecting reimbursements, processing paperwork and struggling with agencies and accountants. When it comes to the nitty-gritty details of elder care, it is hypocritical to envision it as anything but a hard, bankrupting job.

As all the elder care manuals emphasize, guilt is not the appropriate response for those who find themselves overwhelmed by an ordeal like this. The extensive care that the frail and infirm require is uniquely the result of modern medicine. Nobody in any previous culture was expected to handle demands of this magnitude and live a life of their own. We are keeping people alive well beyond any limit for which the family was designed to provide care. Most families still prefer to keep parents at home; they make the effort. But the sooner we recognize the emotional and financial limits of home care for the elderly, the sooner we will begin looking for better alternatives that are bound to take the form of public programs.

Caregiver Politics

It is already possible to make a few confident predictions. When enough people find themselves overloaded by prevailing home care arrangements, there will have to be changes. This is especially bound to be the case with assertive women who have been even remotely touched by feminist values. They could become a dominant electoral factor as politicians come to recognize where the votes are. As a matter of workaday practicality, the women's vote is a welfare state vote. Even archconservatives have had to face up to the gender gap. In the name of family values, women demand more public money for schools, day care, safe streets, food inspection. As if by cultural default in what has long been a "man's world," women care about these realities of everyday life and vote for them. Ideology will not answer their needs. Their vote is a clear cry for help.

Nursing homes are already an issue. The nursing home scandals of the 1980s emerged as a bellwether issue in senior politics. The problem came to public awareness in 1985, when the media and congressional investigators revealed the amount of elder abuse that was taking place in the cheap, unprofessional facilities many families were forced to use.[13] The effort to improve long-term institutional care and make it affordable continues. When in 1992 budget-balancing conservatives in Congress began talking about measures to place a lien on the family home to pay for long-term care, the proposal was quickly dropped as unacceptable — and indeed morally reprehensible.

Full-time, full-scale home care, a burden that is already the blight of many women's lives, is bound to become just as urgent an issue as women find themselves sinking ever deeper into the harsh responsibilities that come with longevity. They will demand relief — and they will get it. With more money allocated for elder care, the caregiving sector of the economy will expand. In turn, caring will become a prominent occupation, even a profession. There are already young people specializing in elder care as gerontological doctors, nurses, and counselors. It is not difficult to imagine this turning into a growth industry, a category of service employment that cannot be sent off-shore or technologically eliminated. In the twenty-first century, geriatric care may take the place of high tech as the unfolding frontier of opportunity.

Will professionalization of this kind compromise the spontaneous kindness that caregiving requires? Hardly. It will institutionalize compassion and reward it as it deserves to be rewarded — not primarily with money, but with recognition and appreciation. Like all jobs, caring takes talent; it requires certain qualities of character, an abundance of patience, an adult sense of responsibility. Above all it takes a gift for impersonal compassion. I have found those gifts in almost every nurse who has cared for me when I have been hospitalized. The caring sensibility they possessed was not trained into them, it was born into them. Nursing happened to be one of the few jobs that called upon that sensibility. In the future there are bound to be more jobs and better-paying careers for those who have that quality. The more compassionately gifted people we have employed full-time as caregivers, the more socially influential their qualities will become. Children will recognize caregiving as a highly regarded vocation and choose it as a life's work, the signature profession of a mature industrial society. Imagine people blessed with the ability to give tender, loving care becoming as important to us as hackers in the era of the computer.

Caregiving is not simply a family affair, nor can it be restricted to a profession. As medical science keeps more sick people alive, caring has turned into a spreading, grassroots feature of our society. It is already transforming neighborhoods, since it is neighbors who often have to intervene in the lives of the seriously ill.[14] Much of this contact is casual and private — a simple understanding between friends that escapes public visibility — but the National Alliance for Caregiving estimates that over twenty-two million households are now caring for neighbors as well as relatives. One federally funded effort called Gatekeepers enlists mail carriers and delivery drivers to learn about the neighborhoods they regularly visit, especially the shut-ins and the elderly who may need their help. They become part of a watchful mobile network of caregivers. Another rough measure: the National Federation of Interfaith Volunteer Caregivers, which trains and supports those who reach out to neighbors, has grown since the mid-1980s from twenty-five local chapters to over six hundred. An important part of that increase has to do with the AIDS crisis in the gay community, many of whose members are taking on the role of traditional families for one another. That example has been appropriated for other forms of care, including elder care.

Increasingly the basic units for elder care, as well as the care of the homebound sick, are the apartment complexes and condos where people find themselves living as age and illness descend upon them. With a few modest arrangements — a doorman to carry groceries, a visiting nurse, some taxi service, a few neighborhood children to run errands — people often prefer to "age in place."[15] The American Association of Retired Persons has discovered that our once-footloose baby boom population has begun to put down roots. Almost half the country's older population has lived in the same place for more than twenty years. Researchers have come up with a quaint formal name for such an arrangement — NORCs: naturally occurring retirement communities. NORCs may become as characteristic of the longevous society as the suburbs were of the early lives of the New People. But while suburbs isolated residents from one another and emphasized high consumption, NORCs and caring neighborhoods unite people and emphasize compassion.[16]

The Aging Opportunity and the Third Sector

When President Lyndon Johnson was formulating Medicare in the 1960s, he also sought to create an Office of Aging at the department of Health, Education, and Welfare. The office would have overseen seniors serving in hospitals as medical aides. The American Medical Association thought this was a bad idea and vetoed it. The department was instead transformed into a little-known program called the National Senior Service Corps. In 1971 the Senior Corps was expanded into the Retired and Senior Volunteer Program (RSVP).

RSVP is a little-publicized, vastly underfunded operation that continues to perform scores of vital services. In the mid-1990s, over half a million seniors in RSVP projects served tens of thousands of sites across the country. They tutored in schools, assisted in clinics and courts, did some environmental watchdogging, participated in rehabilitation and telephone reassurance programs, served as companions for shut-in elders, and took part in intergenerational projects. The contribution made by the Senior Companions Program is particularly valuable. In the mid-1990s, twelve thousand volunteers helped more than thirty thousand frail elders to live independently. With nursing home costs running as high as $35,000 a year, the estimated value of the companion service was $150 million.

RSVP also runs the Foster Grandparents Program, which offers free day care to working parents at minimal cost. There are nearly twenty-four thousand foster grandparents in the United States; their work has been valued at $262 million, but with little in the way of personal remuneration. In some states, as of the mid-1990s, foster grandparents (who are almost invariably foster grandmothers) received $9 a day plus carfare. In short, they are exploited labor, but with time on their hands, they do the job with good cheer.[17]

Marc Freedman, who regards RSVP as a "hidden triumph" of the Johnson Great Society, has called this bare-bones beginning "the aging opportunity." He asks: why not expand it in all directions as a comprehensive, well-funded national service program? He believes that with enough money behind it, RSVP — and similar state and local programs — could turn the retired into the "new trustees of civic life."[18] The possibilities are vast. Retired teachers could become mentors, retired physicians could become medical counselors, retired lawyers could become legal aides available for all the problems people have with employers, landlords, and welfare and entitlement programs. There is a frontier of work and service waiting to be staked out by retired Americans.

But at some point programs like this raise a question of principle. It has to do with the peculiar status of volunteerism in American society. Volunteering is invariably presented as a noble human act that rises above government and the marketplace. President George Bush, who once scored a campaign success by describing the volunteer spirit as a "thousand points of light," praised it as "America's greatness." Like love and motherhood, volunteerism lends itself to many sweet songs. But volunteerism is not politically neutral; it has always been closely linked to conservative values as the glowing alternative to mandatory government programs. Voluntary service is the rich man's substitute for the welfare state and is often falsely opposed to government, as if the two must be at odds. During his presidency, Ronald Reagan contended that the government, following World War II, had actually set out to usurp the fine, friendly things people would otherwise do "out of the goodness of their hearts."[19]

Some among the well-to-do have taken volunteering quite seriously as a personal ideal, but volunteerism can also function as a rhetorically effective riposte to liberal proposals for government relief, welfare, and public works. It can be a thinly disguised effort to guilt-trip those who know that major social problems go well beyond what sporadic, part-time contributions of time and money can handle. We should recall that volunteerism entered American politics as the pet project of President Herbert Hoover, who believed all social problems could be solved by grassroots generosity. The limitations of his high hopes were revealed after the crash of 1929. By no stretch of the imagination could a disaster of such dimensions have been solved by charitable efforts. It was at that point that the first federal entitlements were initiated under the Roosevelt New Deal.

Yet the very fact that Presidents Reagan and Bush turned volunteerism into a talking point on their domestic agenda has sparked ambitious social thought about what is now often called the "Third Sector." Here is where the interrupted dialogue over the guaranteed annual income continues. The Third Sector is the sum total of all volunteer work outside the marketplace, either by individuals or through nonprofit organizations. It would be the main locus of the volunteer work we might expect of retired seniors. When all the people, projects, and assets in the Third Sector are pooled, we arrive at some strikingly large numbers. In the mid-1980s, by one estimate, the money spent by voluntary organizations in the United States for social projects was greater than the gross national product of all but seven nations. As of the mid-1990s, we have more people working in the American Third Sector than in construction or transport or textiles.[20]

Economists give scant attention to the Third Sector, mainly because it tends to operate in informal ways that produce few statistics. It pays little in the way of taxable wages, and it produces nothing that can be measured as "output." For precisely that reason, the Third Sector is a great theoretical challenge to economic theory. The Third Sector is all the work, all the funds, all the resources, that hold communities together in such fields as education, day care, health care, legal advocacy, sheltering and feeding the homeless, and drug rehabilitation. Yet one looks in vain for some recognition of its value in standard economic texts or on the financial pages.

In other lands, the situation is very different. In France, where, as in all the European nations, unemployment has been rising inexorably, the volunteer workforce is seen as one important way to put people to work in what is called the "social economy." The French have been willing to offer a guaranteed income to those who agree to contribute time to that economy. The idea is not far removed from the American welfare reform that puts people to work at community service jobs like cleaning up the streets and parks or wiping the graffiti off walls. But in the United States, such work often goes unpaid and so amounts to a form of servitude.

Conservatives like to see volunteerism as an alternative to government. But the two could work in tandem, exchanging resources and inspiration. Government could empower the Third Sector, often in very simple ways. For example, it could channel what is now welfare money through nonprofit and voluntary organizations to allow them to expand their workforce in the community. It could create a "shadow wage" that allows tax deductions for the value of the time one contributes to volunteer work.

When we identify the retired as volunteers and assume that they are willing and able to work for nothing, we may be badly mistaken. For Social Security recipients who are dependent on family to pay their full cost of living, a paid job makes perfect sense. As we have mentioned, several million Social Security recipients must scramble to supplement their meager government stipend. What they find are usually catch-as-catch-can part-time jobs at meager pay. It would clearly make far greater sense to pay retirees to work at something they know or to assume long-term caregiving responsibilities for members of their own generation. But by far the neatest, least bureaucratic way to achieve that goal is simply to give them higher Social Security payments so they will be free to volunteer. Either way, this would run up the bill for entitlements. All the more reason to begin calling our subliminal abundance to public attention. We are rich enough to pay compassion the wage it deserves.

The "We Generation"

If the senior entitlements should become the model for a guaranteed annual income allied to a growing Third Sector, we would have the basis for a mature industrial economy in America. Such a compassionate economy would lend ballast to our otherwise turbulent marketplace. It would put retired skills to work. It would provide entry-level jobs for the otherwise unemployable young. It would put purchasing power in the hands of those who otherwise have nothing to spend. It would guarantee employment of last resort for all those who lose their jobs owing to global competition. As the pioneers of a robust Third Sector in the United States, the New People would be building a solid economic foundation for entitlements policy and the elder culture that rests upon it. Beyond protecting their own immediate interests in the entitlements debate, they would become the primary defenders of humane social values for all their more vulnerable fellow citizens, beginning with those who most clearly share the vulnerability of the elderly: the nation's children. It should be the highest priority on the senior political agenda to see the same right to a decent subsistence and full medical care granted to the young as to the old. As Maggie Kuhn puts it in calling for a Social Security commitment to children, "We must act as the elders of the tribe, looking out for the best interests of the future and preserving the precious compact between the generations."

In one way or another, every budget-cutting attack on programs created to help the indigent, the disabled, and the down and out impinges upon entitlements. Either the cost of entitlements is used to justify diminishing support to the needy, or continued funding of welfare programs for the needy is used to justify cutting entitlements. As part of the conservative backlash, congressional leaders have been doing all they can to confuse "welfare" (temporary assistance to the unemployed and unemployable) with "welfare state" (Social Security and Medicare) in the public mind, two very different areas of policy that have different histories and goals. The aim of such deliberate obfuscation is to create the impression that seniors are living off of "welfare" and should be ashamed to accept handouts. The very concept of "entitlements" is being called sternly into question, as if to ask: is anybody *entitled* to anything they did not earn in the marketplace? The New People are being forced to recognize that their political fate is bonded to that of all those who are dependent on our common humanity.

As Horace Deets, director of the AARP, reminds us, there has always been another America besides hard-charging, entrepreneurial America.

> One reason for America's greatness is that through our history one generation has helped another. Sometimes it has been through direct family support. Other times, indirectly through programs like Social Security and Medicare, Guaranteed Student Loans or Head Start. With the many problems our nation faces, Americans

of all ages must work together as never before. Those who try to divide us along age lines are doing us a great disservice.[21]

In the 1970s, mordant critics spoke of the baby boomers as the "me" generation, rather as if selfishness had previously been an unknown vice. When they leveled the charge, it was never clear what generation they had in mind as the appropriate ethical baseline. But if that accusation was ever true, the dynamics of the longevity revolution are bound to lay it to rest. Before they leave the stage of history, the New People, the first generation to face up to the challenge of creating an economics of permanence, may translate "me" into "we."

6

The Senior Follies

Elderhood and the Flight from Age

I F THERE IS ONE CONVICTION that every senior in the world shares, it is George Bernard Shaw's melancholy quip: "Youth is wasted on the young." But if the truth be told, age is often wasted on the old.

I have no doubt that, as our society grows more age-dominant, there will be an ever more concerted effort to incorporate everything that is deep and wise about the New People into the dynamics of the marketplace. There may even be those who feel that coping with this great demographic transition is essentially a matter of turning the seniority of our citizens into a sales pitch — just that and nothing more. No doubt there are New People who would welcome becoming a business opportunity; in America, recognition in the marketplace is a form of validation. Being worth money means one officially *exists*.

Generational Hype

Previous generational history has something to teach us about the perils of striking out toward new social values across the great commercial wasteland. In times past, the media and other self-appointed moral authorities might have maligned, censored, or ignored those who made divergent choices in life. The 1960s and 1970s added a new hazard: *assimilation*, which might be a greater threat than repression. No previous protest movement ever had to face so treacherous a strategy. Throughout the period, the radical young themselves worried obsessively about the dangers of "co-optation." As they found themselves reflected more and more in the fun-house mirror of the media, they feared that their rebellion would be absorbed into the mainstream culture as Radical Chic.

The fears were well founded. Gestures of dissent became recognized as hot copy, the big story of the decade. The young were vibrant, innovative, sexy; they quickly became an amazing, wish-fulfilling spectacle. There was never a demonstration, a rally, a teach-in, a love-in, a be-in, but cameras and microphones were on hand. In San Francisco the tour buses soon included the hippies of the Haight-Ashbury District on their itineraries.

The objects of this attention sometimes resorted to extravagant tactics to defend the purity of their stance. People *tried* to look and dress and behave in ways that were unphotographable. It did no good. Grungy rags were soon transformed into grungy fashions. Before the decade was out, expensive Mao jackets were appearing in major department stores and automobile companies were promoting their cars as a "rebellion." Rock, including its various outlaw varieties, became the staple of the music industry. One radical magazine, wanting to make sure no store would display it on the rack, took the title *Fuck You.* At countercultural gatherings, money earned by a book or a record might be scattered to the winds like confetti. Some dissenting voices, especially the rock stars of the era, certainly earned more than enough to be corrupted and probably were. Money is the universal solvent of American society; it melts the toughest ethical armor. I have met few outsiders, radicals, or dissenters who could hold out against a publisher's contract or a network interview. All of us have ways of explaining that the money *we* earn from what *we* do is purer than the money that sellouts and schlockmeisters earn.

When the aged were few in numbers and low in income, nobody rushed to sell them anything except Serutan and funeral insurance. Now, as mass longevity takes hold, the New People are starting to present some attractive market demographics. And they arrive at elderhood with unresolved questions about youth and age that others will rush to answer — for a fee. Already we have a host of commercial interests waiting in the wings to cash in on all the senior follies they can merchandise — and on nothing more so than the flight from age. My local supermarket is devoting steadily more shelf space to handsomely packaged and extravagantly priced longevity potions: various combinations of ginkgo and ginseng, echinacea and chamomile liberally laced with antioxidants. Some carry highly creative copy about the lost lore and secret teachings that went into a rather small, expensive bottle of "rejuvenating infusions." "Age-conscious" producers are finding ways to acknowledge that older people are different, but not — so they hope — in ways that make a difference to business as usual.

The joys of youth — especially as memory wishfully embroiders them — are not easily left behind. Many New People are displaying a clear ambivalence about their role in life. As reaching a healthy age sixty-five becomes commonplace, they are experiencing a peculiar, late-life identity crisis. Having made it that far, one can now envision another twenty or thirty years of life ahead. That is a much longer time to be "old" than most people in the past had to worry about. It takes a moment of concentrated reflection to realize what this means. At the age of sixty, we may now have as much time ahead as our grandparents could expect when they were thirty and in their prime. That is enough life to be put to good use. But how shall those years be spent? A pressing question — especially for those who have enough money to make choices.

Surgical Chic

There are more than enough huckstering voices that want us to believe we should spend our sixties and seventies being twenty or thirty all over again — starting with the physical semblance of youth. The means for doing so are readily available and temptingly proficient. The same ingenious medical science that can keep us vital and alive so much longer can also reshape the body in increasingly clever ways. As of the mid-1990s, the American public that the cosmetic industry refers to as "youth-obsessed boomers" was spending upwards of $2.5 billion on aesthetic surgery. That paid for over two million procedures in 1995, mainly face-lifts, breast augmentation, and liposuction. The numbers are bound to rise; even oral surgeons are tooling up to enter the trade.

Some of the techniques becoming commonplace would have sounded frightening in times past; they still do, but they are now routine and fearlessly endured. In more elevated income brackets where the cost of age defiance is no obstacle, surgical improvement is becoming a painful and costly seasonal routine; procedures are planned in preparation for first night at the opera, the spring round of parties, the year-end holidays, or various openings and galas. One must time the operations carefully to make sure the swelling has gone down before the event —

unless the procedure is breast augmentation. Then the swelling is regarded as a bonus. Some enhancements, like collagen injections to give lips that bee-stung look, may have to be renewed every two months. So too liposuction and skin peels. No longer onetime jobs, these enhancements need to be tended around the social calendar. Aesthetic surgery is becoming a form of maintenance.

Men, who now utilize the skills of cosmetic surgeons nearly as frequently as women, claim their need for age suppression has to do with their jobs. Males represent a growth market for face-lifts, eyelid tucks, and laser hair implants. Keeping their place in the firm and getting promoted, men feel, has to do with looking young. But if everybody does the same, what will come of that? In the 1960s, there was a bit of radical folklore about the Maoist students' meeting where every member of the audience turned out to be an FBI undercover agent. Perhaps one day all the thirty-something-lookers around the conference table will really be sixty-somethings. Will they need to wear the mask of youth then?

We may be creating a new category of beauty in our culture: the beauty of those who have been artfully "made over" and show it. That certain tautly plasticized look is becoming as common a sight among us as stretched lips among Ubangi women. A man or woman of sixty who might (at dusk, with the light shining from behind) be taken for thirty is a makeover; everybody can tell. But perhaps that will matter less as time goes on; it may even become intentional. In his novel *The Bonfire of the Vanities,* Tom Wolfe has a category of well-dieted upper-crust women he calls "social x-rays," ostentatiously lean to the point of emaciation, hoping that thin will pass for young. Similarly, in the anti-utopian movie *Brazil,* society ladies of the future hold parties to announce their surgery, which is meant to be proudly on display. Why hide the makeover when, in itself, it makes the important statement: *I intend to remain vital, active, alert, and competitive. I have suffered and spent heavily for this look. Treat me accordingly.* And if the surgery has been well done, perhaps it should be admired as a kind of living sculpture. Then there need be no serious attempt to deceive. The work may be signed, trademarked, and exhibited. The best surgical talents in the business will hold openings and soirees that are, in effect, living galleries of their art.

And then there are the fantasies, the products associated with vigor and high living. Television commercials are already featuring frisky seniors — perhaps a more acceptable stereotype than the cranky codger, but a stereotype just the same. The problem is a tricky one for advertisers, whose main interest is neither accuracy nor compassion. How they cope with the senior market is less important than how seniors deal with their newfound marketability.

At the extreme, we have the pursuit of age-reversal fads, some little more than the old snake oil decked out in new, scientistic terminology. The magazine *Life Extension* now features an updated "top ten" list of rejuvenating elixirs. Vitamin supplements alone make up a multibillion-dollar industry. Sampling all the remedies, even reading the literature on the products, could easily absorb all the time one has left in life.

All of these pursuits represent understandable human foibles, rather than serious moral failure. Perhaps they would have become common in any society of the past if the aged had not been resigned to poverty, isolation, and early physical breakdown. A bit of hair coloring and cosmetic surgery need not get in the way of social conscience. But it is quite another matter if playing at youthfulness obscures the opportunity and responsibility for making wise use of one's years.

The Productive Agers

The struggle to emulate youth overlaps with another treacherous distraction in the growing culture of longevity. It is called "productive aging." The term was originated in the early 1980s by the gerontologist Robert Butler, who intended it as an antidote for the resignation that surrounded old age. Butler was among the first to recognize that America's senior population was becoming healthier, more active, more competent, and more politically important than politicians and opinion-makers had recognized. The older years were taking on vitality. "The capacity for curiosity, creativity, surprise, and change," he insisted, "does not invariably decline with age."[1]

As a counterbalance to ageism, productive aging may have value, but there are problems with the underlying concept. Productive agers can be seen as those who keep competing and achieving into their late senior years. They include those who run for office at seventy, launch successful businesses at eighty, climb high mountains at ninety, win literary prizes at one hundred. They stay on the job and in the race. These seniors are apt to take on great visibility; they have a special appeal to the media because their stories easily qualify as "feel-good" journalism, combining financial success and inspirational rhetoric. These are often moneyed folk with good social connections who drop all the right names, dress beautifully, and look good on camera — exactly what talk-show hosts are after. Their competitive talents may not, however, be within the aptitude or taste of many others, who are seeking something more in their elder years than a second round of youth. As one group of older women put it in a study of "wise choices beyond midlife": "We are being urged to become politically correct about aging — anything is possible. The elderly Olympics are just ahead. Get Up and Go! . . . Can we still find respect and support for contentment, tolerance, and reflection or for being at peace with ourselves, our friends, our families, and the world?"[2]

Betty Friedan, a commentator whose views have to be respected, is a great believer in productive aging. She was among those who helped Butler shape the concept in the early 1980s. She continues to feel it is the only alternative to the ambience of self-pity and condescension into which elders have tended to decline. She observes that "it was in terms of work that the issue of the personhood of women was finally and fully joined. . . . I welcomed the opportunity to deal with age in such terms." She is impatient with those who do not "want to look at older people in terms of 'work' or 'productivity.'"[3] Friedan's study *The Fountain of Age* is among the most incisive books on the subject of aging in America, and her intentions are the highest, but with respect to the word *productivity*, I would suggest a change of vocabulary. This is language coined in the economic mainstream for purposes of competition and profit. Typically, an executive type who has never met his workforce and who has no idea what, for example, healing or education are all about will push nurses and teachers to increase their "productivity" — that is, demand that they work harder so the firm can lift its profit margin.

"Productivity" derives from the making of products, and products are for selling. That is exactly what hucksters in the senior marketplace are out to do. So they gravitate to those who maintain an air of success and celebrity into their elder years. As a transitional phase in the unfolding saga of the New People, we can expect to see and hear a great deal more about productive aging or some variation on the concept in the years ahead — stories that feature later-life high achievers who might almost pass for thirty years old. This is homage to the cult of youth all over again; we are being told, more and more wishfully, that seniors can keep up with the young at any task. Viewing age this way only makes the phenomenon of the ragged fringe — the point at which physical stamina fails — all the more frightening.

If the New People are to be something authentically new under the sun, competitive achievement cannot be their way of using longevity. It is certainly no form of elderhood. Elders must be a creative force in our culture, not the same old thing in advanced years. Being productive is not the same as being creative. On the other hand, calling competition into question and opting out of the chase for celebrity and wealth — *that* is new and takes both courage and imagination. Friedan is closer to the key question when she wonders whether "there might be life beyond retirement from the power-sex race?" She is right in sensing that the pursuit of power and sex belongs to the market economy. To rise above the race, then, is the beginning of wisdom. But the correct measurement of wisdom is not "productivity."

This is the issue that arises with urgent economic importance when financial entrepreneurs propose to privatize Social Security, turning the national nest egg into millions of speculative portfolios. Such a policy would tie the senior years to the marketplace in ways that would never allow one to detach and grow beyond it. If one's savings have been invested, then one must attend to the mutual funds, follow their progress, choose among them, watch the ups and downs of the economy with an eagle eye. It is retiring into a full-time business: the business of managing one's money. What a nightmarish retirement that could be, worrying around the clock about the fate of Microsoft and the stability of a half-dozen Asian currencies. Of course, fund managers offer to do that for us, but who can trust them to do the job honestly? Certainly not the productive ager who looks after his or her own needs.

The senior follies all trace to the same source: the effort to deny or defy aging, to continue worshiping at the cult of youth. That sad desire ties us to the marketplace and its values: money, success, glamour, celebrity. Moreover, the denial of age is self-defeating, because eventually time takes its toll and that comes as a jolt if one has devoted years to fighting off its claim. If wisdom means anything, it means the ability to see through the illusions of youth. That is the most liberating aspect of age. It frees the mind and enlivens the soul. It is the beginning of the great Socratic adventure of knowing ourselves.

In the Absence of Elders

In one respect the senior follies are worse than merely embarrassing. If the New People lose themselves in trendiness and commercialized hype, they will fail in their prime moral obligation. They will become, not elders, but simply over-aged consumers and fashion plates, as much a part of the marketplace as any American who was ever persuaded to believe that social success is a matter of using the right mouthwash. Elders are not made by doting upon youthful frivolities or by fleeing the responsibilities of age. There is far more at stake in these matters than the wistful longing of the old to be young again. There is what we owe the young who need to grow up. And if ever a generation needed a commanding model of adulthood, it is the generation (and by now more than a single generational cohort) that has come into being since the early 1970s.

The very fact that we now think so much in terms of generations, a slippery historical unit if there ever was one, is the dubious aftermath of the 1960s, which played out as a conflict between older and younger Americans. The issues of that time assumed that shape, not because there was a neat line of demarcation between ages — there never is — but because the most heated issue, the war in Vietnam, saw one generation making life-and-death decisions about another that, at that time, did not even have the right to vote. Against the background of the civil rights movement, which had made voting a burning issue of the day, the injustice of so brutal an assertion of privilege was dramatically clear. As Country Joe and the Fish asked the mothers and fathers of America in their "Fixin' to Die Talking Blues," did they want to "be the first one on your block to bring your boy home in a box?" The debate could become that bitter.

Without planning it that way, the New People in their youth visited upon our society a generationally based reading of history that can do more to distort than illuminate. The media now insist that there must always be a "generation gap"; they see this as an ongoing story. But, of course, the gap in which the media are interested cannot be about anything as substantive as matters of morality or value; they prefer to limit the story to sex, hairstyles, clothing, tastes in music. If these are the characteristics that are to define every generation's place in history, then we are involved in a trivial pursuit. Yet it is precisely this focus on trivialities that has persuaded many of the young who have come along since the 1960s to believe their primary task is to have "attitude," which means above all sticking one's thumb in the public eye.

So we have Generation-X, or the Blank Generation, or the Post-poned Generation, or the Digital Generation, or the Slackers — all hastily concocted Sunday supplement imagery intended to grab attention. But being different for the sheer sake of the difference is a meager project; struggling to be the latest, the hottest, the newest, is a waste of life. It is following fashion, not making history. If all citizens have a first order of responsibility, it is to secure justice and make life fulfilling. That is a project that matters, and it has nothing to do with attitude. In that common human business, we unite across all lines of potential division. It is the task of the young to grow into that role, and the task of elders to help them do that.

Seeking the Inner Child

The relations between generations are apt to be strained under the best of circumstances. There is one respect, however, in which the New People have introduced an odd kink into their capacity to be effective elders. They have invested a lot of time seeking the inner child.

The years following World War II ushered in a new style of child-rearing in the United States. It is usually labeled "permissive" and connected with the ideas of Dr. Benjamin Spock. Because of the unusually liberal parent-child relations that developed during that first wave of permissive child-rearing, a good many baby boomers arrived at their adult years encumbered with a lot of unfinished emotional business — rather as if they were not sure when or whether their childhood was over. Permissiveness taught us all to take childhood seriously, to lavish attention on the young and do all we could to keep them happy. Raising children in that spirit cannot help but bring out narcissistic tendencies, the sort of intense concern for oneself that we associate with children raised as the only child of doting parents. That became the norm in many middle-class families. No society in history has ever run so large and consequential an experiment in raising a generation of narcissists as the United States middle class during the 1950s and 1960s.

Ours is a highly psychological era. We have learned about the penalties of repression; we know there is an alternative we can use to bring shameful truths to light for examination — psychotherapy. And with enough money to indulge themselves in therapy, more and more middle-class Americans have been able to take advantage of the standard advice for all personal problems: "find professional help." That advice was once reserved for the monied few who could afford twenty years of grueling psychoanalysis, which might finally be less than fully successful. So the boomers hired professionals to help them contact the child they once were — and might still be.

Several schools of psychological thought have developed around the image of the child, starting with Freud. Freud's orientation was regressive and reductionistic. He tended to see childhood as a time of illusion and fantasy that must be outgrown. In his eyes, the main reason for unearthing childhood memories was to cauterize the sexual wounds one expected to find there. In contrast, Freud's disciple Carl Jung found something very different in childhood memories. He spent some years hunting for his own inner child, to the point of returning to the game-playing of his childhood. In the spirit of free play, he eventually built an entire toy village, never quite understanding what he was doing until he had completed the task. This playful search became one of the most important episodes in his career. He finally placed the Child among the most powerful of the healing archetypes, a grand "unifying symbol."[4]

In the 1940s, the Stanford University psychiatrist Milton Erickson found his way to "the child within" in much the same playful way and, again like Jung, discovered in his childhood recollections a wealth of rejuvenating new departures for his work. Erickson claimed that great ideas came to him while he rambled through old comic books left over from his boyhood. In his school of thought, contacting the child within is the pivotal moment of the therapeutic relationship. To make that moment as vividly emotional as possible, Erickson recommended the use of hypnosis.

Later, in the 1960s, child-based therapy found its most influential formulation in Eric Berne's school of transactional analysis, which took the "Child" to be a "phenomenological reality" based on the actual "playback" of data surviving as chemical traces in the brain. Berne believed that old experiences of frustration, rejection, and abandonment can be triggered and will replay in the present in ways that put the Child-self "in command." Hurtful memories seem most vivid, but besides such "not OK recordings of negative experiments," there are also memories of delight and deep satisfaction that wait to be discovered. A main purpose of the therapeutic encounter is to reexperience all the old predicaments.

Other schools of psychology took up the same project, sometimes in grueling ways. Primal therapy favored reliving childhood all the way back to a vivid recollection of the birth experience that issued forth in the "primal scream." In the 1990s, the popular television therapist John

Bradshaw was still drawing overflow audiences to lectures whose theme was "reclaiming and championing your inner child." Bradshaw characterized his clients as "adult children" whom he invited to join him in "grieving our neglected childhood development dependency needs." As much as the music, the politics, and the literature of the 1960s and 1970s, the search for the inner child was a sign of youthful times.

Among tougher-than-thou social critics, the image of grown-up people gathering to weep and stew over distant childhood grievances has been an easy target for ridicule. Like all psychological problems that are transcribed to the printed page, consulting with one's "wounded inner child" can be made to seem embarrassingly banal. A middle-aged woman, one of Eric Berne's clients, throws a small fit in her group over her childhood recollection of having to kiss an Aunt Ethel she loathed. The memory still rankles. "Get over it and grow up!" the critics say, as if that were easy to do. Growing up is the purported goal of all these psychologies, though there is room to question how well they do the job.

James Hillman, the Jungian analyst, has concluded that the overarching emphasis on childhood during the 1960s and 1970s returned people to their most helpless condition in life, a position that blocks active social involvement. Moreover, the inner child frequently connects with experiences of victimization that do more to undermine the adult ego than to heal old wounds. "The trip backward," Hillman observes, "constellates the 'child archetype.' Now the child archetype is by nature apolitical and disempowered — it has no connection with the political world. . . . Twenty or thirty years of therapy have removed the most sensitive and the most intelligent and some of the most affluent people in our society into child cult worship."[5]

In fairness to transactional analysis, the school that did most to bring this form of therapy to public attention, the purpose of all the exercises is, in fact, to become a grown-up by resolving the emotional issues of earlier years. The "Child" in question is to be integrated with the Parent-self and the Adult-self. TA, popularized as an affordable form of group therapy by Eric Berne, was designed as "a teaching and learning device rather than a confessional or an archeological exploration of the psychic cellars."[6]

From an unsympathetic perspective, this could look like easy, feel-better psychiatry, which is anathema to those who insist that introspection must be prolonged, heroic, and anguished. It should, however, be kept in mind that as far back as Freud and the Oedipus complex,

working through the traumas of child-parent relations has been the
focus of mental health. In that sense, modern psychotherapy has always
tried to lead us back to the child within. That is what it means to undo
repression. Far from being a trivial, self-indulgent preoccupation, dig-
ging back through one's childhood is among the central tasks of modern
psychotherapy, as well as of the finest introspective literature of our
time. I would not, therefore, be quite as quick as some critics have been
to write that project off, unless one wishes to reject therapy entirely. One
might hope that mothers and fathers who have been put charitably in
touch with their own childhood behavior will avoid the heavy-handed,
moralistic parenting that was the blight of the traditional family. We
should recall that in Victorian times parents were told to play the role of
God to their children, asserting a flattening authority, especially when it
came to self-expression and sexuality. Given that background in our
culture, it is understandable that psychotherapy would at some point
reexamine childhood in intense detail for all that had been lost there.

The remembrance of things past has always been at the heart of
self-knowledge. Coping with the emotional lacerations of early family
life might be the definition of growing up; not coping *well* might make
a passable definition of neurosis. But in the past, people either wrote
great literature about their flawed upbringing or simply buried the
memory as best they could and soldiered on in life — until they had the
chance to inflict the same damage on their own children. This is the
long, sad story that lies behind what some today call "family values."

On the other hand, whatever their theoretical intention, all these
schools run the risk of keeping people so preoccupied with their childhood that they might well fail to get on with their primary adult
responsibility. It seems fair to observe that the peculiar infatuation of
middle-class Americans of the post–World War II generation with
inner-child psychotherapy has left us with an unusual set of dysfunctional family issues. It has also left the task of becoming elders wholly
undefined. Parents, loitering over their inner child too long, may have
left an *outer* child or two of their own waiting for the benefit of wise,
adult counsel.

The poet Robert Bly, a leading figure in the men's movement, has
been especially worried about the inner-child orientation. He reaches
the melancholy conclusion that its influence has left us with a population of "half-adults" stranded between growing up and staying childlike.
He thinks "people of all ages are making decisions to avoid the difficul-

ties of maturity." He even raises the possibility that the neocortex of the parental generation, the locus of civilized values, has been left weakened by too much self-indulgence. Convinced that "the experience of austerity and the experience of maturity are connected," he believes that child-based therapy and the cultural values it induces appeal to "the greedy and lazy parts of the soul." Thus, instead of a normal, nourishing relationship between elders and children, we have a "sibling society" where nobody wants to pay the price and take the risk of growing up.[7]

Bly is surely right in believing that the worst of the senior follies would be to withdraw from the eldering role that no society can long do without. Elders retire *into* responsibility, not out of it. But the responsibility that comes with age is not that of the young entering upon adulthood. Elderhood is what a lifetime of adulthood matures into. In very real ways, it may require outgrowing adult values that block the way to wisdom. That, in turn, may involve one more critical transition in the later years, a rite of passage that we will examine in chapters to come.

Crowding the Young

A letter to *Parade* magazine in June 1996 from a California teenager:

> I am 17 years old, and I am pessimistic about my future. The whole world is so messed up — just look at the news: You have parents beating kids. You have adults molesting and raping children. You have lots of kids on drugs and lots of depressed kids. Our whole generation, "Generation-X," needs help. The X is almost the end of the alphabet. Does that mean that we've come to the end and that we are the ones who will destroy everything? If so, it isn't because we created anything. Everything is already here for us to play with. The flower children grew up thinking that all you had to do is love everyone and smile, and the whole world would just fix itself for you. But Generation-X knows the truth: we are not able to have everything. The odds are against us. Technology is starting to take over America. Jobs are no longer stable. As kids in my generation see it, it's the world against us.
>
> Yes, drug use and sexually active teens have always been around, but their numbers are rising. And now middle school students are having sex. Middle school girls are having abortions. Something's gone wrong. Children are killing each other and themselves. I have friends who have killed themselves. Children are raping other chil-

dren. Either these things have always existed but were never discussed, or our whole generation was raised terribly wrong.

About one-third of our generation doesn't care about anything
important. It's kind of like anything goes. We feel like everything's
changing and we have nothing to do with it, so we'll just sit back
and let it happen. We have nothing stable to grasp. No one to look
up to. No one to believe in. No one to trust but ourselves.

One letter from one sad young person, but a revealing confession of
powerlessness and anxiety. The vision one finds here of the baby boom
generation as a suffocating presence taking up too much social space has
merit to it. On the basis of numbers alone, the boomers were a big
generation, and a privileged one. Now they are enjoying the unforeseen
benefits of longevity and so will be around a good deal longer than their
parents or grandparents. They are not clearing out and leaving an open
field to a younger generation they trust.

These facts radically alter the role of eldering in our time. If generosity is the soul of eldering, then the long-term demographic dominance
of the New People makes generosity all the more difficult. In the past,
elders were far fewer in number and marginal in status. Their wisdom
was all they had to offer. They might have been valued for that, but they
did not necessarily wield power. The young might have deferred to
them, but they did not have to. The deference was based on respect and
appreciation. Now "productively aging" seniors stay actively on the scene
far longer. They have no intention of creeping meekly into nursing
homes. Retirement for this group and for all who follow them may grow
increasingly problematical. If they are fit enough to continue working,
and probably ambitious enough to do so, will they find retirement an
attractive prospect? If so, what kind of retirement will that be?

Meanwhile, youth in their twenties and thirties will be scuffling to
keep employed at *anything*, probably holding more than one job in an
ever less secure job market, accepting employment or independent contracting without benefits, struggling to afford families. How favorably
will they look upon seventy-year-olds who are doing all they can to stay
on the payroll, not least of all for the "psychic income" that comes of
feeling still vigorous, still competent, still competitive? As we have seen,
retired seniors may soon turn into a reserve army of cheap labor that
displaces younger workers.

When anti-entitlements critics propose raising the retirement age to
seventy or seventy-two, they might ask what the young think about

that. After all, the jobs at which people in their seventies are most likely to keep working — white-collar managerial and executive positions or other professional work — are the best paid occupations around. What will the efforts these seniors make to keep fit and appear youthful look like to the young but a cruel trick played by a privileged class? Indeed, these conditions help explain the peculiarly stalled quality of successive younger generations since the late 1970s.

Unless the New People find other places to turn that engage their best powers, they are apt to keep crowding the young for another twenty or thirty years. The result may be an interval when generational conflict grows particularly bitter. The senior generation will not be doing the one thing that could always be expected of it: leaving the stage. Nor, for that matter, will this be true of the New People only. The generation to follow will do the same. Longevity will outlast the boomers. Each older generation from here into the indefinite future is going to stay around longer. The "young" may have no chance to take over until they are well into their middle years.

The Role of the Elder

Those who lived through the peculiar cultural style of the 1960s and 1970s are having their healthy doubts about permissiveness and lifelong narcissism. In my university classes, I now meet students, mainly women returning to school in their late forties, who are struggling with new issues in child-rearing. The experience of their own upbringing has left them acutely aware that parenting is not a talent that one can take for granted. Some who grew up in heavily patriarchal families broke away to live highly rebellious, countercultural lives in their teens and twenties. Rebellion played a liberating, though sometimes bruising, role in their lives. Now they wonder how much latitude to permit their own young. The sort of sex life they knew has become lethally risky.

Others who were raised permissively by Spockian parents are uncertain how to deal with their own children, especially on issues of sex and drugs. They worry about being too unstructured. The more thoughtful parents I meet are trying to steer a midcourse between the authoritarian parenthood they rejected in their youth and an ineffectual leniency that Dr. Spock himself never condoned. As one might have guessed, the remedy for therapy in America is the hair of the dog. In the 1980s a new school of psychology called parent effectiveness training (PET) sought to offer advice to postpermissive parents on questions like these. Essentially, PET has tried to rebalance the scale toward discipline and structure in the family and to give parents a firmer grip on their responsibilities.[8]

As difficult as these choices are to make, an even more demanding role awaits the New People when they reach their senior years. Beyond the dilemmas of parenting their own children lies the task of being an elder within the society at large. Psychology has not come remotely close to mapping this late stage of life. It may well be that many of us will find ourselves face to face with eldering before we have worked it all out with our inner child. Perhaps one day we will have a new school of psychotherapy that starts from the assumption that inner children are destined to remain unfinished business throughout a lifetime. There is a child inside all of us waiting to be cared for, but there is also an elder within waiting to be honored before time runs out.

Just as the 1960s and 1970s generated child-oriented psychotherapy, we are likely to see a plethora of elder-relevant therapy and counseling in the years ahead. One can only hope that this healthy interest does not evaporate into another New Age fad. The scholarly and psychological groundwork for the study of eldering as a distinct phase of human development is under study. The psychiatrist David Gutmann, for example, working from comparative studies of aging in modern Western and Native American cultures, believes that traditional societies have a great lesson to teach us. "In settings in which elders have the social leverage to arrange matters according to their own priorities, we find striking evidence of new development in both male and female personalities in later life." In traditional cultures, the old are often given "great assignments." They may be asked to face formidable "spiritual dangers." Elders, Gutmann argues, are present not simply by virtue of fortunate survival, but because healthy cultures *need* them. "We do not have elders because we have a human gift and modern capacity for keeping the weak alive; instead, we are human because we have elders."[9]

In his study of the male life cycle, Daniel Levinson makes eldering the centerpiece of the senior years. He tells us that in the third era of life (middle adulthood, from age forty to sixty-five)

> we are responsible not only for our own work, but also for the
> development of the current generation of young adults who will

soon enter the senior generation. It is possible in this era to become more maturely creative, more responsible for self and others. . . . Unfortunately middle adulthood is for many persons a time of progressive decline, of growing emptiness and loss of vitality.[10]

As eldering becomes more prominently respected, we can expect the media to feature a steady run of "discoveries" about the emotional contours of the later years of life. No doubt we will be seeing a succession of senior gurus on television and on the lecture-workshop circuit mass-marketing techniques for creative aging. But these schools of psychology may have a strange configuration. Will therapists of thirty and forty take on the job of counseling clients old enough to be their grandparents? Will they presume to know more about chronic disease, grief, and mortality than those who have spent a long life getting to where they are? I suspect I would find it either depressing or aggravating to have someone half my age telling me what life is all about. Or will elders create their own style of peer counseling, forms of spiritual companionship that unite them in facing the great philosophical issues on which nobody is an expert?

7

Maturity and the Media

A TELEVISION WRITER I know was complaining about her difficulties in Hollywood these days. As the years pass, she finds it harder to get penciled in for meetings with studio executives. "Once you're past twenty-seven, you're over the hill and out of sight," she lamented.

She described a common experience. She is asked to sit in on a story meeting with producers and writers who, like herself, are over forty — some of them well over forty. At the table sits a young man in his mid-twenties, who has just been hired. He has no great track record, he is at the bottom of the corporate totem pole, but he is commanding a lot of attention. Why? Because, in a gathering like this, he has an uncanny psychological leverage. Being young and male, he is assumed to be in touch with "the audience." What audience? The only audience that matters: eighteen- to forty-nine-year-olds . . . or, better still, all eighteen- to thirty-four-year-olds, preferably nonfemale. People around the table are taking cues from him. The young are, after all, "with it." People give heed because nobody wants to seem "out of it."

Stalled on Melrose Place

Perhaps this scene explains something I find more and more puzzling with each passing year. The action movies that cost so much to produce and receive the most promotional hoopla are obviously designed for adolescents with nothing more than mayhem on their minds; the television dramas, sitcoms, and soap operas rolled out each season are after an audience of young singles. Confronted with so much media fare that seems stalled on Melrose Place or Sunset Beach, I find myself asking, "What's wrong with this picture?"

The answer would seem to be *everything*.

Productions like these are at war with the U.S. Census Bureau. The audience of high-living twenty-somethings they seek to attract is becoming a phantom population. Singles under thirty are a steadily shrinking part of our society. The number of Americans turning twenty-five peaked in 1986; there will never be that many people entering that age range again. In the twenty-first century, the population over sixty will ever more steadily outnumber the population under twenty-five. Although that has been a thoroughly predictable trend for decades, it was not until President Clinton turned fifty — in the mid-1990s — that the media suddenly registered the demographic facts of life. When, in March 1997, the *New York Times* devoted an entire issue of its Sunday magazine to the "Age Boom," it began by reporting that "America Discovers a New Stage of Life." Meaning, of course, that the *New York Times* had just discovered a new stage of life — and decided to compliment itself for so doing.

The word *discovers* underscores how demographically illiterate we have become. By simply glancing over the census figures or following the calculations of the Social Security Administration, one could have learned twenty years ago that ours was a rapidly aging society. "Discovering" that fact is like discovering that a plane flying due west from anywhere in the United States is getting closer to the Pacific Ocean. When facts like this have to be announced with banner headlines, it is not because they were so hard to see, but because those who make the announcement have been looking in the wrong direction.

Who would guess from watching what goes out over television these days that Americans over sixty are now the largest viewing audience in the United States? They report spending half their free time watching.[1] Perhaps they might wish to have better things to do with themselves, but if the media and the advertising image-makers elect to continue ignoring such elementary demographics, that is not because they enjoy privileged access to some inviolable first principle of marketing science. It is, rather, an impressive indication of how embedded the stereotypes of youth and age are in the folklore, cultural symbolism, and wishful thinking of our society. So stubbornly embedded, in fact, that even when money — a great deal of money — is at stake, people who are otherwise single-mindedly preoccupied with profit cannot see the obvious: namely, that our society is getting older and the young are getting poorer.

Demographic Illiteracy

Before the advent of mass media that could be privately owned and exploited, popular culture was an accurate expression of what most people in a society believed, liked, and valued. "Popular" might mean commercial, but the quality of the cultural offering could range from P. T. Barnum's circus all the way up to Shakespeare's tragedies and the liturgy of the church. In any case, what people sought out and enjoyed was a direct reflection of their taste. With the growth of an "entertainment industry" in the twentieth century, we now have contingents of middle men and women who pursue high-paying careers brokering culture between the public, the advertisers, and the sprawling conglomerates that monopolize ever more of the means of communication.

What "popular" means in our time is decided in boardrooms by people who claim to be professionally equipped to know what the public wants and who can talk the polling statistics to prove it. They hold august titles (Vice President in Charge of Planning and Research, Head of Programming, Director of Corporate Advertising, Chief Media Coordinator) and have staffs of eager young assistants with university degrees in marketing and mass communications who review the microdata and shuffle the demographics. The problem is not that they cannot read the numbers, but that they have more than one master to please. Even when they work from supposedly reliable data, they may be trying to appeal to what a corporate client or sponsor thinks the public wants rather than to the public itself. So they trim and tweak the numbers to please the people who pay them — and doubtless they do a lot of guessing. More and more frequently, they guess wrong because they are reluctant to face an unsettling truth. Youth is becoming a thing of the past.

In their adolescent and college years, the New People were the stars of an ebullient and colorful youth culture that has left its mark on media and advertising. More than representing immense purchasing power, they appealed to a certain restiveness in the business community that wished to break free of the Organization Man conformity that had often stifled the liveliest new minds. Youth, even in so inane a formulation as the famous "Pepsi Generation" sales campaign, was the image that liberated these stymied energies. In his study of "business culture, counter culture, and the rise of hip consumerism," Thomas Frank chronicles this remarkable transformation of corporate America in the

1960s. "What happened in the sixties is that hip became central to the way American capitalism understood itself and explained itself to the public." And "hip" meant pushing the "young demographic." "Suddenly youth became a consuming position to which all could aspire. . . . The conceptual position of *youthfulness* became as great an element of the marketing picture as youth itself."[2]

What Frank overlooks is that the "young demographic" of the 1960s was freakish and transient. Demographers remind us that the United States began growing collectively older as early as 1800. Nobody was taking serious note of the statistics then, but in Thomas Jefferson's time half the white European population was under the age of sixteen, a ratio of young to old that the country was never to see again. Throughout the nineteenth century, despite the demographic ups and downs that resulted from industrialization and the massive influx of impoverished immigrants vulnerable to killer epidemics, life expectancy grew slowly longer and the society grew steadily older.

The one great exception to the gradual, long-term aging of America was the reproductive surge that occurred between 1946 and 1964. Through those years, the American birth rate ballooned to 3.7, well above the replacement rate of 2 and very nearly what we consider a Third World level of reproduction — but of course with many more of the babies surviving. Then, as if in a fit of exhaustion almost immediately following that brief birthing spurt, total fertility dropped off sharply to reach a record American low of 1.7 by 1976 — well below the rate needed to replace mothers and fathers. Since then, as in many industrial societies, our rate of population growth has hovered around the replacement number, with immigration playing an ever greater role in our population growth.

It is the unusual and unforeseen bulge of the baby boom that has obscured the long-term trend. Within a larger historical context, we might almost say that what the baby boom produced was a massive contribution to the continued aging of the nation. As of the late 1970s longevity had more demographic raw material to work upon than ever before. Yet as aberrant as the baby boom was, it induced a wishfully delusionary state of mind that continues to distort demographic reality. It gave one last infusion of vitality to an age-old fascination with youth — and not simply because of the numbers involved. There was also the role played by politics, the media, and the marketplace. As early as the 1940s, the young came to be recognized as a lucrative market; accordingly, advertisers skewed their appeal toward them. Then, as the babies grew up to become more politically obstreperous through the 1960s, the media paid them inordinate attention. They were identified as a prime indicator of changes "blowing in the wind." But the media, which continue to treat youth as the primary force for change, are making a serious mistake. While they have been looking longingly backward toward a social style that was set during the 1960s, the future belongs to a longevity revolution.

Not only are Americans above the age of fifty the fastest-growing segment in our population, but their share of the national wealth vastly exceeds that of their children and grandchildren — a fact that one would assume to be of considerable interest to the media. The one-quarter of the American population over fifty years old as of the turn of the twenty-first century has an annual personal income approaching $1 trillion. This age group controls half the disposable earnings in the country. That includes 75 percent of financial assets (worth over $8 trillion) and 80 percent of all savings and loans accounts. With a long life expectancy, the boomer generation will get richer as it gets older. It will inherit some $10.7 trillion from its parents.[3] There are still too many seniors who fall below the poverty line, but thanks to personal savings, Medicare, home ownership, and tax breaks, the Social Security Administration estimates that, as of the 1990s, Americans over sixty-five years of age have the largest amount of discretionary income in the nation — more than twice as much as that of young people between twenty-five and thirty-four.[4] Among postmenopausal women alone we have what the columnist Ellen Goodman calls "a marketeer's dream" — an alert, book-buying, culture-consuming population heading toward fifty million in the early years of the twenty-first century, many of them working women who have earned well in their careers.

In contrast, as we enter the twenty-first century, the eighteen-to-twenty-four-year-old population will shrink by four million, down 15 percent from its 1990 total, and lose $3 billion a year in discretionary income. "There will always be a youth market," observes the editor of *American Demographics*, "but it won't always be powerful relative to other markets. In the future, American business has got to learn to love the middle-aged."[5]

The trend is clear. In every coming decade, the same population that is now fifty to sixty — minus an ever decreasing percentage who die along the way — will report in at an older age, still there, still numerous, still moneyed. Unless another baby boom occurs — and that is nowhere in sight — the ratios of old to young with respect to numbers and wealth will remain "senior-skewed." Eventually the people now in the eighteen-to-forty-nine population whom advertisers want so desperately to reach will be affluent enough to respond to their messages, but by then they will have moved on into the senior ranks. The marketing trend away from youth and toward age is irreversible.

A moment's reflection explains why things have turned out this way. Americans of fifty years and over are the chief beneficiaries of the Great Affluence, the greatest economic boom in history. That boom saw the wealth of the nation more generously distributed than any labor leader or social reformer of the past had ever thought possible. The years that stretch from the beginning of World War II through the later 1970s have been called — now with an increasingly melancholy nostalgia — the era of the "Great American Job." Now that privileged generation is carrying its wealth into its retirement years.

Here, clearly, is where our society's financial center of gravity lies. These are the people who own homes, shop for luxury vacations and cars, and pay off their credit cards on time. Nevertheless, the media have long regarded them as "consumer zombies."

Why?

Generational Myopia

One team of marketing analysts describes the problem as "generational myopia," meaning a "shortsighted application of the values and attitudes of your own generation to the development of strategies for marketing to another generation." In other words, the over-fifty population is written off because it is simply not the youth market that once mattered. Instead of being an easy mark for glitzy goods and trendy novelties, older consumers — in this analysis called "matures" and "boomers" — are seen as a tough sell. The matures (with a Great Depression–World War II background) are "slow to embrace new products," and the boomers (Great Society background) want "the kind of sophistication and impertinence that has always appealed to them."

"To advertisers, youth is excitement and pizzazz," says an advertising copywriter in the New York Times special issue on age. "It all goes back to one of those unwritten rules of marketing: Don't target consumers who are 50 and over because they're beyond reach."[6]

Of course they are "beyond reach." That is because they *know better* than to let themselves be too easily reached by commercial rhetoric and imagery. There is at least a bit more skepticism and a lot less gullibility to be found in older heads. So by way of a self-fulfilling prophecy, older people are out of reach because advertising itself has placed them there. They pay less attention because the advertisers prefer lifestyle fantasies that have little to do with being postadolescent. And yet, though the job market may fluctuate by the season, the jobs available to most younger workers have been steadily trending toward lower pay and less security since the mid-1970s. The hard-bodied teens and twenty-somethings most avidly courted by the media are the same job-worried youth who sell us ninety-nine-cent tacos and hamburgers and think of themselves as "slackers."

To be sure, one can always find youthful high achievers: Wall Street wheeler-dealers, million-dollar athletes, rock stars, genius hackers. The networks and the news weeklies routinely run stories about the hot young talent of the "digital generation" about to "take over" the world. It is the usual American success story that is meant to convince anybody who may be taking a hard hit from the economy that it must be his or her own fault. But one need only look at the course of real wages in our economy to realize that the income of younger workers has been steadily downscaling to the cheap jeans and six-pack level. If these young people display nice teeth, you can be sure they were not the ones who paid for the orthodontics and caps.[7]

Is it possible that the media elite, now in their middle and senior years, cling to fond illusions of the lifestyle they most want to emulate: wrinkle-free skin, endless parties, easy (apparently AIDS-free) sex? An older television director interviewed in 1995 on the subject of the "Hollywood Greylist" contends that there is "an abnormal obsession with the young, white boy . . . a male youth fantasy syndrome.[8] This is the "diaper brigade" of young producers and young audiences that accounts for the biggest film budgets, namely, those spent on action movies that lose any semblance of coherence after the first fifteen minutes.

Besides consoling personal fantasy, there may be another explanation for this fixation on youth. The people who produce our popular culture may have certain inadmissible limitations. Those who have earned their living for so long selling silly products to mindless millions may have lost the capacity to deal with a more discriminating audience. An older audience may look daunting in comparison to the ditzy world of adolescent–young adult tastes and fashions, where the attention span is so

brief that no one can track through thirty seconds of commercial soph-
istry. Perhaps it is easier to dismiss those who think twice about the cost
and quality of what they buy and move on to less demanding targets.

There are now highly paid "coolhunters" who study the youth market
in microscopic detail, reporting on trends in speech, dress, cosmetics,
haircuts, entertainment, food, lifestyle — effluvia that come and go so
rapidly that there may not be time for the goods to reach the market
before they have lost their cachet. Coolhunting clients include some of
the largest corporations in the global economy: franchise food and
clothing chains, software manufacturers, theme park operators, media
producers. As clever as it is meant to be, coolhunting produces the same
boring result over and over: lists of arbitrary weird things observed on
the streets or in the clubs of major cities. Teenagers wearing their pants
backwards, dying their hair saffron, chewing tobacco . . . a "trend" is
anything done, said, worn, eaten, drunk, listened to, or laughed at by a
twelve- to eighteen-year-old that nobody remembers hearing about
before. In this bizarre ambience, changes in sneaker and jeans design —
for example, a switch from fake grease spots to pastels — inflate to
cosmic importance. Age brackets are exquisitely refined: fourteen- to
eighteen-year-olds, nineteen- to twenty-four-year-olds, twenty-five- to
thirty-year-olds. Often what is "cool" is a revival of a period the young-
sters know only from television reruns — something "totally fifties,"
"absolutely sixties." Even "old lady" clothing can be cool — if it is worn
by girls of fifteen.[9]

These merchandising strategies are not limited to the United States.
In Japan the business community has developed a fascination with the
"ko-gal" population: teenage schoolgirls whose preferences are carefully
monitored by the media. They have been identified as Japan's trend-set-
ting consumers. Highly brand-conscious and willing to squander hundreds of dollars a month on ephemera like Fendi bags or Tamagotchi
virtual pets, the girls are rounded up into focus groups and hired as
temporary consultants on "what's hot." One marketing analyst calls the
ko-gals "the incubator for any product boom." If they go for the item, it
will be promoted first to twenty-somethings and then to thirty-somethings before being rushed into the export market as a likely prospect.
The girls are reported to be so addicted to consumption that a certain
number of them stray into prostitution to find more money to spend.[10]

This is almost the stuff of comedy. One imagines that somewhere at
the dizzy top of the global-corporate pyramid, serious-faced men in
expensive suits meet with deeply studied marketing specialists to plan

the investment of billions. And what is the topic under discussion? The latest rage among fifteen-year-old schoolgirls: cell phones wrapped in panda skin, cone-shaped hamburgers, Beavis and Butthead underwear. There cannot be a single person in the meeting who does not know this is unworthy of grown-ups. But they are driven to it by the money they want to make.

Coolhunters . . . ko-gals . . . is this what Adam Smith, David Ricardo, and John Stuart Mill had in mind when they hymned the glories of the free market?

There may be people who are brilliant at selling zany clothes and novelty soft drinks to intellectually challenged adolescents. But those who have worked throughout their careers in so mind-numbingly vapid a world may be in no position to retool and switch over to maturity as if it were simply another transient style. So one adjusts the statistics and pretends the audience out there is really still eighteen to forty-nine years old. If that is the case, then "18-to-49 rules" only apply for as long as the media remain in the hands of people who cannot themselves outgrow that age range. Others will have to take their place.

And in time that will happen. Money will make it happen. We may safely assume that the media will at last develop a marketing strategy aimed at a mature public. One already sees signs of the change: cover stories about "ageless beauties" in film and television, fifty-something superstars modeling panty hose and lingerie, press-agentry about bringing back all the once-popular stars who have joined the Over-Sixty Club. Some advertising agencies already specialize in reaching senior consumers. At some point, there will be an accelerated shift, rather like an earthquake fault responding to pressure that has been building for years. Suddenly products and programs galore will surface for those who have the discretionary income to spend. Tremors have already registered. Early in 1998 the Kellogg Company noted a sharp drop in the sale of its principal brand. Research revealed that the middle-aged female market it was after was repulsed by the cute, young, size-four models the company was featuring in its commercials. Kellogg ordered new commercials and new models. When enough sales resistance of this kind accumulates, advertising may even be forced to use intelligence and honesty to gain the attention of grown-ups — though that may be too much to hope for. If that happens, no doubt opportunistic industry leaders will rush to claim credit for waking up to facts that should have been apparent years ago.[11]

As the New People make their presence known, we may expect to see the media adjust by fits and starts, trying this and that to cope with the unprecedented task of meeting significantly more mature standards. One can predict what the changes will be. There will be more stories about *old* lawyers, *old* cops, *old* teachers, and *old* divorced singles starring comeback actors as aging studs, sexy moms, and randy grandmas; there will be tales that mix and match older men with younger women, younger men with older women.

But does maturity mean that the next phase in popular culture will feature a cult of age to replace a less and less profitable cult of youth: older faces, older actors, stories about age and its problems? Let us hope not. The young, always touched with a certain adolescent narcissism, may be eager to see themselves constantly mirrored in the culture, but not so the old. What a truly adult audience wishes to find in books and films is a decent reflection of its judgment and experience: material that reflects knowledge, a sense of significance, coherence, imagination, a grasp of the way of the world. Otherwise, what have they to show for the years that take such a physical toll?

While maturity might mean wisdom at most, it must surely mean intelligence at least. Intelligence is a broad category; there is no limit to the cultural content that can fit within it. Certainly it is not dependent on the age of characters. *Huckleberry Finn, Alice in Wonderland,* and *Catcher in the Rye* are adult novels just as much as *War and Peace.*

M for "Mindless"

One comes across a report in the papers. The networks have run the annual sweeps that determine which will draw the most lucrative advertising. CBS has scored the highest ratings. But CBS is the loser. The winners are NBC and Fox. Why? Because they have drawn the most viewers in the eighteen-to-forty-nine age group, "deemed the most valuable by the advertising community." The programs that drew the younger crowd for NBC and Fox are the standard run of sitcoms and police procedurals. So what does "younger" mean in this context? The term has little to do with subject matter; it has to do with tone and quality. Producing for the younger audience means the stories will be filled with more action than plot, more sex than substance, more violence than dialogue. It means nobody is going to take much trouble making the stories coherent or the scripts crisp, so there will be more clichéd lines, more flabby reaction shots, more slack and vacuous scenes filling time between commercials, more running, chasing, punching, and shooting, more footage of cars pulling up or pulling away, more quick cuts to keep viewers from asking embarrassing questions about continuity — not to mention more gross-out material, more toilet humor shot in the actual toilet, more graphic vomiting and dismemberment, and more slow-motion montages of bodies spurting blood.

We need a new television ratings category. M for "Mindless — unsuitable for IQs above 50." The networks need not fear. There is a lucrative audience down there below IQ 50. It consists of all the little boys and ex–little boys who grew up on *Power Rangers* and *Mortal Kombat.* That audience would probably search for the rating. They will watch the M-rated shows all the way through, including the hamburger commercial where the cute babe drips the ketchup down her cleavage. And because they are *the* audience, the rest of us will be expected to watch what they watch — or turn off. So perhaps searching for maturity in the media is hopeless. Perhaps television, like the summer movies, is destined to be a preserve of whatever audience it can find in the lower intellectual depths. After all, the baby boomers have brought some seventy million children of their own into the world. They may not be as affluent as their parents, but for as long as they are in the eighteen-to-thirty-four range, they will be seen as an easy mark, meaning their tastes will continue to dominate the media.

Meanwhile, the authentically mature audience that is worth more both financially and intellectually drifts steadily away toward other sources of entertainment and education — public television, cable, videotapes, pay TV — and takes its money with it. The share of the eighteen-to-forty-nine television audience that major networks are squabbling over is a diminishing prize. But momentum keeps the system going; it is always easier to coast than to rethink and revise.

In chapter 12, we will note how the New people are opening up a promising educational frontier in our universities and colleges. It may well be that in the years ahead the major competition faced by popular culture purveyors who want grown-up dollars will not be the next television channel but the lectures, book clubs, seminars, theater productions, symphonies, discussion groups, and museum tours that a mature audience finds far more appealing.

Can material of this quality be drawn into mainstream culture? That is what public radio and television were intended to do and still sometimes do, despite ever greater commercial incursions. But even before content can be revised, there is a more intractable issue to resolve. The greatest change our media-masters will have to make to attain maturity has nothing to do with quality of content. Given the state of our popular culture, something else needs to be talked about first, something that underlies and permeates content. Marshall McLuhan believed that the medium was more important than the message; I would rephrase the idea. *Context* is more important than content. And the context here is commercialism — the media's greatest offense to maturity.

Cézanne's Baseball

Punctuated every eight and a half minutes by two minutes of spot commercials, even the best television drama or documentary becomes intellectual mush. No "in-depth" news report that has to be wedged into the two minutes available before the anchor intones, "When we come back . . ." can be more than a snippet. On television, commercials dictate the pace, the timing, the continuity, the emotional impact of everything. What is the effect, for example, of following a report on famine in Africa with a thirty-second spot for antacids or diet pills? What is the psychological impact of following a brutal rape on a police drama with a pretty young woman modeling panty hose? If we are reading an article about endangered species or environmental crisis, what does it do to the meaning of the report if the magazine pages are sprinkled with screaming advertisements for lip gloss and running shoes?

Why did anyone ever think that such assaults upon attention, coherence, and meaning were acceptable? Clearly those who carry out the assault have never cared about content or continuity of any kind. The material between commercials is a nuisance to them, at best something to be used as bait. By now many of us may have become inured to these witless intrusions. We are like those tribal people we see in the news who are inured to having flies creep over their faces; they no longer bother to brush the pests away. Nevertheless, in the midst of any honest effort to instruct, inform, or entertain, intrusive commercialism violates the adult intelligence of our society. It cuts a hole in our attention and inserts the unrelated, money-driven antics of hucksters. What could be more basically immature than that?

By commercialism I do not mean simply advertising. Advertising may be the major manifestation of the vice, but it at least declares itself for what it is. Worse, because less obvious, are the corrupting choices made behind the scenes on the basis of money: how many will watch, how many will come, how many will buy? How can we get another few dollars out of them? Rigorous marketing strategies that turn on questions like these are just beneath the surface of every cultural event that is out to make money, if only enough to pay for itself. It may be the symphony, the opera, a major art exhibit. We now have an entire profession of people trained at arts promotion. They study tie-ins and spin-offs that will sell T-shirts, toys, gimmicks. If they were not promoting Beethoven, they would be selling real estate. No blockbuster movie is *just* a movie any longer: it is a deal about hamburgers, soft drinks, and trinkets; the actual work may be a mere adjunct. No art museum can do without its gift and souvenir shop. The result is an air of silliness and avarice that cannot help but permeate the exhibits.

In the summer of 1997, a friend of mine returned from a trip that had taken her through Philadelphia, where she had managed to attend the year's biggest art-show success: the traveling Cézanne exhibit. As a lark, she had brought home a souvenir: a multicolored baseball bearing Cézanne's signature.

Cézanne's baseball. Doesn't that say it all?

To be mature in the arts or media is to do what one loves to do with the hope of excellence foremost, doing it all the way through with decent concentration and clear purpose. It means caring that the work is well done as an end in itself. This is a natural human behavior, an instinct of workmanship that can infuse cooking a meal or washing the dishes as well as painting a fresco. We are so sunk in commercialism that many have forgotten that this form of behavior was once as true of popular as of highbrow culture. Excellence is not elite; it is within the reach of everybody. The work may be a Brahms symphony; it may be a dance routine by Astaire and Rogers; it may be a Raymond Chandler detective story; it may be a Krazy Kat comic strip. The work can be done to make money, as most popular culture has always been done; Molière and Shakespeare worked for companies that turned a handsome profit. But the money does not have to crowd out the quality; the creator does not have to be lost in a promotional scramble that swamps the work.

Maturity means one does not adapt the work to the preexisting advertising copy; one does not fit the play between the commercials, or paint the picture with a view to how it will fit on a coffee mug. That, for example, is the difference between the clever and modestly inventive early creations of the young Walt Disney and the schlock that rains down upon us under the Disney name today, all of it stamped with logos, franchised and syndicated to the hilt, wrapped up in deals concocted by agents and promoters in whose eyes the movie is an afterthought.

Infantilizing the Millions

A common complaint from media critics is that advertising tells lies. That was once true, but less so today since class action law has found ways to hold companies responsible for their claims. Advertising still lies when it can get away with it, but that is no longer the preferred strategy. Effective lying, after all, assumes or encourages some degree of adult intelligence on the part of the person lied to. The ability to deal in lies appears well up on the evolutionary scale — from about the mental level of chimpanzees. To lie, one has to tell a story and back it up with claims and facts; one has to expect that the person being lied to can follow along and be persuaded. But for advertisers, calling on even that much adult intelligence is hazardous. The safer tactic is not to awaken intelligence at all, but to lull it to sleep. There is a better way to sell a product. Simply steer clear of the mind and aim at rudimentary reflexes built up around the simple commands "need," "want," and "buy." In brief, deal with the public the way we deal with babies.

The main move in contemporary advertising is to get attention — not an easy assignment given the amount of competition from other advertisers. Just as the sound level keeps rising in a restaurant as each person tries harder to be heard, we have come to expect advertising to assault us with noise, bright lights, and sensational or irritating images — in the same way we try to attract a baby's attention. On rare occasions, this is done cleverly. For the most part, however, television commercials begin with people making fools of themselves to get us to look at them. Whether cleverly done or not, it is always the same attention-grabbing move. And that move is inherently infantile. Children rush into a room uninvited, breaking the flow of conversation, shouting, "Look at me! Look at me!" and demanding to be heard, seen, responded to. We forgive children for being intrusive. Advertisers expect us to forgive them as well.

After that, all that remains is to lodge one's message firmly and portably in the audience's mind. How does one do that? First of all, by being so brutally simple that no intelligence whatever is necessary to register and retain the content. Indeed, often the message is nothing more than a logo or a slogan hammered into one's skull like a nail. Hit hard, be loud, repeat, repeat, repeat. This is not lying, this is imprinting, as with newly hatched birds. Some advertising is a bit more imaginative; it drives its message home by associating the product with an image that will win instantaneous approval. The images are selected from a small, obvious repertory: sexual delight, health, wealth, happiness, success, social acceptance, mastery. The point is to leave the audience with a simple equation: our product equals that image. For example: Here are happy people. Here is beer. You-want-happy. Buy-beer. Since no intelligent human being will believe that happiness equals beer, advertisers have to play upon the lowest susceptibilities of people to present messages like this. Advertising has a vested interest in infantilizing its audience. It cannot work unless it is dealing with numb, passive, childish mentalities.

This is the real obstacle to reprogramming the American media for a mature audience, and the reason the advertisers are apt to resist maturity as long as possible. Their work is predicated upon an audience of infants — or as close to it as one can come. Lose that audience and advertising becomes a very different project. The commercial media may be bonded to immaturity by irrational forces that cannot be overcome even when those forces make no financial sense. Thomas Frank's analysis of "the conquest of cool" leads him to just that conclusion. He believes that advertising and the media have been won over permanently to the young demographic. "Youth must always win," he tells us. "The new naturally replaces the old." "We will have new generations of youth rebellion as certainly as we will have new generations of mufflers or toothpaste or footwear."[12] If he is right, then we will never have a truly mature popular culture unless the New People succeed in closing down Madison Avenue.

The one alternative would be advertising based not on novelty and fashion but on the enduring quality of the product. Quality does not need to be lied about; it does not need to force itself on the attention. It actually suffers for becoming a silly spectacle. Quality can tell the truth; it is its own best advertisement. Advertising that sells quality can therefore be tasteful, courteous, honestly informative, intelligently balanced, and respectful of the content it sponsors. There is no such advertising in the world today. Maybe nobody knows how to do it. But if anybody finds the secret, there will be a market ready to hear and buy. One need only have the eyes to see it on the far side of the longevity revolution.

What If Sex Stopped Selling?

At the rear of my neighborhood video shop there is a cramped, airless little cubicle. The videocassettes that line the walls of this tiny den bear pictures of young women in various contorted sexual postures, leering, winking, drooling. Some wear leather and chains, some wear nothing at all. The sign above the door reads "Adult." It might just as well read "Abandon Intelligence, All Ye Who Enter Here." If a child wandered into a place like this, I suspect he might be traumatized by images of sexuality that offer no hint of love or pleasure. But he might be even more troubled by being told that this is what "adult" means.

Adult, mature . . . like all age-related words in our culture, these too cry out to be redefined, especially as a category in our popular culture. In film and television programming, *mature* or *adult* refers to some combination of heavy-handed sexual titillation, excessive violence, endless profanity, and off-color jokes. Add smoking cigarettes and driving fast cars to the list, and we have "adulthood" as a twelve-year-old boy might understand it. Yet that is the mentality that now earns the most and spends the most in producing films and television.

I have no way to prove the point, but I suspect there is one more reason the media and the advertisers flee from maturity, something about it that arouses a peculiarly deep anxiety. It has to do with the kind of sex on display in the room at the rear of my video shop.

The new demographic reality touches upon sex in a way that may secretly panic the media and those who buy their merchandising services. This may be the point where the New People deliver their most decisive challenge to the ingrained habits of the marketplace. Sex, after all, is the most potent weapon in the arsenal of commerce, the one come-on that can sell anything — or so the advertisers hope. Sex sells cars, beer, clothes, movies, medicine. The business of advertising is very largely the business of manipulating sexual promises.

In my childhood, the sexual imagery in advertising, though just barely subliminal, was comparatively innocent. The pretty girl on the swing in the Coca-Cola adds of that day, her skirt wafted to the inner thigh, seems tame by contemporary standards. But she was still meant to offer a kind of peekaboo thrill. These days the imagery is over the top and aggressively obvious, served up lavishly enough to suggest that its effect is rapidly fading. So the dosage increases as the subjects build up tolerance.

Where would the media be if sex — I mean that *kind* of sex, blatant, puerile, unsubtle, essentially adolescent — lost its power to sell? For all we know, the American economy would collapse. Perhaps the entire structure is supported by cheesecake. In fact, that kind of sex surely will wane in its influence — if not tomorrow, then soon and inevitably. As we will see in chapter 9, age deconstructs gender and reconfigures sexuality, possibly to the point where it ceases to function as a psychological hot button. Doubtless people of all ages entertain sexual fantasies and hidden desires, but it is insulting to assume that the fantasies never get beyond the mental age of fourteen, and that, in their grip, grown-up men and women lose all capacity for intelligent judgment.

One would expect advertising aimed at teenagers to be sexually saturated. But the New People, the bulk of the spending public, are finding a very great deal more to occupy their attention and their energy. Life moves on and sexuality matures. I suspect that many in the media would feel their sexual identity as well as their careers threatened by that fact. The images they deal in are apt first of all to be attuned to their own responses. Question those responses, and people fall into an anxiety that is both erotic and financial — a potent mix. If sex stops being a compulsively adolescent glandular reaction, how will they move all the merchandise? So they try harder, cranking the sexual signals up to maximum, never realizing that they are working against the demographic and cultural grain.

Sex has an odd political and commercial history in our time. The Western world spent most of the twentieth century freeing itself of sexual repressions that reach well back into our Judeo-Christian past. Getting out from under that dead weight has been a commendable struggle, not simply with respect to private sanity. As the New People learned in their youth, the shame that attaches to sex can be a powerful form of social control. Shame disempowers people and mutes their public voice. Defying sexual shame was therefore both a personal and a political project.

But the sexuality that was brought out into the open through the early years of the twentieth century was *infantile sexuality*, highly charged erotic impulses that grow out of unresolved childhood frustration and the child's search for an adult identity. This was the sexuality that preoccupied Freud, and it was an explosive enough issue in its time. Liberating sex at that level shook the structure of families and marriage; it undermined gender roles and public authority. But people pass on in life, and the cry of the wounded inner child steadily fades into the past. New needs arise that are more demanding.

There is now a clear consensus among psychologists and sexual counselors; it can be found reflected even in the countless how-to and self-help sex manuals in the bookstores. We are learning that sex as pure performance, as push-button pleasure, as macho/bimbo role-playing, is emotionally crippling. Everybody who purports to have studied the subject now speaks out in behalf of intimacy, depth of feeling, companionship, meaning. The consensus deepens as sexual counseling moves into the years beyond menopause, both male and female. Indeed, the discovery of a stage of life that is being called the "male menopause" is a key insight in contemporary psychology, one I will address in chapter 9. What emerges from this growing body of psychological practice is a vision of sexuality that is complex, many-sided, and subtly related to the whole personality.

As the society grows more authentically mature, we are leaving behind the compartmentalization of sexuality, the notion that sex is a repertory of images and actions disconnected from the rest of life. But compartmentalizing the sexual response is exactly what merchandising requires: the programmed stimulus that never fails to catch the eye, grip the mind, trigger behavior. There may be a time in life when sex can be enjoyed as impersonal recreation and pursued as a succession of one-night stands. But if contemporary film and fiction are any measure, that kind of sex belongs in long, sad stories of alienated and fragmented lives. It almost invariably is the sex of very young, very confused, and very unhappy people.

Candor about sex deserves to be respected as one of the great achievements of our time. Through the middle decades of the twentieth century, that project helped free the young from a backlog of old, life-denying repressions. But being candid about sex has to include a possibility that few adolescents can imagine: namely, that sex isn't everything. Our popular media are in debt to commercialism, and commercialism is bound to the mentality and the sexuality of the very young. The longer that constellation remains intact, the greater will be the division between our cultural life and demographic reality.

8

The Planned
Obsolescence of Elders

*Cultural Skirmishing at the
Cyberpunk Edge*

INNER-CHILD PSYCHOLOGY, the distinctive psychological style of the 1960s and 1970s, may pose a serious problem for the eldering responsibility of the New People. But another, more troubling obstacle has appeared that makes it even harder to define the relationship of youth to age in our time. The obstacle is a machine, and not just any machine, but one that is linked to the signature technology of our time.

These days, it is commonplace to hear anybody above the age of forty who is not a professional hacker say, "I'm so stupid about computers." They are convinced that "young people are much better at it." That is more than a confession of some minor incapacity. The computer has become a generational landmark. Behind it stands "high tech," a multibillion-dollar industry that dominates the heights of the economy.

Growing Up Absurd, High-Tech Version

Since the early 1980s, when the personal computer began to sell in significant numbers, the high-tech industry has been touting it as an epoch-making invention comparable to the steam engine, if not the wheel. The young — the *very* young — have been the special target of this sales pitch. Some high-tech enthusiasts come close to identifying all children born since the early 1980s as the first mutant generation of the Information Age. One of the first PC television commercials showed a bright-eyed baby reaching out in delight to stroke the keys. He might almost have been the Starchild who appears at the end of *2001*, finally midwifed into life by IBM.

Not only is high tech presented as inherently youthful, but the hackers and investors behind it are invariably identified as young — exuberant kids who caught the wave of the future and joined the ranks of what *Time* magazine calls "instant billionaires." The implication has been that children are now *born* computer-proficient — and that they are therefore leaving their hidebound parents and teachers far behind. The latter assumption is crucial. Blocking out parents and teachers is integral to the sales campaign. It is not enough for children to see themselves as innate hackers; they must also see the parental generation as technologically retarded.

Paul Goodman analyzed the problems of youth in the increasingly technocratic society of the post–World War II world and concluded that the young were "growing up absurd."[1] The substance of that absurdity was considerable. The contretemps between baby boomers and the older generation — as voiced by such sources as *Catcher in the Rye*, *Catch-22*, the Beat poets, *Mad* magazine, the satirical comedians of the day, the early Bob Dylan folk-protest songs — had to do with serious politics and the greater purposes of life. Parents were accused of failing as citizens by becoming the docile pawns of a military-industrial complex that was undermining basic American institutions. The accusation was high-handed and hurtful — though to a significant degree true. It was at least an important line to draw across the culture. The very act of drawing that line had everything to do with becoming an adult and a citizen.

In contrast, the current younger generation is being encouraged to draw a very different line of generational demarcation. Elders are now to be denigrated because . . . they cannot defrag their hard drive.

With the passage of time, one might expect this marketing gambit to wear thin. The baby boom generation has, after all, been living and working with computers longer than their children have been alive. Yet a recent study of the "N-Generation" (Net Generation) cites research to tell us again that 85 percent of children aged four to twenty know more about the World Wide Web than their parents.[2] But what is there to "know"? One clicks, one scrolls, one stares. With a credit card, one buys. And with a slow modem, one waits and waits. Having little time to waste clicking, scrolling, staring, and waiting might be a working definition of being grown-up.

Those who trouble to probe the claims that lie behind this promotional propaganda might find that there are about as many children born computer-proficient as there are born violin-proficient — but nobody is seeking to turn the violin into mass merchandise. Why, then, are we being told that children take to computers the way ducks take to water? There is a treacherous sales strategy behind this claim. It plays upon the difference in intelligence between children and adults — but *at the expense of intelligence!*

Adults, assessing the personal computer with a reasonably mature eye, have seen the obvious. The technology is being vastly oversold. The machine's actual utility in the home falls far below what it is advertised to be. High-tech promoters have tried again and again to persuade the public to adopt the computer as a substitute for everything in their lives from television to the family dog. (The latter is no exaggeration. Consider the "virtual pet," a cunningly computerized novelty that needs care and feeding.) Hence the industry's desperate effort to invent problems for the computer to solve — like storing recipes or balancing the checkbook. If one believed the info-hucksters, people would need computers to turn off the lights and start the coffee. The older one is, the more childish it seems to have a computerized interactive gadget intruding into every aspect of one's life. But kids, equipped with far less sales resistance, are an easier mark. They see the blinking screen, they hear the bells and whistles, and they register the proper amazement. They become the market.

Meanwhile, the skepticism of their elders is written off as a generational liability, and the well-placed reservations of their teachers, who sometimes resist spending scarce dollars to wire the classrooms of the nation, are ridiculed as stodgy. The young, as the high-tech industry would have it, may have to haul their parents and teachers kicking and screaming into the digital future.

What, then, is the subtext of this pitch? Clearly, that this buzzing box on the table has more to teach the young than real people speaking from living experience. Degrade the value of experience and elders have nothing left to offer.

At War with the Boomers

The Internet, destined to play the role that radio and television played for earlier generations, carries a great deal of traffic from Generation-X, the Slackers, the Cyberpunks, the Ravers — newsgroups where those in the fourteen-to-thirty-four age range gather to exchange joys and sorrows.[3] If one samples what youth of the Information Age are doing with the computer power at their disposal, the experience is disheartening. Much of the problem is in the medium itself, which encourages a cyberbabble that becomes ever more barbaric — a patois compounded of abbreviations and catchphrases that has so little connection with structured language that it might as well be a system of runes. Many newsgroup messages are off-the-top-of-the-head outbursts hurled blindly into empty, impersonal space. On the screen they look like a chaos of sound-bite-sized fragments, usually laced with profanity in capital letters.

The Internet, where one can find a newsgroup on nearly every subject imaginable, may not be an adequate sample from which to generalize about an entire generation, but it reveals something of importance about a reasonably good-sized subculture within that population. Because online communications are so spontaneous, unstructured, and anonymous, they arrive on the screen as unguarded emotional outpourings, streams of consciousness at once cathartic and confessional. There is also much role-playing, which no doubt liberates schizophrenic tendencies and all that they reveal.[4] Hostilities flash out online, as do fears and insecurities, all bubbling up too rapidly for the keystroking fingers to bother with spelling, syntax, or often even minimal coherence.

At its murkier depths, the Internet has rapidly gone from being a valuable communications asset of computer technology to a slough of youthful despond, featuring groups like alt.life.sucks, alt.angst, alt.suicide, alt.bitterness, alt.depressed.as.fuck, and alt.galactically.pointless. Most troubling of all are the social animosities one finds there: nasty, frat-house swipes at women, gays, and — of special interest here — the boomers. Efforts by those who have come of age since the early 1980s to assert their historical identity often take the form of backlash against what they understand of the protest and countercultural experimentation that came before.

But their sense of history lacks depth; the issues that once provoked that protest are only dimly remembered. One would never guess from reading what young people have to say on the Internet that America of the 1950s and 1960s was a Jim Crow society, that the military-industrial complex had ever abused its power, that political dissent had to fight to make itself heard against McCarthyite witch-hunting, that thermonuclear annihilation was a serious threat, that there was a war in Vietnam. With no clear realization that dissent in America once related to real moral dilemmas, the younger generation has only a blurred perception of protest as a theatrical gesture, something done to gain attention, rather like an outrageous set at a rock concert. If, then, the young seek to be "different," either they opt for ever more shocking exaggeration, as if history were a contest judged by media-grabbing sensationalism, or they discount protest and just go slack. It is hard to say which choice is worse.

Writing to the editor of the *San Francisco Chronicle* in 1996, one twenty-four-year-old commented mordantly on the Slacker option. Observing that "misery has become a cottage industry" among members of his generation, he went on to say:

> Any grunge rock concert or coffee shop will reveal thousands of young adults wallowing in self-pity and despair — and loving every minute of it. Faces chiseled in pain, these twenty-somethings sing along with lyrics attesting to their crushed dreams, worshipping at the altar of despair. . . . It all adds up to one Mount Everest of Misery.[5]

A contributor to alt.bitterness strikes the same tone: "At 27, life is seen as it really is — too much damn work, pain, suffering, boredom, and maybe if you're lucky one or two good days a year. At this rate I should be fat, arthritic, toothless, old, and (if I'm lucky) dead within a year or two." But just as often the tone is angry, as in this posting to alt.punk:

> I remember being excited around 1990–91 when I first started seeing books and articles about "us kids," just because nobody'd ever bothered to fucking care before — the media was so fascinated with the Baby Boomers, and noting their every pathetic milestone. Yeah, the Boomers had it better, and the whole country played, and continues to play, indulgent-parent-from-hell with them. Yeah, it sucked coming of age in the 80s. (I'm waiting for "THE BOOMERS CAN NO LONGER GET IT UP" issue of *Time.*)

It would be a mistake to write off rancor and self-pity like this as mere posturing. There is a resentment here that can be easily enlisted against the "Woodstockers." Nobody seems more eager to believe the generational accountants than Internet adolescents, with the result that they are more apt to identify the American Association of Retired Persons as their enemy than the corporations that have mangled their wages and benefits. Accordingly, business-financed lobbies like Americans for Generational Equity, acting as stalking horses for private insurance companies that want to move in on Social Security and Medicare, have recruited younger voters by playing upon their sense of victimization.[6] "The baby boomers took all the jobs," complains one message posted to alt.society.generation-x, "polluted the Earth and left us with an enormous national debt and no Social Security."

One need not look far to discover where the younger generation has acquired distorted notions like these. Their fears and frustrations are being expertly fed by those who purport to defend their interests. A 1996 syndicated newspaper feature bearing the headline "Mind-Boggling Disaster Looms in Medicare, Social Security" offers the usual doom-laden scenario of our entitlements future. The principal figure in the story is, once again, Laurence Kotlikoff, leading voice of the generational accounting movement. When he was asked what he would say to the president of the United States if he had the chance, Kotlikoff replied, "How can you sleep at night, given the fiscal disaster you're constructing for the next generation?"[7]

The "next generation" will face no greater test of its political intelligence than seeing through corporate propaganda of this kind. Neither *Yahoo!* nor *Encarta* will help with that job. A few good history books might, with a few basic economics texts, some sociology — plain words on the page, no links, no screaming multimedia, no animation.

RL Is Getting Weirder

I am talking to a bright young woman who works for a slick new New York magazine oriented toward an under-thirty readership. We are talking about high tech and the younger generation. She cautions me. "*My* generation wasn't much into computers. That's really the *younger* generation — like seventeen . . . in high school. I don't understand *them*." She is, as of 1997, age twenty-five.

The generations seem to be passing more rapidly. Maybe they are being "archived" like the compressed data on computer disks. Certainly young people have become aware of fine distinctions among themselves; even more so the media, which need a new youth culture every other year to back up their regular cover story on the "takeover" generation. As of the late 1990s, the teens and twenties young, taken as a whole, clearly find themselves deeply conflicted both culturally and morally, especially those who are "into" computers. They — or at least the more sensitive among them — are torn between a near-mandatory optimism and an instinctive cynicism.

Optimism is the official cultural line that the high-tech industry has been disseminating to young Americans since the day they were born. It is a tale of amazing possibilities and limitless opportunity in which the digital generation is the star of the show. High tech, the young are told, is serving up a "techno-feast of goodies." It is "enabling and empowering" them; it is an "ultra-personalized intimate technology — everything made to order."[8]

But they — or many of them — seem less than fully convinced. They sense that the very technology that supposedly enables and empowers them is also the source of the alienation they reflect so vividly in their own youth culture. Some may even suspect that, if it were not for this technology on which they lavish so much time reaching out to one another across the lonely night, they might actually have durable, nonautomated jobs that deliver a decent standard of living. If one recent analysis is correct, they have yet to register the effect on their wages and hiring prospects when the younger generation in Singapore, Bangalore, Taiwan, and the Philippines — young people trained in American universities to be every bit as computer-proficient as Americans are — begins reporting for jobs with multinational firms.[9]

High tech functions as both devil and deliverer for the young in their uncertain future. For example, one young woman logs on to alt.bitterness to say, "I have no fucking idea what I want anymore. You begin to wish to join the fellowship of productive citizens once again, even if it means processing workman's compensation claims which your employer hopes to be able to get out of paying." And another, posting to alt.cyberpunk: "Is our one force to break free from the corporate monsters that try to control information going to be completely swallowed by that which we strive to escape? It all bores me to death. Maybe I lost the energy to search hard."

Another, realizing that were it not for this machine, he might be out in "RL" (real life) enjoying the sun and the moon and the sky, not to mention other people, posts his resignation to alt.angst: "I am now spending more time communing with my single, square-eyed brother than with any human type. No offense, but I like all of yous out there as he configures you for me on the screen better than if I had to meet any of you in RL. In fact, this ***is*** RL for me from now on."

There is, however, a hopeful sign. Though they remain enthralled by the glowing screen, America's recent younger generations have gravitated toward movies, music, and literature that reveal serious misgivings about their high-tech destiny. Trapped between the ennui of the suburbs and the violence of the inner city, adrift in a world of menacing scale and intimidating power, some begin to suspect that, unless they are gifted hackers out of MIT or financial wizards out of the Harvard Business School, they will have to scheme, scuffle, and grovel to find even mediocre temporary jobs. Hence, from punk rock forward (through heavy metal, death metal, grunge rock, gangsta rap, and so on), the music that fills the youth clubs has grown steadily more anguished and ugly. One typical group bills itself as "specialists in apocalypse, annihilation, psychedelia, immolation, loss of ego and vertigo." Even allowing for some theatricality in the advertising, one can surely expect neither hope nor tenderness in the music that speaks for the young. When the movies need a cheery tune or a love song these days, they have to reach back a long way to find them.

The music of the young also grows progressively louder, unmistakably with the intention of *hurting*. One rock group called Biohazard actually begins its concerts by screaming at the audience: "Are you ready to receive your punishment?" The bands, sporting vile names (Cradle of Filth, Napalm Death, Slayer, Virginkillers) and vying with one another to be as gross and gruesome as possible, reach out toward ever more extravagantly amplified expressions of depravity and fury. At raves, teenagers, as if to go the boomers one better, deliberately dose on far more damaging drugs — and combinations of drugs — than anybody knew existed in the 1960s. Heroin, sniffed in near-lethal amounts, has become the suburban favorite. A high school student preparing for the next rave posts a message to alt.rave, asking for advice from anonymous online experts about a narcotic recipe he is brewing:

> I have 3 questions which I hope somebody will answer before Saturday (but later is OK too). (1) Did anybody try the "new" antidepressant called Aurorix (moclobemid) with LSD or Shrooms? This antidepressant is a reversible MAO Inhibitor. Would it work to potentiate the trip? (2) I'm taking 20 mg of Paroxetine and 75 mg of Anafranil. I know mixing TCAs with MAOIs is dangerous, but would 150 mg of moclobemid really be a risk? (3) Should I discon-

tinue Paroxetine and/or Anafranil for any other reason (do they interact with LSD/Psilocybine)? If yes, how long does Paroxetine/Anafranil stay in the body?

Medical friends tell me these are lethal mixtures, yet such mad pharmaceutical improvisations are a prominent thread running across the Internet, as is advice about suicide. Among the most common themes is the "woe is me" morning-after lament for the aches, pains, and mental dislocations of masochistic self-medication. One is reminded of the late nineteenth-century decadents, who turned dissipation into a fine art. The current version all but amounts to a romance of brain damage.

A posting to alt.drugs:

> mushrooms make you sick as a fucking dog for a couple of hours, then you're home free acid is a great trip if you can stand the speedy/metal-in-the-veins feeling acid is a walk along the razor's edge with every step pushing the razor deeper into your brainstem interesting the way being raped is interesting

And another:

> i forget things that i'm trying to learn, they just won't stick. i don't have any new ideas anymore (if i ever did), every paper i've written this semester has been like self-inflicted brain-surgery, first, rooting around inside to find something that was still alive in all that dead tissue — then, finding the words to say it with — making the letters all hang together one after another so they look like english and lining the words up in the right order so they come out like a thought. pleeze! how is this done? i have a dim memory of once actually considering the kinds of things that should matter to a college student who's supposed to want to go off to grad school at some point. all i know is that RL is getting weirder for me by the hour like messages in a language i never learned.

The Future as Nightmare

I cannot say how typical this taste for punishing, life-endangering experience may be. I doubt that anybody can, because the cries for help from these troubled young go largely unheeded — except as occasional disciplinary or legal "problems" if they lead to riot, arrest, or front-page scandal. Some, like Tipper Gore, have sought to censor ugly and violent rock lyrics. I can understand why one would want to do that. But it is quite as important to ask why ugly and violent things are being said in the first place, especially when so many young people are saying them at the top of their voice or crowding into concerts to hear them. The possibility that ugly and violent remarks are significant, if halting, statements about our cultural condition has yet to be widely appreciated.

I know of some concerned members of the liberal clergy in England and the United States who have provided advice and friendship by hosting "rave masses" for the young. Their hope is to win them away from their seemingly self-destructive and nihilistic tendencies by offering a drug-free, humane alternative. Matthew Fox, the maverick Catholic and now an Episcopal priest, has been hosting such gatherings in San Francisco since the mid-1990s. He calls his religiously eclectic rituals Techno Cosmic Masses; they are usually dedicated to "Gaia Our Mother." One small effort to provide responsible eldering and a sincere one, but there is something about the abrasiveness of such events, even in the absence of drugs, that needs understanding. Why the volume and the frenzy? Why the need to shock, batter, and brutalize the nervous system?

I think it is this: rather than growing up absurd, many of the young seem to be growing up *numb* — as if there were some narcotizing process at work in the collective cultural consciousness that deadens the senses of those who were raised on television and constant commercial stimulation. Is this, possibly, a defensive response to the scale, pace, artificiality, and intensity of urban life, as well as to the "normally" delusionary state of mind the media induce? Psychologists have identified a neurosis for our times: the "highly sensitive person" feels the stimuli of daily life too much.[10] Maybe more of the young than we realize are caught between feeling too much and feeling nothing at all. So they seek in the music, the mania, and the deadly drugs some way to spark a vital sensation and so awaken themselves to life.

Some raves try valiantly to promote themselves on the basis of "good vibes and positivity"; sponsors insist that the event will be about love and respect. There is also a Christian rock movement, which was deliberately launched to counter the widespread negativity. The music scene is becoming like a battleground for the souls of the young. Does the young man who posted this sad little message to alt.evil represent many or few? "Life holds nothing but pain and death, but don't look for love, there is none left. There is only Scum, Napalm Death." Bad enough if there were but a few who feel this way; I suspect from the size and dynamism and earnings of the rock music industry that there are many. The only numbers that indicate which way the audience is trending are ticket and CD sales. Everything seems to sell, but hard rock, as it continues to reach for the extreme beyond the extreme, outsells all its competitors.

Those who came to their adolescence in the 1980s are more fully integrated into high tech than any generation before; the technology has been hyped to them as "theirs" in ways that cut them loose of parental ties. For as long as they can remember, corporate America has been leading cheers for an Information Age that promises endless electronic stimulation — a thousand channels of television, the excitement of ever faster, ever more eye-popping World Wide Web sites with bandwidth galore, virtual realities beyond number, stereo that can be heard from here to the moon. And how do the young respond, at least in sufficient numbers to be of concern? They rush to offer themselves for a thorough mental and emotional battering at the hands of sadistically oriented rock groups like Nine Inch Nails . . . just to feel something *real.*

Here is a problem for which the high-tech industry seems not to have found a solution: *Why aren't these kids happy with all they have been given? Why don't they just quiet down and enjoy their nice electronic toys?*

It is no coincidence that young people whose lives have been radically shaped by high tech are telling us that they are going numb. The cyberpunk resistance is a desperate cry from those who feel the wave of progress closing over their heads. They may not have found more to do about their plight than to suffer and cry out, but thanks to some surviving organic instinct, they know that what the high-tech visionaries are pitching at them is a lie. When it comes, then, to imagining the future, what they find most credible is the antithesis of the world according to Microsoft and the Media Lab. They see the future — their high-tech future — as a nightmare.

Down Among the Cyberpunks

Now he slept in the cheapest coffins, the ones nearest the port, beneath the quartz-halogen floods that lit the docks all night like vast stages, where you couldn't see the lights of Tokyo for the glare of the television sky, not even the towering hologram logo of the Fuji Electric Company, and Tokyo Bay was a black expanse where gulls wheeled above drifting shoals of white styrofoam. Behind the port lay the city, factory domes dominated by the vast cubes of corporate arcologies. . . .

By day, the bars down Ninsei were shuttered and featureless, the neon
dead, the hologram inert, waiting, under the poisoned silver sky.

— WILLIAM GIBSON, *Neuromancer* (1984)

Some cyberpunks bristle when they are associated with punk rock.
"Cyberpunks aren't about PUNK MUSIC," insists one highly upper-
case contributor to alt.cyberpunk.movement. "Cyberpunks are about
FREEDOM OF INFORMATION because INFORMATION IS
POWER and by god — POWER TO THE PEOPLE." But in fact
there is a significant overlap of sensibility between the groups. The
shared word *punk* serves in both movements to reveal an identity born of
victimization. Both punk rock and cyberpunk express a spirit of resistance; both are made up of those who see themselves as marginal
insurgents in a culture gone wrong. Cyberpunk takes its cue from science fiction literature rather than rock music, but the literature is every
bit as dismal and despairing as the music. Like the hyperamplified howls
of anger and anguish that blare from the stage at a death metal concert,
it reminds us that, besides the yea-saying techies at *Wired* who see an
endless frontier of technological wonders and amazements ahead, there
are the grunts, the malcontents, the delinquents of the high-tech workforce, the hacker proletariat working out of coffin-sized cubicles with
their phone calls and e-mail monitored to ensure quality service. Their
view of the future runs to alarm, if not desperation. Leave them out and
the picture is incomplete.

The most influential of the cyberpunk authors is William Gibson.
His jackhammer abrasiveness suits the harsh landscape of his world, a
vista of gargantuan corporations and monolithic institutions where em-
battled anti-heroes can survive only as outlaws plotting clever ways to
sabotage a system they cannot own or control. Gibson's cyber-cowboys
are marginalized bottom-dogs so sunk in narcotic fantasies and halluci-
natory worlds that they have no reality principle to cling to. They
inhabit a fictive zone where nothing is certain and everything can be
manipulated. Anybody you meet might be a hologram. Not even their
minds are their own. What the powers of modern technology have
finally brought them is ecological doom in an empire of unlivable cities
dominated by the high-rise towers and emblazoned logos of the reigning corporate elite.

Gibson's cities are the private property of ruthless American-Japanese-German-French multinational companies. "Sprawls," as Gibson calls the urban eyesores of the future (BAMA sprawls from Boston to Atlanta), are as squalid as any factory town of the nineteenth century — yet they are congested with advanced technology. Nobody draws a breath or dreams a dream without the use of "derms," or "entertainment modules," or "simstim" implants. In the sprawls, an underclass of demoralized billions struggles to survive in conditions of hopeless moral degradation. For them, the media offer, at best, forms of sad, mindblowing escape or, at worst, techniques of psychological control. People have themselves been reengineered from their DNA up; they have been transformed into near-cyborgs equipped with internal processors and microbiotic spare parts. It is a world where nothing is real, nothing is human, nothing is gentle, beautiful, or noble. The only love Gibson's cowboys find might be a few drug-laced hours with a company whore in an overnight sleeping coffin.

A young man logs in to alt.cyberspace.rebels to utter a word of anguish. His entry may fall short of literary elegance, but he is giving a voice to the cyberpunk vision of things to come:

> LOOK at us and look out there we are living in the world dominated by corporate marketing machine. These guys eat up just every opponent out there. Nothing is existed beyond corporate world. These guys are GOD. These guys have the real consciousness. These guys eat you and me. These guys slowly take over our existence and body and mind. We have no power to fight against these fascist gigantic monster ever created by human race.

Cyberpunk fiction's literary genealogy traces back to early anti-utopias like E. M. Forster's *The Machine Stops* (1905), the novel and film versions of *Metropolis* (1920s), and Huxley's *Brave New World* (1933). All these works saw the bright promise of science and industry being swallowed up by fanatical social engineering and profiteering interests. At that early stage, the future depicted in these works was, on the surface at least, clean and elegant. (One exception: in *Metropolis* the proletariat is inexplicably confined to a dingy underworld.) Cyberpunk redesigned anti-utopia by adding just the right touch of corporate philistinism and ecological disintegration. The films *Alien* (1979) and *Outland* (1981) helped embed images of futurist noir in the public perception. They show industrial life under the control of interstellar corporations reverting to the grubby drudgery of early Manchester. The cavernous and clanking space stations have lost their luster; they are lightless, dank, and dripping. Everything is built cheap and chronically malfunctions; underpaid technicians sweat, scowl, and grumble; cutthroats skulk along the garbage-strewn air shafts and docking bays. The screenwriter Dan O'Bannon, who invented the style for *Alien,* calls it "the used future." That is what the future will look like if it is owned by the same forces that own the world today.

It is a new and jarring insight — a hell of a different kind. In earlier anti-utopias — Zamyatin's *We* (1920–21), Orwell's *1984* (1949) — it was universally assumed that only the central state could ever be powerful enough to rule the world. The dehumanized future would be the product of collective planning. But there is another possibility. What if corporate elites, with their insatiable appetite for profit, shape our destiny? Then we will have regimentation, but without the least concern among these selfish, competitive giants for cleaning up the mess or preserving order. Under the hegemony of triumphant market forces, pleasure gardens for the rich may survive under heavy guard, but the rest of the world will become a garbage dump.

It was, above all, the 1982 movie *Bladerunner* (directed by Ridley Scott, based on the Philip K. Dick novel *Do Androids Dream of Electric Sheep?*) that most effectively exposed the decadent underbelly of corporate high tech. Both the film and the novel have since acquired a mythic stature on the Internet; there are three or four highly active *Bladerunner* web sites. *Bladerunner* envisions a future where quasi-human replicants — patented products of the Tyrrell Corporation, one of the industrial giants that rule the future — have more humanity to them than "real" human beings. The tale, played out in the thronging, smog-shrouded streets of a decaying megacity, is a study in the ultimate criminality of corporate power. The fact that younger people are learning these facts of life from science fiction rather than sociology should not undercut the validity of the lesson.

Elders in the Reign of Anti-Life

A snatch from a preconcert harangue by a death metal group whose performances usually end with punch-outs and riots in the mosh pit:

> Power, rage unbound because been pounded by the streets. Cyanide blood burns down the skyline. Hatred is purity. The bullet connects at last. Let freedom ring with a shot-gun blast.

Words howled by twenty-somethings at an audience of teen-some-things. Not teens who have suffered through a holocaust or the horrors of ethnic cleansing or thermonuclear war, but kids from suburban homes. The performance, with its super-amplification and programmed light show, is supremely high-tech. But the audience is wearing T-shirts with slogans like "Get Up and Kill" and "Hail, Satan."

It is difficult to take young people seriously when they immerse themselves in a nihilism they have not earned and cannot fully understand. Yet, as presumptuous as the cyberpunk vision may be, it is an expression of the life impulse, still there, still struggling to make its way forward. If that impulse is left uneducated and given no creative means of expression, it will finish where it began — as a howl of indiscriminate rage drifting toward the madness or suicide with which the young too much confabulate. Either that or it will become mere show business — a marketable act, tolerable because it has no target and no strategy.

The cyberpunk vision is so extreme that it is tempting to dismiss it and hope that it will simply be outgrown. But the first thing that one must say is how *true* that vision is. It has a great deal more history and culture behind it than the young realize. That in itself is a healing lesson, for it brings perspective. William Blake saw the smoking mills of his day as dark and Satanic. Were he around today, he would very likely see high tech as *sleek* and Satanic. He would surely recognize the same inhumanity and sacrilege at work in the most ingenious of Silicon Valley's achievements. He would also see the genius, for he celebrated the inventor's skill as much as the artist's.

I suspect much of the angst and bitterness the young reflect in their online messages to one another stems from their sense of isolation — which also imbues their words with an annoyingly self-congratulatory sense of originality. That is an error of ignorance on their part. That is why seeking to make elders, if not the entire pre-high-tech past, obsolete is so crippling. These wrongs need the voice of experience. Misguided science, the abuse of wealth and power, technology in the wrong hands . . . these are issues that connect to the countercultural movement of the 1960s and back at least as far as the Romantic artists. What the cyberpunks have done is to press those issues to new, histrionic extremes, as if to warn us that, like Hollywood's indestructible Alien, this thing is still *here*. Blake called the thing Urizen ("a shadow of horror"), and Allen Ginsberg named it Moloch — a suitably ancient name that reminds us how old the horror is.

What sphinx of cement and aluminum bashed open their skulls
   and ate up their brains and imagination?
Moloch! . . .
Moloch whose mind is pure machinery! Moloch whose blood is
   running money! Moloch whose fingers are ten armies! Moloch
   whose breast is a cannibal dynamo! Moloch whose ear is a smoking tomb!

— *Howl* (1957)

Some of our children are having bad dreams about Moloch. With a
prophetic clarity beyond their years, they see the monster now as the
alien, the cyborg, the android, caricatures of humanity that cannot love
or understand us. They see it as the Tyrrell Corporation, as the *X-Files'*
cigarette-smoking assassin, as Darth Vader in any number of his sword
and sorcery/science fiction variations.

The first step in effective eldering is to make common cause with the
dread and disgust of the young. But we must also recognize that their
despair is a measure of their immaturity. The nihilistic hysteria that fills
their music and literature simply tells us that they cannot make their
way alone. They need the competence of elders to find their way out of
the bad dream we are in together. Left to their own devices, they come
up with poor solutions. Some contributors to the cyberspace newsgroups spend much time exchanging ideas for a liberating "people's
technology." But what they have in mind — railgun specs, bioluminesc-
cent LCD implants, perimeter defense droids — is just more science
fiction.

Others identify a cyberpunk as "a highly intelligent person who likes
to spend 120 percent of his available time in front of a terminal doing
something to test his brain." Such people are losing all touch with real
life. Robert Bly, speaking with a poet's wisdom, believes there will be no
growing up in what he calls "the sibling society" unless children find
their way beyond the machines and the systems and back into the
sustaining natural world to learn from the trees, the stars, the beasts.

The elder who taught me the most through my college years about
the use and misuse of technology gave Moloch another name, perhaps
the best choice of all. Lewis Mumford called it "Anti-Life." Anti-Life
was the psychic distortion that Mumford believed was at work behind
megatechnics, seeking to replace all things organic with mechanical
substitutes. The inventions of Anti-Life might be as modern as the
latest computer program, but Mumford believed they traced back to the

divine kings of the River Valley civilizations with their compulsive appetite for power over man and nature. His vision of our destiny under the dominance of Anti-Life was grave in the extreme, and more deeply studied than any cyberpunk fantasy. But he knew that the true measure of wisdom is hope, and hope is what the competence of elders brings to the dilemmas of the young.

> On the terms imposed by technocratic society, [Mumford observed] there is no hope for mankind except by "going with" its plans for accelerated technological progress, even though man's vital organs will all be cannibalized in order to prolong the mega-machine's meaningless existence. But for those of us who have thrown off the myth of the machine, the next move is ours: for the gates of the technocratic prison open automatically, despite their rusty ancient hinges, as soon as we choose to walk out.[11]

9

Longevity and Gender

The novelists never told us that in love, as in other matters, the young are just beginners and that the art of loving matures with age and experience. Furthermore, while many of the young believe that the world can be made better by sudden changes in social order and by bloody and exhausting revolutions, most older people have learned that hatred and cruelty never produce anything but their own kind. The only hope of mankind is love in its various forms and manifestations — the source of them all being love of life, which, as we know, increases and ripens with the years.

— ISAAC BASHEVIS SINGER, *Old Love* (1979)

A S THE FOLKLORE of the world would have it, age and sex are poles apart. Almost by definition, the old are beyond passion as well as reproduction. The famous reports by Kinsey and by Masters and Johnson that did so much to launch the post–World War II sexual revolution gave scant attention to sex after sixty — as if there were little to be found. It is only since the mid-1980s that the media, registering a growing audience of over-sixties, have discovered sex among the seniors, though usually with a certain coy astonishment. Inevitably, as with all matters sexual in the United States, there has been research on the subject, followed, just as inevitably, by workshops at the university extension, earnest documentaries on television, and how-to manuals in the bookstores.

The Game of Sex, the Rules of Gender

As one might imagine in a popular culture still dominated by the fascinations of youth, the focus of this belated attention has been almost wholly on sexual techniques and habits. Frequently overlooked is the crucial distinction that social scientists make between sex and gender. "Sex" — the biology of being male or female — is what we are born into; it is of the body. "Gender" is of the mind; it is learned from the culture and usually rigidly restricted to just two behavioral choices: masculine or feminine. If we think of sexuality as a game whose goal is reproduction, then gender lays down the rules of the game as enforced by the umpire called "society." Gender, for example, decides who initiates a sexual encounter, how courteously or aggressively, with how much mutual consent, under what circumstances, with what responsibilities, and with how much personal improvisation. Gender in fact prescribes an entire personality and way of life that might, paradoxically, make sexuality more of a chore than a joy. Gender as Victorian ladies knew it actually defined females as angelic beings who found sexuality distasteful.

Raw erotic energy may always be more insistent in hard, young bodies primed for reproduction, but when it comes to gender, the cultural amplification of sexuality, youth might be the last place to look for enlightenment. What goes unmentioned in most media surveys of senior relationships is the intriguing possibility that viewing gender from the other end of life may teach us how much we got wrong in our youth.[1]

The courting rituals of young love invariably exaggerate the dissimilarities of male and female, often seeking maximum contrast in clothing, hairstyles, makeup, and behavior. It seems to be universally part of the mating game for man and woman to see themselves as polar opposites, though there is reason to doubt that this tendency arises from some underlying glandular agenda. Homosexual love clearly does without such extremes of contrast. Whatever the reason, the role-playing and reproductive maneuvering that preoccupy the young all but obliterate the human continuities between feminine and masculine. Male and female become almost alien breeds, different in every possible aspect. The differences are mythologized until they take on cosmic proportions: all nature — the sun, the moon, Earth, the heavens — opposes masculine to feminine.

For all its exciting tension, this is a psychologically grueling way to see life — grueling because, as time and experience reveal, it is untrue. With the passage of years, perception has the chance to soften the contrast and blur the edges. Both the older woman who discovers that the girlish and eye-catching fashions of the day are no longer being designed for her and the older man who discovers that he is no longer (and may never have been) a superstud are bound to rethink the stereotypes they have honored all their lives. Hard knocks, the ordeal of disease, the approach of mortality — facts of life that must be faced when careers and child-rearing are left behind — offer men and women the chance to find their common humanity. They may begin to feel more comfortable with the idea that the genders are *adjacent* rather than opposite, a realization that opens the way for durable friendship and authentic intimacy. It is one of the rewarding discoveries of age that the other gender has the mind, the inner life, the aspiration of another human soul and is in all these ways very like oneself.

With so many healthier seniors pursuing love, sex, courtship, and even parenting decades later in life than anyone ever imagined possible, we might expect to find the youthful gender roles prolonged into deep old age as people strive to stay young longer. I have talked to therapists who tell me — with a sigh of resignation — that they are seeing clients in their sixties, women mainly, who are still struggling to keep up with the dating and mating game. At the same time, when it comes to matters of sex and gender, the New People are a special generation. Exploring what it means to be a man or a woman returns them to a project that began in their youth. Challenging the gender stereotypes was a staple part of countercultural teach-ins and love-ins, rallies and rock festivals, where young men and women came together in rebelliously unstructured encounters, eager to throw off the repressive parental culture. In those years, when it was a daring gesture for men to wear their hair long and for women to do without bras and makeup, they launched (and suffered) a sexual revolution that still rolls through our society.

In the 1960s, Mick Jagger performed onstage dressed in a skirt; in the 1990s, we have gay liberation parades in the streets and lesbian sitcoms on prime-time television. And we are discovering unimagined sexual identities. Some sexologists now believe there are at least *five* physically defined sexes, including three hermaphrodite variations that have long been altered at birth to enforce gender orthodoxy. Accordingly, there has been an organized rebellion among "transgenders," aimed at keeping everybody's sexual equipment just as it was originally furnished, on the grounds that androgynous infants have a right to their own gender orientation.

I can think of only one aspect of sex and gender that has not been explored over the course of the last generation. That is the role that age has to play in deepening sexuality and taking it to the threshold of mortality.

The Six-Year-Old Beauty Queen

If the New People finally succeed in bringing greater maturity to our understanding of gender, the contribution of women will vastly outweigh that of men. Even more than it has been changed by the struggle for racial justice, our society has been revolutionized by the redefinition of gender brought about by the women's movement, which has transformed every institution in our lives. The New People are, indeed, unimaginable apart from the *new women* who make up more than half their number.

And yet . . .

Even as I write, the police are investigating a gruesome murder in Boulder, Colorado. Late in 1996, a six-year-old girl was found strangled in her home. As terrible as such a crime would be under any circumstances, this case took on a macabre twist that played across the front pages of the nation's tabloid press. The little girl was a "beauty queen." On television and in magazines, we have been treated to pictures of her tarted up to look like a teenage seductress. The story out-Lolitas Nabokov's *Lolita*. The child at the center of this story was raised to emulate that same helpless, utterly vulnerable sexpot who filled the movie screens in my boyhood. A child mimicking women who are playing the role of overgrown children, she was the cult of youth and the female-as-victim rolled into one. Worse than functioning as a salacious male fantasy, she was part of something that still haunts the sexual psychology of women. The main role in promoting little girls as beauty queens seems to be played by their mothers, who are apparently living out a fiction of virgin-vamp sexuality through their daughters. All the toxic images of femininity that the women's movement has labored to expunge have survived like a resistant virus in some corner of our popular culture.

Every year Miss America walks the runway, bikini-clad and wobbling on stiletto heels. Gaunt and girlish supermodels dominate the pages of the fashion magazines that women still buy and peruse. Salesmen take their customers to lunch at strip clubs confident that they will find women at work enacting fantasies straight out of Victorian pornography. Books that tell us men are Martian hunters and women are Venusian homebodies still rank high on the best-seller list.

The columnist Maureen Dowd, wondering whatever happened to women's liberation, bemoans the persistence of "bimbo feminism," which gives "intellectual pretensions to a world where the highest ideal is to acknowledge your inner slut. I am a woman, see me strip." Can we confidently predict that the next turn of the cultural tide will finally carry such sexist flotsam out to sea? Or will it wash in still more of the same? At the very least, it would seem that feminism has a long way to go in achieving its primary goal of deconstructing gender in order to bring women their equality.

Though they have accomplished much over the past generation, women, who make up the majority of the New People, have some unfinished business with the men in their lives. Age is at the core of that business. For their own good and the good of the culture, female New People will have to help male New People grow up as well as grow old. They have special qualifications for that role. By physiological default, aging belongs to women as it has not thus far belonged to men. Menopause announces a dramatic end to a woman's youth, and after menopause women live longer, for reasons that cannot be wholly explained by genetics. Women, as Royda Crose puts it in her study of gender and life expectancy, are "winning the game of life." Not that it needs to be that way. "It's time," Crose believes, "for men to break out of the life-threatening bonds that traditional masculinity places on their lives and their longevity."[2]

If there is one clear reason why inherited gender stereotypes continue to plague our lives, it is the domineering self-image to which men, especially men of great influence, continue to cling. It is an image that constellates social power and wishful thinking. It promises status, but at the risk of sorrow and early death. Most treacherously, it promises youth, or at least the fond reminiscence of youth. But what it brings men is a life-threatening folly.

The Peculiar Problem of the Alpha Male Human

In the late 1940s, the film star John Wayne was at a crossroads in his career. Approaching his midforties, he would soon find it impossible to continue playing a conventional leading man. He was in sight of the age at which romantic leads of that period either retired from the movies or segued into character parts. But as it turned out, Wayne's best years as a he-man lover were still ahead of him. In 1948 he appeared in a movie that would give him a second career; it would also introduce a new male type into our popular culture. In the western *Red River,* Wayne plays a father, a brooding widower, and a successful cattle baron. A distinctly senior figure, he is nonetheless the domineering stud, possessed of potent sexuality and capable of awing younger males into submission. Wayne would play that role for the next thirty years, never once giving up his claim to glory, dominance, or women. At about the same time, the slightly older French matinee idol Jean Gabin was staking out a similar film persona for the remainder of his career: the lonely, hard-bitten, older male, the survivor of a dead wife or a hard divorce, perhaps a kingpin criminal who carries on with as much erotic power as ever, feared by the men around him, pursued by lovely younger women.

In the movie world, older actresses still tend to drop by the wayside after forty. If they survive into romantic roles, it is by way of some awkward concession to their age. Wayne and Gabin, however, created an enclave for over-age leading men that opened new possibilities well beyond the movie screen. They embodied a masculine fantasy that cast its spell over men in all walks of life: the patriarchal male who grows sexier and more formidable with age. Many others have followed in their footsteps: Clint Eastwood, Sean Connery, Paul Newman, Robert Redford, Anthony Quinn, perhaps most definitively Clark Gable, who died playing the part opposite an adoring Marilyn Monroe in *The Misfits.* The strangest version of this normally he-man role is the film persona that Woody Allen has developed, the nerdy Romeo whom gorgeous young women — sometimes *very* young women — cannot resist. Watching actresses throw themselves at Allen is not actually an exercise in the willing suspension of disbelief. One simply recognizes that the man writes and directs his own movies — though in Allen's case the fiction has overflowed into whatever "real life" means in the movie world.

In primate groups, such dominant figures are called alpha males: grizzled, old veterans who monopolize the females and stand as a target for eager young males who must prove their selective advantage by overthrowing them. Freud had something like this in mind when he invented his fanciful notion of the prehistoric primal horde. He imagined there were once elder males who ruled by taking all the women into their harem and suppressing (Freud thought castrating) their rival sons. Working more from dramatic license than reliable anthropology, Freud thought this was the distant origin of the famous Oedipus complex. If the notion had any intellectual validity, it nevertheless had to wait for Hollywood to give it popular visibility and, at least for the men of the world, popular appeal.

As age-denying as our culture is, senior men obviously continue to wield great power in our politics and economics. We see them in the news of the day giving speeches, attending VIP conferences, making deals, announcing policy, getting richer. As heads of state and as high corporate chieftains, they have succeeded in moving the John Wayne image off the screen and into the real world, where they become the political equivalent of the old gunslinger, the veteran cop, the battle-scarred military hero. The prominence of this figure might seem a paradox in a society that grants age so little respect. Does it represent a significant exception to the long history of shabby treatment that the old have suffered?

Not at all.

Men who continue competing for power into their older years are more the problem than the solution to age discrimination. They are, in the area of age, what token women have been in government or corporate life. Women, in order to qualify for positions of leadership in institutions that are shot through with stereotypic masculine qualities, often must become honorary men. While it is now generally recognized that the positions women must compete to hold in the political and corporate worlds are saturated with masculine qualities, what often goes unnoticed is that these are *young* masculine qualities — very young. Like ambitious women, men who cling to power must also become "one of the boys." As Betty Friedan was among the first to observe, "in the debate about women and men, sex roles and sex, over the last thirty years, it is never pointed out that all our assumptions and definitions of masculinity are based on *young men*."[3]

Even when it is older men who play the role, they are enacting the part of adolescents. In the world of power, the "king of the mountain" game-playing that every boy learns in the schoolyard remains the rule. Like the wild boys in William Golding's *Lord of the Flies*, old men in the power elite continue to compete for supremacy as if to prove that they are not *really* old. They play the role of targets for the young men coming along and bucking for dominance.

In his approach to the psychology of older men, David Gutmann includes a comparative study of the alpha male in industrial society and elders in Native American cultures.

> The elder rulers of "advanced" societies are only older versions of successful young men, those who have laid down the bases for their economic and political power early in life. They receive little honor, title, or credit on the basis of their age alone. For the rest, for the majority of undistinguished older males who have not laid up power and riches in their early years, personal and social prospects can be bleak, making for a striking and disheartening contrast with the typical older man of the folk-traditional assemblage.[4]

Few men in their fifties and sixties have what it takes to be ideal alpha males — namely, a professional makeup artist, all the right camera angles, a stunt man to take over the running, jumping, and fighting, a director to call "Cut!" when your toupee slips, and a million-dollar publicity department. Nevertheless, all men to some degree feel the weight of that image. It stands over them like the looming threat of failure — as failure is judged by a cruelly unrealistic standard.

Women sometimes complain how unfair it is for men to fixate on nubile movie queens. It is as much of a heartache for men to be held up to the Sean Connery criterion. Sometimes the movies that created this image reflect upon its pathos in real life — though rarely. In the 1950 film *The Gunfighter*, Gregory Peck, as the old gunslinger, yearns to give up the game and reclaim his life as husband and father. But he cannot. Wherever he stops, younger versions of himself insist on calling him out to prove that they are the fastest gun in the West. And at last the old man is gunned down by his youthful successor. John Wayne finished his career with a similarly pathetic story in *The Shootist*.

There are signs that things are changing in the film world, slowly drifting toward greater reality as the society ages. Paul Newman, in his seventies, is exploring roles that rather gracefully combine maturity and subdued masculinity. In the films that are finishing out his acting career, Clint Eastwood openly shows his years; his declining physicality is worked into the story line. Of course, when the script requires it, he can still leap from windows, run a mile, and bed the female lead. But in *Absolute Power*, he announces his AARP membership as a sixty-six-year-old retiree and turns fatherly toward his estranged daughter.

A small glimmer of reality perhaps, but in the far more consequential world of business and finance, alpha males have yet to make even that much of an adjustment. There, pretensions of youthful vigor and agonistic prowess reign supreme. Just as little boys play compulsively at gory and sadistic video arcade games, hoping to set the record for wiping out more planets than anybody else in the universe, big boys play for money and titles and status.

They also play for women, a sure indication of the adolescent orientation of the game. "Power," as Henry Kissinger once said, "is the ultimate aphrodisiac." The successful sixty-something CEO with a twenty-something trophy wife on his arm (and perhaps a well-advertised mistress or two) is like the alpha male chimp who must constantly display sexual prowess to the adolescents of the pack lest he lose everything he ever fought to achieve.

From time to time we get listings of the current alpha male standings: CEOs who are ranked by salary, stock options, bonuses. A few years back, a box score in *Forbes* magazine reported that even Bill Gates of Microsoft, though not old enough at the time to qualify as an alpha male but well on his way, might be in danger of falling behind in the money race. "Asian Billionaires Gaining on Gates," cried the headline. There followed a list of the pursuers who might soon "dethrone" him, the "poorest" of whom had a personal fortune of $10.5 billion. One woman was listed, the usual token, identified as "heiress" to a cosmetics empire and thus not a self-made man. In any case, she lagged well behind the pack with a mere $5 billion.

What is the meaning of money like this? It is more than a man can spend and enjoy, more than his family needs to remain secure for centuries to come. It is an abstract score, the grown-up version of a computer game: meaningless points that simply tell the world who the lords of the universe are. Yet as silly as that ambition may seem when viewed in the clear light of mature judgment, the alpha male model of masculinity links Darwinian self-interest to sexual potency in a way that makes criticism too threatening to tolerate.

The Separative Self

Down among the primates, alpha masculinity is a sad role for an old ape to perform; many die playing it. It is their only way out of this world. It is sadder still to see alpha male humans playing that part as if it were instinctually mandated. Sad for the men, sad for the women, but saddest of all for the planet Earth.

In one of the first books to probe the psychological dimension of human ecology, Paul Shepard described the males of our society as "ontogenetically crippled." They grow from a protracted adolescence into a false adulthood saturated with "juvenile fantasies." At that point, "irrational feelings may be escalated into high-sounding reason when thrown up against a seemingly hostile and unfulfilling natural world. The West is a vast testimony to childhood botched to serve its own purposes, where history, masquerading as myth, authorizes men of action to alter the world to match their regressive moods of omnipotence and insecurity."[5] As the women's movement discovered early on, gender stereotypes have more than social consequences. They determine our relationship with the Earth itself. Real women groan beneath the power of the alpha male human, but even more so the woman called Mother Nature.

The new school of feminist psychology has done much to illuminate the structure of the "separative self," the typically stunted male psyche. Feminist psychologists most often describe the masculine ego as a tightly bounded, autonomous, self-regarding module that permits of no penetration, no union, no warmth of feeling. In Catherine Keller's words, men (and all psychological schools modeled on the masculine norm) "identify development itself with separation, and attachments appear as developmental impediments."[6] This is a character type that permits the maximum aggression, acquisition, dominance, and ruthless competitiveness.

In her science fiction novel *Woman at the Edge of Time*, Marge Piercy imagines the ultimate example of the male separative self. He — or more accurately *it* — is called a "cybo," a semirobotic, seven-foot-tall warrior that never removes its body armor, even when indulging in violent sex with the prostitutes provided by its employer. "Instead of a sex drive," we are told, cybos "have a basic killer instinct." The futuristic employer is, significantly, a global conglomerate called Chase-World-TT. "We embody the ideal," the cybo proudly announces. "We can never be deflected, never be distracted." This semi-mechanized, single-mindedly aggressive male is now a film standard: images of *Steel*, *Robocop*, and *The Terminator* fill young imaginations. I know that comic-book heroes played a major part in shaping my boyhood ideal of manliness; their literary quality was no higher. But I recall that Superman and Batman lived up to a certain chivalric ethic in their treatment of women. The cyborg has none of that. He — it — has evolved beyond sexual warmth and tenderness.

The separative self is the man that every little boy is encouraged to become as he breaks free of maternal influence. In the life of the male, the nonrelational ego is a thing-in-itself; it never becomes a person-in-relation that would lack identity outside of relationship. The feminist psychologist Jean Baker Miller puts it this way:

> The concept of a "self" as it has come down to us has encouraged a complex series of processes leading to a sense of psychological separation from others. From this there would follow a quest for power over others and over natural forces, including one's own body. . . . Our tradition [has] made it difficult to conceive of the possibility that freedom and maximum use of our resources — our initiative, our intellect, our powers — can occur within a context that requires simultaneous responsibility for the care and growth of others and of the natural world.[7]

Mainly in response to the women's movement, a vigorous and many-sided men's movement has grown up since the late 1970s that seeks to meet the need that many males feel today for other identities. Unfortunately, this quest often continues to turn up patriarchal images. The Christian Promise-Keepers, whose leader insists that "God is a Man-with-a-capital-M," meet in numbers that can fill football stadiums. Their goal is to reimpose paternal authority in their homes — an unlikely prospect. Even in the evangelical community, women hold jobs and enjoy access to education. There cannot be many among them who will accept the subordination that an antiquated biblical ideal requires. Other men's groups place more emphasis on liberating the repressed emotional ("feminine") side of the male personality, allowing fear and kindness to show through. But even these movements are frequently based on images of the warrior and hunter, roles freighted with excess historical baggage, all of it having to do with some repertory of supposedly exclusive masculine traits. Typically, the literature of men's groups touches not at all on aging but emphasizes ways to maintain virility. Sometimes compassion is mentioned, but there is always much histrionic rhetoric about experiencing wildness and fire in the belly.

The problem with these efforts is that they remain age-biased and therefore will not last out a full lifetime. The age bias cuts deeper than the gender bias because it ties men to an essentially adolescent phase of life when their main psychological project was to differentiate from the mother — and from all that is identified as feminine. But as the lives of women come to include more social space, what is the point of that task?

There was a time when dominant males enjoyed privileges rooted in the control of property, political office, education, official authority. Stripped of that backlog, the alpha male role becomes a kind of pathetic macho-lite that is apt to wilt at its first confrontation with any self-possessed woman. I confess that I have found myself embarrassed to be in groups where men gather to search for "manly" ways to be sensitive or caring. Trying to find "the warrior within" sounds too much like situation comedy. But then I never found alpha male "manliness" all that appealing. At school I was the boy who ran for cover when fighting broke out in the schoolyard. And when I didn't run fast enough, I got beaten to a pulp and had to drag myself home in tears. I can still hear the cries behind me, "Mommy's boy! Mommy's boy!" Being manly always seemed to mean hurting or getting hurt. I hated that game and longed to be free of it. Of course, I envied the he-man movie stars of my time — the Clark Gables and Gary Coopers and Errol Flynns — but I always hoped the girls I wanted to impress would prefer the attentions of gentlemen like Leslie Howard or Ronald Coleman.

The Missing Male Elder

Alpha male humans may grow old, but they are not elders. They are over-age adolescents, geriatric boys. They do not lead by virtue of wisdom, but by cunning and ruthlessness. The historical and mythic talents they draw upon are not those of the sage, but those of the hunter and the warrior. They may take pride in holding their own with the young blood, but in truth, clutching at power until it is torn from one's grip makes for an unbecoming end to life. If they were as wise and brave as their years should make them, they would long since have put the strenuous pursuit of salaries, status, and sexual dominance behind them and moved on to other, better things.

Not that it is obvious what those "better things" might be. In our society, where money controls so much of the media, it is inevitable that moneyed men will try to hold center stage, crowding out the alternatives. What they want to see in the culture at large are reflections of themselves. To take a telling contrast: in the Hindu tradition, there is a stage of life, called the *sunyassin,* that is reserved for men who retire after their family and business duties are at an end. It is meant to be a phase of contemplation and completion, a time to put one's spiritual house in order. Since the near-demise of the monastic life in the Western world, our society has had no equivalent to such a phase of spiritual retreat. At the beginning of the modern period, that wise and gentle male identity was obliterated. It is difficult to imagine a society as dynamic as ours generating anything like it again, not for as long as the alpha male model remains dominant.

But then we need not assume that a man or woman needs to leave the world in order to become a true elder, especially at this point in our history. As we lay the foundations of a postindustrial moral order, it is essential for elders to assume a greater role in our affairs. That role ought not to be a mere extension of midlife getting and spending. Far more challenging is the task of remaining involved and responsible, but in a new key, one that sounds a note of gentleness and ethical responsibility.

There are now any number of books, many of them growing out of men's therapy groups, that reveal the soul-searching men have undertaken. *The New Man, The Sensuous Man, The Liberated Man* . . . all focus on the cultivation of emotional warmth, counseling men to open to their feelings and risk being vulnerable in relationships. Among counselors and therapists, there is a clear professional consensus that the role of the alpha male has become a burden that more and more men need to unload and want to unload. Alpha male masculinity has been blamed for the ruination of sexuality, marriage, family, and social conscience. It is also plain unhealthy for men to drive their aging bodies to keep up with a handful of wealthy business tycoons or with movie images of compulsive masculinity. If the pace and strain of the macho lifestyle does not kill them, depression and despair will.

Suicides among men over the age of sixty-five are several times more common than among women in their age group. Elderly white males have by far the highest suicide rate in the senior population; they are unique in being the only group of Americans more likely to die by their own hand than in an automobile accident. In contrast, the lower suicide rate for women over sixty-five has been traced to their greater flexibility and more developed coping skills. Women spend more time building the relationships they need for support.[8] Men can be so good at hiding their emotions that they conceal even suicidal despair from professional counselors. And unlike women, for whom attempted suicide can be a cry for help, when men elect to kill themselves, they use the means most likely to do the job: guns, hanging, or car accidents. "Men," as Royda Crose observes, "are more at risk of early death because they are taught to ignore weakness, illness, and health concerns. . . . They not only don't listen to their bodies, but they are applauded for the denial of pain and discomfort."[9]

Men become especially suicide-prone after their wives die, an event that often leaves them with no close friends, nothing to occupy their time, nothing to give meaning. Like Willy Loman in *Death of a Salesman*, if they have not proven themselves to be a success in their careers, they give up on life, feeling they are worth more dead than alive. They have outlived the role that sustained them since adolescence. A psychiatric social worker I know tells me he once organized a widowers' support group for men who had recently lost their wives. Discovering that most of the men could not find their way around their own kitchens, he brought in a woman to teach some basic cooking. To his surprise, the men resented what he had done. They felt embarrassed to be taking lessons from a woman so late in their lives.

The search for a way out of this masculine trap has produced the quaint concept of the male menopause. Technically speaking, there may be no such thing as a male menopause that fully corresponds to a woman's later-life transformation, but emotionally, as a psychological stage of life, there is something very like it. Since menopause is not as decisively announced by the male body as it is for women, men have been able in the past to override the crisis. No longer. "Putting the men back in menopause," as one therapist cutely puts it, is now an established psychological and cultural project among the New People. At its heart lies the search for intimacy, a word that always requires another to be intimate *with*. That other is usually understood to be a lover, in most cases female. But liberating the male capacity for intimacy may also awaken another male potentiality, one that has to do with other men — younger men. Becoming intimate in love may be the gateway to becoming an elder to one's children and to one's society.

In his studies of the human life cycle, Erik Erikson, among the first psychologists to see aging as "a stage in the growth of the healthy personality," coined the word *generativity* to refer to the eldering project of our later years: "the interest in establishing and guiding the next generation," as he defined it. When that important task is left unattended, "regression from generativity to an obsessive need for pseudo-intimacy takes place, often with a pervading sense of stagnation and interpersonal impoverishment." Erikson, however, saw generativity as primarily a parental responsibility toward one's children and gave little attention to the collective responsibility of the whole senior generation in society.[10]

That is precisely the orientation that Daniel Levinson has sought to provide in his broader study of male developmental psychology. Referring to eldering as "mentoring," Levinson takes this defining responsibility out into the society at large, where men must deal with one another in school or the workplace. It is a complex role, combining the function of teacher, sponsor, guide, exemplar, and counselor. "The mentor represents a mixture of parent and peer; he must be both and not purely either one." Significantly, Levinson regards mentoring as a social task that had best take place outside the parent-child relationship. Parents, he feels, are "too tied to their offspring's pre-adult development (in both his mind and theirs) to be primary mentor figures." At his most challenging, Levinson identifies mentoring as "a form of love relationship." But love between men, so long shadowed in our society by fears of homoeroticism, is a difficult emotion to cultivate, especially for the alpha male. Some cultures, like the Greeks in the time of Socrates, saw no problem. Ours does. The alpha male is compulsively heterosexual, needing what he hopes will be a yielding woman to validate his sexual domination.

Levinson believes the ideal age differential for mentoring is about a half-generation; however, "a person twenty or even fifty years older may, if he is in good touch with his own and the other's youthful Dreams, function as a significant mentor."[11] "Dream" has a special, technical meaning for Levinson. It is the self-chosen life task that ushers the adolescent into the world as a man or a woman. Not all young people form a Dream; not all are allowed to have one of their own. But the job of the mentor is to connect with the passion of the Dream and help make it real. The Jungian psychologist James Hillman echoes Levinson when he tells us that "mentoring begins when your imagination can fall in love with the fantasy of another."[12] And so too the poet Robert Bly, who defines the "true adult" as "one who has been able to preserve his or her intensities . . . so that he or she has something with which to meet the intensities of the adolescent." Both Levinson and Bly remind us that cynicism and despair make for the worst kind of old age; such negativity leaves us unable to nourish the lively aspirations of the young. The essence of youth is *beginning*. If those who have lived longest cannot resonate with the adventure of beginning, what will the young want to learn from them?

Bly has made eldering the principal focus of his highly influential male consciousness-raising work. He has concluded that the rampant wildness of young men, their difficulty with commitment and responsibility, has only one cure: older men must show the way. "The fundamental problem in the continuation of a decent life everywhere in the world," he insists, "is this question of the socialization of young males. . . . It is not women's job to socialize young males. That is the job of the older men." But, he wisely fears, "we are losing our ability to mature. . . . We are always under commercial pressure to slide backward, toward adolescence, toward childhood. With no effective rituals of initiation, . . . young men in our culture go round in circles. . . . Observers describe many contemporaries as children with children of their own."[13]

The eldering task Bly and Levinson have in view is nearly impossible to carry out in a culture that has taken the alpha male as its model for social leadership. The inherent bad faith of the marketplace, its cynical strategies, bullying habits, and low opportunism cripple the power to mentor. The business community has nothing to do with gentle or loving qualities; it does not encourage men to be mentors, only winners. The "commercial pressures" Bly cites as an obstacle to maturity are the creation of world-beating entrepreneurs whose goal is running up a score measured in dollars. Their way promises wealth, power, and status. Where values of that order are at stake, it takes more moral courage to stand *against* the alpha male than to *be* the alpha male.

Because the alpha male role licenses irresponsible uses of power on the part of men, reconfiguring gender is part of a larger social task. This, as the women's movement realized long ago, is the place where the personal and the political intersect.

Learning from the Invisible Woman

Historically speaking, old age is very new. As far as we can tell from the bones they have left us, early humans rarely survived beyond the age of forty. "Life after 40," Daniel Levinson observes, ". . . has been a significant part of man's collective experience for but a moment in our history."[14] In the past, the relatively few men who outlived their active young male adulthood might, at best, carry on as alpha males for another few years, but the charade was soon over. They did not have to maintain the pretense for as long as twenty or thirty more years into deep old age. But however long their lives may last, alpha maleness has given men, whether in reality or fantasy, the option of eluding the facts of aging longer than women can. Older women may find that men their age are frequently a full stage behind in life, still seeking things in women that are fast passing, still seeking things in themselves that are not there. There are few studies by men seeking wisdom in age, but there are many by women. The new run of men's magazines may spend more space on health, toiletries, and aesthetic surgery, but they are a sorry spectacle. The tone must still be gruff, the content overwhelmingly concerned with sexuality. Literature for older men is largely mired in an unresolved postadolescent struggle with the women in their lives, as if men read them with their eighteen-year-old self looking over the shoulder and snickering. Even the more enlightened fringe of the men's movement is still trying to find better ways "to be men." Older women, on the other hand, have gone on to finding better ways to be human.[15]

The alpha male blights the life of the older woman. Women must often wait for men their own age to play out their fantasies with younger women. A man can go to his grave still enacting some version of that role; in doing so he helps to strand the women of his generation. So the women are left to think things through for themselves: what does age take from them, what does it bring to them? Women, like it or not, have more experience with aging than men; age comes to them with a physical decisiveness — and for most of them will last longer. Most decisively, they have no equivalent of the alpha male role awaiting them in their senior years to hold off the great changes brought about by age. In the past, the dominance of alpha males threw women into social eclipse. In the eyes of a patriarchal society, older women became devalued and invisible. But these once invisible women are now doing most of the thinking and discovering that will make longevity worthwhile.

In this they have some support from evolutionary history. The best explanation biologists offer for menopause becoming a feature of our species is that it enabled women in early human society to stop having babies and thus save their strength for raising the children they had already borne. But as the life span has grown, women's postmenopausal years have taken them well beyond child-rearing. They are left with time on their hands for other matters — something approaching what women of early times would have considered a full lifetime. That punctuating event of menopause — a built-in rite of passage — causes women to give serious thought to aging long before men have to think about it. A woman may be undergoing that transition while men her age are still fiercely on the job, competing away, battling it out with younger rivals, hopelessly immersed in a male stereotype that has no future.

If wisdom about sex and gender begins on the far side of the inherited male and female stereotypes, then it is clearly women who are doing most to create a wisely nongendered identity for the New People. "How do we *live our age* as simply a new time of our life, a new period of our humanness, a new stage?" Betty Friedan asks. "The clue lies in those individual differences that increase with age for both women and men. The clue is the *personhood of age*." With age, we are, as she observes, "defined less by biological programming . . . than at any other period of our lives, [and] not necessarily programmed at all by the social roles and norms that defined our youth and middle age." She calls this "at once the terror and the liberation of age."

Thanks to the women's movement, especially as it becomes the *older* women's movement, we are learning that human qualities, whether good or bad, simply are *not gendered*. There is nothing genetically "male" about courage, forcefulness, daring, creativity, decisiveness — nor about harshness and insensitivity. There is nothing genetically "female" about caring, nurturing, gentleness, compassion. That is why we find young and middle-aged women these days up to their eyes in the cutthroat competition of boardroom politics. As much as insecure adolescent boys in various military academies may flinch at the fact, the U.S. Marines are training women for combat and finding they can do the job. On the other hand, I have known a surprising number of fathers and "house-husbands" who cook, do the dishes, and diaper the baby with no sense of humiliation. And in the streets and parks each day I see more and more young men tending their children with some delight. But even progress of this kind in the home and on the job may leave lingering vestiges of gender in the personality, the woman's concern for her femininity, the man's longing for virility. Maybe some sense of balance and civility in expressing those needs is the best one can expect at midlife. But beyond that initial insight lies the uncharted territory of deep maturity where all talk about "the mystery of gender" and "the ineradicable differences between the sexes" rapidly loses meaning.[16]

As we learn in every basic anthropology survey, gender roles vary from culture to culture. That is precisely what calls all the roles into question. But we also know that there have always been roles of *some* kind. It is as if our inborn division of reproductive labor has to be seen as more than a purely physical difference. All our fellow mammals respond to signals and cues in their mating; arousal is the inevitable prelude to procreation. To that extent, gender game-playing may have been necessary for as long as fertility has mattered. If fertility still mattered, then it might make biological sense to keep the old game of boy-girl going. But reproductive success has come to play less and less of a role on our overpopulated planet. Indeed, I suspect that the very fact that people in the industrial societies — the women especially — have come to challenge gender roles, as I do here, is some reflection of our greater biospheric condition. We are at a point where discovering the person who lies beyond masculinity and femininity — as age offers us the opportunity to do — has become an ecological necessity. Longevity is becoming a greater fact of planetary life than fertility.

It is time to call off the game.

10

The Disease Called Aging, the Mistake Called Death

The Disruptive Wonders of Biotechnology

L UIGI CARNARO might be regarded as the first celebrity elder. A Paduan who died in 1565 at the age of ninety-eight, Carnaro was a wonder of his age. As far as anybody knew, he was the oldest man since biblical times. When he had reached the age of eighty, people across Italy wanted to know how he had managed to live so long. He obliged their curiosity by authoring periodic discourses on longevity. Since he had restored his health after living through a dissipated middle age, Carnaro's counsel was all the more coveted. He recommended temperance and moderation in all things. He also believed in preserving the "innate moisture" of the body, which, he felt, kept the humors in balance.[1]

Genetic Roulette

Ever since Carnaro's day, the oldest old have been objects of popular interest. After all, the oldest old define our life span, the maximum number of years that a fortunate few of us can hope to live. As of the turn of the twenty-first century, the consensus among physicians and actuaries is that the life span can reach no further than 125, and even so only for a very few.[2] While we can expect to see an increasing number of people reach 100 in the years ahead, few are expected to live much longer than that.

In recent years, the oldest old have become a special medical study — and not just the oldest human old. Geneticists are carefully studying the longest living of every species, from rodents to elephants, to see whether we share genetic factors with other animals. Even the lowly nematode has contributed a few "candidate longevity genes" for research. But so far, as remarkable as the endurance of the very old may be, it tells us little about our generic prospects in the years ahead. When doctors quiz the oldest old about their habits, the results are notoriously inconclusive, almost comically so. Probably bored by the question, elders over ninety tend to give flippant answers, as if they were beyond caring. Some say they smoke cigars, some that they drink wine; some lead active lives, some do not.[3]

About the only conclusion that researchers have reached about the oldest old from studying them directly is that most of them are female and most remain relatively lean. Their caloric intake is modest. Is this because abstemious eaters live longer, or simply because, with age, appetite drops off? George Roth, a molecular physiologist at the National Institute for Aging, has kept lab animals alive for abnormally long periods by underfeeding them until their metabolism drops to "survival mode." Though he believes caloric austerity alone might lengthen the human life span to well over eighty, it remains uncertain why this should be.[4] Some researchers believe it has to do with slowing down cell division, others that it diminishes the damage done by free radicals in the cells — a hypothesis that receives support from other lines of investigation mentioned later in this chapter.[5]

In one respect, the longevity of the oldest old might be seen as discouraging. After all, these supremely senior people were born and raised before there was much reliable knowledge about nutrition or aerobics or the damage done by saturated fats and smoking. They knew nothing about cholesterol or antioxidants. Yet they have outsurvived millions of clean-livers. This suggests that long life is simply a matter of genetic roulette.

If that is true, then the natural human life span still remains to be discovered. That cannot happen until today's healthiest people pass beyond one hundred. It was only after World War II that the population at large began to understand about the basic risks posed by saturated fats, tobacco, and toxins; it was only then that better nutrition and physical exercise became widespread. Thanks to these more enlightened practices, some among the New People, those who happen to be blessed with the right genes, may be giving themselves the chance to live far longer — and in better condition — than the oldest old today. That result will not be reported in the *Guinness Book of Records* until the middle of the twenty-first century.

The Last Older Generation?

Both medical science and common sense have long shared a basic theory of aging and death. It might be called the "wear-and-tear" hypothesis. Bodies simply give out the way cars give out after a certain amount of mileage. One rheumatologist puts it this way: "You've got an automobile that has a carburetor, wheels, valves, a water pump and all these different parts that are built to last beyond a warranty period. . . . The human body expires when enough of its components have collapsed."[6]

This mechanistic image of aging and dying has been with us since William Harvey first likened the heart to a pump in the seventeenth century. Call the heart a pump, and you can expect it to wear out as all pumps do. The venerable Thomas Jefferson, writing to the more venerable John Adams in 1814 (both men were in their seventies), observed, "Our machines have now been running 70 or 80 years, and we must expect that, worn as they are, here a pivot, there a wheel, now a pinion, next a spring, will be giving way."

As this imagery would have it, people run down and finally die of a "natural cause" called "old age." Eliminating those familiar phrases from the medical vocabulary has been a major advance in the science of gerontology. We have come to see that dying of old age is a self-fulfilling prophecy. The terms are left over from an era when no one troubled to perform autopsies on the very old. Doctors simply assumed that old people died of old age and would record "natural causes" as the cause of death. Statistics compiled from such records would therefore confirm the assumption that old people died of . . . being old.

Today we can be more precise about the wear and tear our bodies sustain through a lifetime. We can trace the damage to numerous sources. In one respect, death may be a cosmic process: the radiation that streams in from outer space may eventually scramble the genetic data in our cells; or all on its own, the DNA containing that data may, after years of replication, simply accumulate so many random mistakes in transcription that the result is an "error catastrophe" large enough to prove fatal. Once we have identified such causes, however, the mechanistic model of aging at once gives rise to the hope that we will be able to fix the damage the way we fix any machine.

As we learn ever more about the specific sources of senescence, the word has gone out: future generations need not age as fast as generations past. For example, Dr. Steven Lamm, who practices "vitality medicine," prefaces his book *Younger at Last* with the admonition: "Discard the tired, outdated, and inaccurate notions of how we're supposed to be at 40, 50, or 60. You are not your parents; you are not doomed to age the same way." His prescription for fending off the incursions of age is a balanced combination of several new anti-aging medications: yohimbe (from the bark of an African tree), testosterone, L-arginine (an amino acid), pycnogenol (an antioxidant), plus some "nootropics" like ginkgo biloba and deprenyl to offset memory loss.[7]

Lamm's approach to rejuvenation is becoming ever more widely practiced. Find a substance that we produce naturally in youth but that drops off with age. Then replenish the supply or find a substitute. Several hormones diminish with age, among them testosterone, melatonin, and DHEA. In our youth, for example, the adrenal gland secretes DHEA in high quantities; by the age of eighty, we have 90 percent less in our blood than at twenty-five. Is one or another of these the substance that once kept us young?

Since the early 1990s, we have been involved in a massive public experiment with just such a hypothesis. Female hormone replacement therapy (HRT) to replenish estrogen is now a routine procedure for postmenopausal women, and one of the most commonly prescribed treatments in American medicine. The benefits, which may include a declining incidence of heart disease and various signs of rejuvenation, are well documented. So too is the effect of estrogen on the brain's cognitive functions; it has been found to enhance learning and memory even in those suffering from Alzheimer's disease.[8] Estrogen replacement seems, then, to retard aging.

Among other leading candidates as a cure-all for aging is human growth hormone (HGH). Ronald Klatz, president of A⁴M (the American Academy of Anti-Aging Medicine), believes that aging is essentially a pituitary deficiency disease. He points out that people who suffer from that deficiency manifest all the signs of age. The pituitary gland can, however, be revived by dosing on HGH, the "fountain of youth" hormone. The result, he is certain, will be the reversal of natural aging. It is as simple as that. Klatz, who writes articles in the popular press under headings like "Can We Grow Young?" answers the question with an emphatic yes. Other researchers believe the most astonishing results with HGH have been placebo effects achieved with participants who were highly motivated to regain their lost youth.[9]

It is an odd feature of American medical culture that, for all its closely guarded professionalism, anti-aging, the most crucial of fields, remains in the realm of do-it-yourself folk medicine. The public usually learns about anti-aging medications from one of the television news magazines or from pop medicine best-sellers (bearing titles like *The Melatonin Miracle*) that now arrive in waves, always accompanied by extraordinary claims. Once a promising supplement has been publicized, it becomes a product. Since many hormones are not subject to FDA control, health food stores are free to stock and sell them; so too every local drugstore and supermarket. They are casually on sale alongside hair spray and aspirin tablets, or they can be ordered in bulk from merchants everywhere.

But self-administration can be risky. There have been few reliable tests on the effect of these hormones on human subjects; taken in large quantities, some have adverse effects in lab animals. DHEA, for example, can cause liver tumors in mice. Then there are the more benign immunity boosters, mainly antioxidants, that promise to arrest the aging process. Echinacea, an extract from the purple coneflower, cat's claw from the Amazon rain forest, shark's cartilage, goldenseal, ginseng, or plain garlic . . . each has its following as a way to restore the vigor of our younger years. Along this line of research, an astonishing new idea about aging has emerged. Rather than accepting old age as fate, researchers now define it as a *disease* — or rather, as a collection of mainly deficiency diseases. If that is so, then perhaps aging is also curable, if not all at once, then in the same piecemeal way we have gone about curing other sicknesses and extending life expectancy. It is simply a matter of going through a checklist of lethal or disabling ailments and eliminating them one by one, as we have very nearly eliminated smallpox and scurvy.

The ability of medical science to reverse or prevent diseases once thought to be invincible is very nearly an article of faith. Recently I came upon a children's AIDS project in the local YMCA. It was a quilt the children had sewn to wish AIDS sufferers well. At the center of the quilt was a large patch that said, "Hang on! Scientists will invent a cure." That conviction is among the major reasons we may never be able to agree upon the moral permissibility of euthanasia, even for the very ill. Who can say what medical miracle waits just around the corner? If we can believe what life-extension researchers are telling us, perhaps one day soon it will not be necessary to age at all. This generation will be remembered as the last older generation. And if aging can be cured, the same might be possible for the ultimate result of aging, death. People who do not grow old do not die — at least not of "natural causes."

In Search of the "Death Gene"

Rejuvenation in its various modes is a "stochastic" theory of aging. That is, it holds that aging is due to the buildup of random damage in the organism. As optimistic as rejuvenation therapy has become in its claims, it is fast becoming the conservative position in life-extension medicine. There is another, more radical hypothesis. The extreme wing of anti-aging research sees the entire complex of characteristics we call "aging" as *a single physiological phenomenon* that is controlled by a core genetic mechanism. Rather than seeing aging as stochastic, this approach maintains that senescence is "programmed." The very terminology suggests a line of therapy. Find the flaw — or bug — in the program and fix it.

The guiding image here is the oldest model of nature in Western science: the clock. We are to imagine a genetically determined clock ticking away in the organism; it counts out our hours until it runs down and stops. The first researcher to use this image was the Russian biologist Vladimir Dilman, whose book *The Grand Biological Clock* was published in 1955. Dilman theorized that the metaphorical clock in question was a neuroendocrine mechanism based in the hypothalamic-pituitary axis of the body. This clock, which at first facilitates healthy growth and development, begins falling out of balance at about the age of twenty-five. To correct that imbalance, Dilman recommended the use of phenformin, an antidiabetic medication, plus several hormones, among them estrogen, to fine-tune the organism. Dilman's proposed cure did not work, but ambitious life-extenders have adopted his clockwork image, believing that it makes obvious what route medical science should take. Find that clock, reset it, and aging will be at an end.

As far-fetched as this sounds, the goal stems from a curious fact of life that calls the wear-and-tear theory of aging into question. Aging is not a universal phenomenon among living things. In a sense, the oldest of life forms — the microbes — are immortal: they go on and on dividing with no sign of age. At a more complex level of development, creatures do indeed die, but rarely by aging. With the exception of a few long-lived species like the elephant, the parrot, and the Galapagos tortoise, very few animals have the chance to grow old in the wild; they are hunted down or they die by starvation, freezing, or any number of fatal accidents.

Before zoologists began keeping animals alive to study them in captivity, aging was a rare experience in the nonhuman world. Until the twentieth century, there has probably never been such an animal as a very old chimpanzee. We now know that rockfish, mollusks, sharks, tortoises, and sturgeons may go on for decades longer than humans, showing no signs of physical deterioration; even their fertility lasts to the end of their days. The flounder female grows larger rather than older; the male reaches a limit and then shows signs of age. The bristle-cone pine lives for millennia, though only at the growing edges. The creosote bush has clocked in at ten thousand years of age. Oddly enough, many of these creatures are distinguished by how primitive they are, as if a long, perhaps immortal life were the original design from which "higher" types have deviated. It is, in any case, the fact that we cannot say of every living thing on the planet what we can say for our own species: that their clock runs down and that they finally die of old age.

Can this human evolutionary departure, then, be reversed by reengineering the genetic apparatus?

In working with yeast cells, researchers have been able to identify fourteen genes that are directly related to aging. By manipulating the genes so that they "overexpress" or "underexpress," aging in yeast has been increased or decreased by as much as 30 percent. No one has yet discovered timekeepers that govern aging in the human cells with that precision, but progress in that direction represents one of the most impressive lines of research in modern science.

At the Hayflick Limit

Until the early 1960s, the dogma among microbiologists was that, given proper attention, a cultured human cell might live indefinitely. The implication was that cells do not themselves age; aging must originate in some other process. Then two researchers, Leonard Hayflick and Paul Moorehouse, discovered that cells do indeed register the passage of time. There is in fact a limit to how many times a cell can divide in the body. This finite replicative capacity gives out after about one hundred divisions.[10] This means that the cells of a young person will survive in a petri dish longer than the cells of an older person. Eventually, however, after a certain number of divisions — now called the Hayflick limit — the cells stop dividing, begin to malfunction, and soon die.

Here we have a landmark discovery in modern medicine. *Aging happens at the cellular level* and presumably works out from the very foundations of life.

In 1978 the site of the Hayflick limit was discovered to lie at the tip of the chromosome. There we find an expendable stretch of DNA called the telomere. Each time a cell divides, a small amount of the telomere flakes away, leaving less to lose the next time the cell divides. The telomere is a buffer that protects the rest of the DNA from growing shorter. A great many of the effects we see as the aging of the body actually ensue when the telomeres begin to break down at their tips. In aging cells, molecular debris accumulates, membranes get ragged, some genes stop functioning, other genes, capable of doing great damage, begin to run rampant. The malfunctioning of senescent cells that have used up their quota of divisions causes brittle bones, parched skin, declining memory.[11]

This cellular model of aging is now the prevailing paradigm in medical research. It has that empirically mechanistic quality that always proves highly attractive in science: specific mechanisms causing specific effects by way of chemical reactions. Images like this invite tampering and possibly improvement. In a typically mechanistic metaphor, the gerontologist Vincent Giampapa puts it this way: "The blueprint of aging is in the DNA under the hood of the telomere."[12] Obviously, then, if the telomeres can be kept from breaking away — better still, if damaged telomeres can be restored — aging might be stopped, even reversed. At the cellular level, this is called "immortalization."

There is an enzyme that does exactly that. It is called telomerase. In 1984 the microbiologists Carol Greider and Elizabeth Blackburn, working along the lines Leonard Hayflick had charted, discovered that telomerase can actually render a cell immortal by keeping it dividing seemingly forever. But there is a problem with telomerase. It is the enzyme that causes cells to keep growing beyond control. That is called cancer. In that case, the immortalized cell kills the all too mortal organism. Finding a way to make controlled use of telomerase is among the most active areas of anti-aging research.[13]

Early in 1998, biotechnicians at the Geron Corporation in California took the first significant step toward that goal. They identified the gene that manufactures telomerase and used it to "immortalize" aging human eye and skin cells. Once the gene had been inserted, the aging cells began to divide vigorously once again. Leonard Hayflick, whose limit had thus been surpassed, greeted the achievement as a "monumental advance in the understanding of the molecular genetics of aging."

At this point the most likely application for the new technique is in cell biology. Long-lived human cell cultures will diminish the need to use laboratory animals; they may also help grow customized tissues for spare parts surgery. At some still distant point such cultures may be used to rejuvenate selected organs and tissues, but the prospect that this method can be used to switch off aging in the entire organism before birth is still in the realm of fiction. As one critic puts it, "To think that aging is caused by a single clock ticking away inside cells is almost as naive as thinking that homunculus-like figures control your brain."[14]

Radically altering the genetics of aging lies a long way off, but in the meantime there may be ways to protect the telomeres from the daily damage they suffer and so keep the cell in good working condition. Some longevity researchers think this may be quite easy to do. Grace Wong of Genentech Corporation was among the first to suggest the deleterious role played by oxygen free radicals in our organism. The free radicals, molecules that lack an electron and go hunting for it in other molecules, eventually damage DNA and RNA. Wong showed that antioxidants like vitamins C and E tame the free radicals. Several other dietary supplements also do the job. Beta-carotene, selenium, and coenzyme-Q10 all block the extensive damage done by the cellular burning of oxygen and may be most effective when they are coordinated to work as a team. Selenium and CoQ10 can be synthesized by our bodies, but they are among the substances whose presence in our blood declines with age. Their deficiency may play a role in aging.

Immortality Inc.

If there was ever a line of scientific research that needed advice from outside science, it is biotechnology. Any significant advance in this field that abolished aging or simply gave us decades more life would radically alter the human condition. Youth would become a matter of some fifty years, and retirement would stretch out over as much as eighty years, not for a lucky few but for all who did not die of accidental causes. At that point, every death below the age of eighty or ninety would be as great a tragedy as we now regard the untimely death of a teenager. The economic disruption that would come about is obvious. The current entitlements debate asks us to worry over baby boomers who may live some twenty years longer than their grandparents. What if the entire human race were demanding access to medications that would *double* life expectancy?

Medical professionals and biotechnicians have only lately begun to give serious thought to this daunting prospect. Writing for the *Journal of the American Medical Association*, Dwayne Banks and Michael Fossel have called for a review of all public policy based upon conventional population projections. "The possibility of extending the maximum human life span," they warn, "has gone from legend to laboratory. . . . Predictions of the costs of aging will be hollow unless they factor in the ongoing, nascent, and fundamental changes in our understanding of aging and age-related diseases."[15] But can we imagine calling a moratorium on life extension research, or fixing some limit to its pursuit? The rough rule of thumb that Leonard Hayflick has suggested will hardly do. He advocates calling off research when life expectancy reaches one hundred, long enough, he feels, for a good life. Pressing beyond that opens up "grotesque scenarios" of overpopulation.[16] But his choice is little more than arbitrary. That proposal might be endorsed by everyone below the age of fifty — and it would just as surely be rejected by any healthy ninety-year-old. Other researchers wash their hands of all responsibility for social consequences. Some make an optimistic appeal. A race of healthy elders, Ronald Klatz believes, will find the wisdom to solve any problems that arise.

Biotechnology could be the gateway to our evolutionary future. It might bring us an expanding repertory of scientific knowledge, medical skills, and social values that we culturally transmit to our progeny as the secret of longevity. Eventually, if we ever discover the biological basis for aging and incorporate that discovery into the human genome, the genetic transmission of longevity might take over from cultural transmission. Longevous traits would then become as much a part of our physical constitution as hair or eye color. Someday, looking back, our ancestors may regard the twentieth and twenty-first centuries as the great watershed when longevity made the transition from cultural ideal to genetic characteristic.

Or . . . biotech may be summoning us to a delusionary and ultimately fruitless quest, rather like the search for the proverbial fountain of youth. But the quest could take a tragic turn; it might leave the human race impoverished and perhaps genetically crippled in ways that cannot be repaired.

How could this terrible result come about? One need only survey the growing literature of biotechnology to sense where the flaw might lie. It has to do with the very exuberance that drives research in the field. The hubris and hyperbole that now characterize popular writing in biotechnology, even that of leading professionals, comes worrisomely close to the commercial hype that surrounds computers and high tech. The reason is the same in both cases. The research, far from being "pure," stems from corporate sources. The lion's share of biotechnology is being financed by private laboratories. We are dealing here with entrepreneurial science. In search of venture capital, it is selling longevity like a product.

No, not *like* a product — *as* a product. The treatments and medications that yield longevity are taking the form of merchandise: pharmaceuticals, vitamin and nutritional supplements, lifestyle accoutrements, and, most controversially, patented genes. The result is exactly what we have come to expect in other dollar-driven fields: exaggeration, misleading advertising, and frenzied, competitive jockeying — none of which precludes the possibility of genuine research breakthroughs. High tech promises machines that will be smarter than people; biotechnology promises us the life of the gods. But in the case of longevity, we are dealing with a product that impinges upon the deepest yearnings of the human heart.

A television series on biotech takes the title *Man Immortal.* A survey of the field calls itself *No More Dying.* Ronald Klatz announces that we are in "a life-extension revolution" that "will soon make human lifespans of 120 years and beyond a boring reality." These are intoxicating promises. They carry with them the resonance of an age-old cultural ideal that lends them almost religious significance. They are the life impulse raised to its highest power. Wisely or not, people want those promises to be true. If limitless longevity is now to be made available from corporate America, what charge is too high? And if the profits are also limitless, then what claim is too great to make?

But to pursue the evolutionary metaphor a bit further: commercialism could prove to be the flawed gene in our *cultural* transmission of longevity. Profiteering may very well corrupt the message and produce a monstrous cultural mutation.

In August 1997, the front page of my daily newspaper carried a jarring juxtaposition of reports that illustrates the problem we may one day face. One story recounted a great new breakthrough in our understanding of telomerase, the enzyme that plays a central role both in cancer and in aging. The story indicated that we are getting ever closer to the ability to manipulate the aging process and thus extend life expectancy by many years. That same day the news from Washington was that the Congress had cut thousands of retarded, dependent children from the welfare roles as part of a budget-balancing campaign. The Social Security Administration explained that it had been mandated to save the money. In effect, the society was declaring that it could not afford to maintain these children. Consider what the burden would be if these children were the beneficiaries of a revolutionary enzyme therapy that gave them another century of dependent life.

The Ultimate Nightmare

Imagine that we achieve a dramatically increased life span, but not the health and vigor we want with it. To be sure, vitality is always intended to be an integral part of life extension. But can we be certain that we will get what we want? Will profitable advances in life-extending technology be kept classified and off the market until it can be demonstrated that the procedure guarantees twenty or thirty years of vigorous, disease-free life? If we are mistaken about a matter as consequential as this, there will be no obvious fix. The "mistakes" will be people clinging to a life that may not seem worth living to most of us, but not for that reason volunteering to take themselves off society's hands.

Or suppose we discover that there is an *older* old age waiting somewhere beyond the present life-span horizon; suppose it brings with it forms of disability we cannot imagine, a sort of hypersenility. In a recent survey of progress on the genetics of aging, the researchers conclude with a dark rumination upon the "polymorphism" of the genes. Polymorphism means the ability of genes to express themselves in unpredictable ways over the life span. "One might consider that, if the human life expectancy should approach the present record of 122 years, some existing gene polymorphisms that may be 'lying in wait' could rise up to challenge the quest for health in the advanced years."[17]

Hopeful as this progress is bound to seem as it is reported in the media, we should remember that enthusiasm can blind as readily as it can inspire. In their 1976 book *No More Dying*, Joel Kurtzman and

Phillip Gordon confidently predicted "the conquest of aging" and "freedom from death . . . the last enemy." A breathtaking prospect. But one looks in vain in the pages of the book for any mention of Alzheimer's disease. Why is the disease not there? Because, as of the early 1970s, too few people had contracted the disease to make it a significant feature on the medical agenda. Indeed, as of the late nineteenth century, when life expectancy was much shorter, we did not even know that Alzheimer's disease existed.

Those who offer glowing predictions of an ever extending life span may be as wrong as those who predicted intelligent computers by the year 1990. But even to raise such possibilities has an impact upon the culture of longevity; indeed, research, investment, and development are rushing forward on the basis of those expectations.

Considerations like this return us to the dilemma of the ragged fringe: the declining physical condition that awaits even the most long-lived among us at some point in the future. That dilemma is with us now and is already contributing to the rising cost of Medicare. Biotechnology could make that problem even worse. Currently, the oldest of the old — those who reach ninety and one hundred — seem to require little medical care and die quickly when their time comes. But biotechnology could allow many more people who reach the seventy-to-ninety-year-old range to die very costly deaths. The result could be the ultimate nightmare: a society in which the hospitals and nursing homes are filled with decrepit but superlongevous seniors in need of ever more long-term, expensive care.

This is the "terrifying prospect" Sir George Pickering raised in the 1960s when he warned that "those with senile brains will form an ever increasing fraction of the inhabitants of the Earth."[18] That sad scenario is, of course, as speculative as anything the biotechnicians are brainstorming. Life beyond 125 is terra incognita. That does not mean the research should cease, but only that it ought to be guided by a certain prudence and caution. We should be feeling our way forward. We are not. Market forces are rushing us into the demographic frontier as if nothing could go wrong. The main reason for the optimism is money. Everybody involved in the research has an eye on the prospective profits and the glory of the discoveries to be made. This is hardly a prescription for objective scientific work.

Life/Death, Yin/Yang

"To be" and "not to be" arise mutually.
Difficult and easy are mutually realized.
Long and short are mutually contrasted.
High and low are mutually posited.
Before and after are in mutual sequence.

— from the *Tao Te Ching*

There is a philosophical conundrum hidden away in the more optimistic lines of life-extension research. Some of the most promising ideas about reversing aging and staving off death share a perplexing characteristic. They link aging and death to otherwise necessary functions of the living organism.

Consider what we have discovered about glycosylation. Glycosylation results from the way sugars are metabolized, or caramelized, in our bodies. It is known to contribute to cataracts, the blocking of arteries, and the stiffening of joints — all characteristics of old age.[19] The same process underlies the wrinkling of the skin in old age. As we grow older, our aging cells do a less and less effective job of producing the enzyme that eliminates the sugar, which then begins to gum up the functioning of the cells, and so the skin begins to age.[20] Perhaps, then, this most basic of cellular chemical processes is implicated in aging.

But cellular use of sugars, like the burning of oxygen, is the cell's main way of gaining the energy it needs to do everything. The wedding of oxygen and vitality is one of the great turning points in the evolution of life. By virtue of this ingenious cellular chemistry, it became possible for life to develop a complexity far beyond the microbial level. Now, at a much later stage of life's evolution, human beings have developed a science that can study the chemistry of our organism. What we have discovered is that, over time, the bonding of sugars and protein produces harmful side effects that resemble aging; so too the burning of oxygen produces free radicals which eventually damage the cells of the body and kill them. Thus, while learning how to use oxygen was among the basic achievements of life on Earth, in the form of free radicals oxygen becomes a life-shortening menace to the organism. Our efforts to eliminate free radicals that come of oxygen combustion amount to reaching a few billion years back in evolutionary time and revising how life works.

While there are many other directions in life-extension and anti-aging medicine, I mention these for a particular reason. At least to my layman's eye, this situation has an intriguingly paradoxical character. We now know that one promising way of reversing senescence leads us to a process that both nourishes and kills. It is almost as if the human organism were booby-trapped. Our perception of death as an "enemy" leads us to believe that it can be eliminated as the "opposite" of life. But is it possible that life and death are intertwined, not as "opposites" one can choose between, but as a radically coupled, mutually defining phenomenon resembling the yin-yang relationship in Taoist philosophy?

Is it possible that life and death are not an opposition but a *polarity?* The answer makes a great difference. One can choose between opposites, but not between poles. One cannot, except under exotic experimental conditions, have a positive pole without a negative pole; the two are companions that define each other. So too one cannot strip certain quarks of their companion particles. What if death is rather like the shadowed ground that makes the bright figure upon it visible?

Apoptosis and the Death Instinct

One new area of medicine seems to be flirting with just this ancient spiritual insight in its biological translation. "Apoptosis" is a process that accompanies life throughout its course, serving the needs of the living creature. Apoptosis is defined as cellular suicide, or more colorfully, as a "cellular death wish." Research now suggests that life is as much the beneficiary of that death wish as its victim. One of the experts in the field, Martin Raff, actually refers to the process as an "existential drama" and connects it with Albert Camus's conviction that suicide is "the only truly serious philosophical problem."[21]

Apoptosis is a process of self-destruction programmed into cells. It is there from the beginning of life; it appears in the embryo where it acts systematically to kill off cells by the millions in order to shape the newborn. For example, the human fetal hand first appears with webs between the fingers. The cells that constitute the webs kill themselves so that the hand can have the right shape. Similarly, if a cell is infected by a virus or expresses mutated DNA, for safety's sake apoptosis sets in, nudging the cell toward self-destruction.

Throughout life, cells are constantly proliferating, but their numbers remain constant, again owing to apoptosis. Some scientists believe this process might be susceptible to manipulation for the purpose of saving lives, say in the case of heart attacks or strokes. Left alone in such crises, damaged heart muscle or brain cells may opt for self-destruction. But if that response can be stalled for days or even hours, it may be possible to preserve the cells and repair the damaged tissues.

Like all microbiological processes, apoptosis is intricate. It involves the production and carefully orchestrated interaction of enzymes whose behavior adds up to a suicide gene. The enzymes carefully repackage dead cells so that neighboring cells can consume them. Unlike necrosis, which is the untimely death of a cell due to trauma or disease, apoptosis is neat and efficient. It leaves so little waste behind that it wholly escaped the notice of scientists until the 1970s, and even then its function in the normal course of life was unremarked for another decade. In a sense, the role played in our healthy functioning by dying cells was invisible because there was so much of it going on.

Our bodies are filled with death, but the dead cells are neatly scavenged and recycled by the organism. It is now understood that without apoptosis life would not be possible. In fact, when cells lose their ability to die, they run rampant, assuming the life-threatening form we call cancer. Thus, every cell has to be able to die for the good of the organism. The result is a cell carefully "balanced on a knife edge with death on one side and growth on the other."[22]

The process of apoptosis as a whole is profoundly communal, or cooperative — though, of course, these metaphorical terms have to be used with some allowance. The signal each cell needs to keep growing and living comes from adjacent cells. Martin Raff speaks of this as a "social control" exercised by "cellular neighborhoods." He goes so far as to suggest that cells behave as if death were their "normal" state; suicide, he thinks, is their "default setting." Cells are kept alive as long as their "life-affirming partners" signal them to stay alive. That is why no cells — except for a cancerous one — can survive long in isolation. They need to be "encouraged" to live.

How did such a process get started in evolutionary history? Some scientists believe apoptosis is a primitive defense mechanism against disease that can be found very early in evolution; the process has been located in some microorganisms. Single-celled parasites have been observed performing apoptosis. The parasites apparently use apoptosis as a way of controlling their growth as a population in their host and thus surviving.

Because of its mysterious links with both cancer and aging, apoptosis is one of the most active areas of inquiry in medical biology. However complex the chemistry of the process, there is no doubt that apoptosis is a primordial feature of all organisms and deeply embedded in the evolutionary history of life on Earth. It bears a haunting resemblance to Sigmund Freud's purely speculative Thanatos, the death instinct, the deeply conservative psychic force that seeks to return life to the inanimate state from which it arose. Freud wrote quite lyrically about Thanatos; he called it the "equally immortal adversary of eternal Eros," one of the two "heavenly forces" that govern the human soul.

None of these thoughts is meant to suggest that we should not do all we can to control free radicals and harness the powers of apoptosis. As deeply ingrained as they are in the evolution of life, these may be processes that we can modify or put to use. On the other hand, they at least suggest that we may eventually discover, somewhere in the foundations of life, a figure and ground unity that so tightly combines the polar companions life and death that it cannot be altered — and that we will not want to see it undone.

Longevity at the Darwinian Limit

This same distant, prehistoric background has been invoked in a new field called Darwinian medicine. It too has something to teach us about the paradoxical relationship between life and death.

Developed in the 1980s by Randolph Nesse and George Williams, Darwinian medicine raises the prospect that there may be a limit to age-reversal research that has yet to be fully appreciated. Darwinian physicians believe that some of the diseases and disabilities of our species may represent adaptations carried forward from the deep historical past.[23] These adaptations once served a good purpose; they allowed life to survive and prosper and so became embedded in our genes. Perhaps they still benefit us, but we have lost sight of that beyond the historical horizon and now see the adaptation as the symptom of disease. Fever, for example, may be the body's primordial way of making itself inhospitable to infectious agents. Stop the fever, as doctors are inclined to do, and the germs may do more damage, not less. Similarly, the swelling that surrounds a break or sprain may be the body's way of immobilizing the injury. Even some lethal diseases may have once played a very different role in life. A good example of this is sickle-cell anemia. A deadly disease among African Americans, sickle-cell anemia evolved out of a beneficial adaptation to malaria. Those who carried the trait in certain malaria-infested areas of the world — mainly Africa — benefited and survived. But now, in other times and places, it shows up as an inherited liability. This is called "negative pleiotropy."

Is it possible that senescence has something of this quality, that it confers adaptive benefits early in life but later claims its price in the form of organic deterioration? Those pursuing this line of research have found creatures whose capacity for reproduction seems tied to traits that age them rapidly as soon as they have mated. The salmon and the Australian marsupial mouse are examples of this; they mate and reproduce in a frenzy, then almost at once show signs of age and die from an accumulation of diseases.

We cannot say. But if it should turn out that there are diseases linked to positive survival traits, we may find ourselves unable to remove them from our constitution. Darwinian medicine is still in its infancy, but it may lead to a new kind of medical science, one that works with evolution and so brings unexpected benefits. Among its discoveries may be one possibility that will undermine the most ambitious goals of biotechnology. The bodies we inherit out of the evolutionary process are intricately woven into the history of life on Earth. That history has been preoccupied with the evolution of life forms that are viable just long enough to reproduce and bring offspring into the world. In achieving that much, the process of evolution may have had to make compromises in the structure and function of organs — trade-offs, as we might now call them, that limit our life span. That fact may be so deeply embedded in our development that it can never be changed short of replaying the entire process.

The Readiness Is All

If it be now, 'tis not to come; if it be not to come, it will be now; if it be not now, yet it will come; the readiness is all.

— SHAKESPEARE, *Hamlet*

The current wishful fascination we are coming to develop for survival and longevity could be an invitation to staggering disappointment — like a rash investment in a highly speculative enterprise. That is literally so in the biotechnology industry, where the value of the companies fluctuates with each new breakthrough or failure. The more credence we give to such chancy prospects, the more we are distracted from the great truth: that all of us, long-lived or not, confront a common fate. Whether death comes sooner or later, it nevertheless comes. "The readiness is all," as Shakespeare wisely said. If that is so, then the wonders of biotech may be treacherous indeed. Once again, like so much of Western science, we find ourselves pitted against nature as if we were face to face with an adversary whom we must outsmart. Moreover, with the promise of near-immortality somewhere in the future, how can we help but feel cheated that we do not live to see the time?

Playing upon that fear, some impresarios of immortality are hawking their cure-alls as if they were street-corner vendors applying the hard sell. One of the newsweeklies, sporting a cover picture of a glamorous young lady, runs a major feature titled "How Science Is Searching for Ways to Keep Us Forever Young," and making that promise seem very close at hand. Ronald Klatz, whose research in longevity has a distinctly entrepreneurial bent, announces (as of 1996) that "within five to fifteen years . . . we will have true age-reversal. . . . But the train is leaving the station and anyone who is past age 35 or so will have to clamber on now." Another anti-aging enthusiast, Vincent Giampapa, warns that "if you don't limit cellular damage and treat the DNA now, . . . you will have so much extra damage to chromosomes and DNA that you won't be able to benefit."[24]

Here is one respect in which earlier generations may have been more fortunate than us, despite their briefer life expectancy. They lived with no eager predictions of endless physical survival to inflate their expectations. They knew earlier on in life than we do that the time was at hand to prepare. *Memento mori* had a far more persuasive meaning for them.

Under the pressure of treacherous commercial blandishments, the New People may finish by giving more attention to pills and medications than to matters of mind and spirit. What a shame it would be if we became a society that spent more time combing through "how to live forever" best-sellers than acquiring the wisdom that is appropriate to elders and our only true consolation in the face of death. Fleeing mortality is no way to make ready for it.

11

The Future of Death

The idea of death, the fear of it, haunts the human animal like nothing else; it is the mainspring of human activity — activity designed largely to avoid the fatality of death, to overcome it by denying in some way that it is the final destiny of man.

— ERNEST BECKER, *The Denial of Death* (1972)

WHEN BECKER WROTE those words in 1972, existentialism was the reigning philosophical style in the universities. Like Sartre and Camus, Becker saw the willingness to face our inevitable annihilation without flinching as the only dignified stance in life. He called it "cosmic heroism." But as medical science finds ever more ingenious ways to keep the body alive, the relationship between Sartre's "being and nothingness" is changing radically. We may soon discover a greater dread: *the fear of life*.

Cosmic Heroism and the Right to Die

In the era of the New People, death is becoming a new kind of problem. More people are going to have to choose when and how and at whose hands they or those they love are going to die. Or they will have to choose someone to make that decision for them if they cannot. For the first time in human history, ordinary people — not existential philosophers — will have to decide whether life is worth living. That is one hard result of having more life: the quantity of years we may have ahead of us forces us to ponder the quality of the life we will be living in those years. No image more typifies the meaning of philosophy than that of Socrates in his prison cell electing to drink hemlock rather than live on as an exile from Athens. Few of us may have Socrates' greatness of soul and acuity of mind, but we are going to be *forced* to be philosophical about the greatest question of all.

That question has already passed beyond philosophy and into politics. Wherever euthanasia initiatives have been placed on the ballot in the United States, the debate that ensues reveals that many people (and I count myself among them) regard thwarting death at all costs as a frightening prospect, one that grows more horrifying as our power to keep people alive increases. While modern medicine can now stave off death longer than ever before in history, the result is not a dream come true but, beyond a certain point, a deepening nightmare.

During the 1990s, Oregon voters twice approved doctor-assisted suicide ballot measures that legalized euthanasia for the terminally ill. The debate, which was heavily covered by the national media, rapidly became a bitter confrontation between "right-to-life" and "right-to-die" factions. Those who supported the proposition may have been defending "death with dignity," but not far below the surface they were sounding a distinct note of terror. They protested passionately against being kept unwillingly alive and made a burden to all around them. In highly charged television commercials, they pictured themselves being trapped in a vegetative state with images that recalled Edgar Allan Poe's dread of premature burial.

The fear they were invoking is age-old. It is the fear of the dungeon and the rack that was once the stock-in-trade of Gothic tales. But the images evoked to express that fear are new: the hospital bed, the intensive care ward, the nursing home. They force us to imagine ourselves as prisoners of our own bodies, bound to an existence that must be lived out to the last gasp in pain and helplessness. Instead of thumbscrews and iron maidens, we have the IV tube and the respirator. Instead of hooded torturers, we have doctors and nurses in clean white uniforms at the bedside scrutinizing dials and gauges.

As long ago as the seventeenth century, Francis Bacon speculated that a day would come when the fluids and organs of an infirm body might be replaced by healthy ones. In this way, he believed, life might be prolonged indefinitely. Since then, the "conquest of death" has been one of the defining features of scientific progress. Bacon actually flirted with the heresy that science would reverse the fall of man by lifting the curse of death under which the human race had groaned since being cast out of Eden. He referred to this as the "restitution of man to the sovereignty and power which he had in the first state of creation." By the age of the

Enlightenment, champions of worldly progress had made the defeat of death and disease part of their revolutionary agenda. There was no telling how long life might be extended. "A period must one day arrive," proclaimed Condorcet, the great eighteenth-century prophet of progress, "when death will be nothing more than the effect either of extraordinary accidents or of the slow and gradual decay of the vital powers; and that the duration of the interval between the birth of man and his decay will have itself no assignable limit."[1]

How ironic, then, that so many now live in dread of becoming the involuntary beneficiaries of the highest reward that science can offer.[2]

Gothic Medicine

I have had a firsthand encounter with Bacon's promise. I found it chilling. Several years ago I was caught in the sort of medical crisis that forces one to rethink the meaning of life and death. Told I was likely to be suffering from an incurable malignancy, I was assured by my physicians that they would make every effort to save my life. I did not feel encouraged. What I saw ahead of me was months, possibly years, of medical dependency: an endless regimen of tests and procedures that would make the hospital my home, and all of it possibly leading to a protracted state of helpless delirium. The terror that gripped me was relieved only by one conviction: if it all became unbearable, I would take my own life. I went out in search of a suicide manual (no easy item to find) and was relieved when I finally discovered Derek Humphry's *Let Me Die Before I Wake*, published by the Hemlock Society. Suddenly death appeared to me, not a curse, but a deliverance. As for my concerned physicians, so heroically determined to keep me alive, they took on a most unpleasant aspect. Distorted in the mirror of my fears, they began to look like mad doctors, not because they were out to kill me, but because they were so intent on saving me — like it or not. Could I depend on them to take my worst fears into account? Or would I become an intriguing challenge to their medical expertise?

These days doctors can keep their patients alive under physical and mental conditions that approach the grotesque. They can prolong the lives of the disabled and demented for years. Their decision to do so may spring from many motives. They may honestly feel that there is reason to hope, perhaps that some unexpected cure or palliative will appear. They may fear that anything less than heroic measures will open them to lawsuits for malpractice. They may know of no way to explain the bad news to their patient or the patient's family. They may be doggedly determined to fight to the last as a matter of professional pride. Sherwin Nuland, whose book *How We Die* offers a rare insight into how physicians deal with death, believes that many doctors take the death of a patient as a defeat. "Physicians accept the conceit (in every sense of the word) that science has made us all-powerful and therefore the only proper judges of how our skills are to be used. The greater humility that should have come with greater knowledge is instead replaced by medical hubris: since we can do so much, there is no limit to what should be attempted — *today* and for *this patient!*"[3]

This fixation on success may finish by delivering patients into an ethical hell. Doctors can keep alive hopelessly sick people who may be using up the financial, emotional, and spiritual resources of their families.

I had another occasion to reflect on these matters in the course of writing a sequel to Mary Shelley's *Frankenstein.*[4] As I worked back through the original text of this familiar classic, I realized that Shelley had anticipated the fears I speak of here. The dread of unnaturally extended life is the prophetical subtext of her novel, underlying the gore and violence of the tale. Seen in this light, the story becomes a moral analysis of the flight from mortality. Frankenstein's monster is monstrous, not simply because he is ugly, but because he is a living corpse. The ultimate achievement in life extension, he is a collage of dead body parts stitched together and forced to return to life. Endowed with the high intelligence of his transplanted brain, the creature soon learns of his origin and rebels against his enforced immortality. The epigraph to the novel anticipates the horror of his condition. It is the poignantly rhetorical question that Adam asks of God in Milton's *Paradise Lost:* "Did I solicit thee from darkness to promote me?"

From this point of view, the horror of the story is first of all *his;* our fear is the prospect that we may become what he is.

Recalling my own condition as I once lay in intensive care with as many as five tubes plunged into my body to deliver and extract fluids, I realize how much like the familiar image of the monster on the laboratory table I must have looked. Yes, I was grateful to have survived the crisis. But what if this were to go on and on until I became the comatose appendage of some relentless machinery of survival? Only recently doctors at a Virginia hospital managed to keep an anencephalic baby alive for over two years; in days past the child's life span might have been mere days. It was an astonishing achievement — and absolutely horrifying. In this instance, the doctors might claim they were simply following orders since the mother had demanded that the child be kept alive. But in 1992 an anencephalic baby born in Florida was placed on life support against the parents' wishes until it died. In both cases, the disturbing fact is that such a thing *could* be done and was. How many of us would welcome having our bodies kept breathing and metabolizing years after we were brain-dead? In video reports, the poor brainless baby we are shown is an even more grotesque monster than Mary Shelley's brute. With no mind to register its condition, it has become a mere physical lump, completely helpless in the clutches of curious doctors.

Even more grotesque, in the fall of 1997, an American laboratory managed to engineer a headless frog that could be used to produce spare parts for other frogs. The "animal" was little more than a circulatory system used to keep the parts alive until they were harvested. There is no reason to believe the same might not be done with a headless human carcass. If it ever is, more and more people walking the streets of the world will be assemblages of borrowed anatomical equipment. A medical ethicist, asked about the matter, could see no issue, since nobody had been hurt by the procedure. Nevertheless, images like these strike me as exercises in Gothic medicine.

The same theme can be found in the work that has become *Frankenstein*'s companion in horror: Bram Stoker's *Dracula*. *Dracula* works from the other direction. Frankenstein's monster survives as a crazy quilt of cadaverous parts: many dead bodies adding up to one live one. Dracula's victims are many who take their collective life from a single source: the legion of the undead is forced to share the demonic elixir of the master's blood. The terrifying effect is the same: the undead are denied the peace of the grave and driven to endure an anguished existence. Yet both the monster and the vampire cling desperately to life even when they despise what they must be to survive.

Several years ago, a cardiac patient with no chance of surviving more than a few weeks was attached to a huge artificial heart, a blood-pumping machine the size of a horse that he had to drag about his home to keep alive. The cruelest part of this is simply that such choices should be forced upon us in the first place. For how many can refuse the chance to ward off death a little longer? By the time the man's exhausted organism was ready to give out, he confessed to being relieved that his ordeal was over. Surviving had become hell.

That is the true underlying terror that the monster and the vampire embody. Both are torn between drives that work on two distinct evolutionary levels. At the most basic level, they are driven by an undiminished biological instinct for self-preservation. That instinct all but defines life itself; we assume it characterizes all living things. Except for the most sentient of the mammals, who have been known to will themselves to death in zoos, the "lower" animals struggle to survive under all conditions. Were it not for that drive, no individual, no species would have been selected for survival.

But at another level, intelligence comes into play. And at that point, our species, having evolved the capacity for foresight and aspiration, transcends biology; human beings set an independent cultural value upon survival. We can conjure up fears that our fellow creatures cannot — specifically, the fear of a valueless life. This intellectual gift introduces a terror that does not exist in our primal nature. At the level of instinct, human beings find themselves driven to survive like any other animal. But they can also find themselves longing to surrender their existence.

Such a divided state, psychologists tell us, is the essence of horror. In his analysis of nightmares, Freud observed that "anxiety is an indication that the repressed wish has proved too strong for the censorship and has accomplished or is about to accomplish its fulfillment in spite of it." We recognize this state vividly with sexuality. We experience horror when a deep sexual taboo begins to crumble in the face of an insistent desire to enjoy what is forbidden. Similarly, in the flight from mortality, horror sets in when we feel ourselves wanting what our instinct for preservation forbids us to want. The ghouls and walking corpses invented by an earlier generation of Gothic novelists were initially meant to frighten by their ugliness and menace. But now we can see them in a different light. They embody a tragically conflicted condition that is surely more real and more fearful to modern readers than their traditional fangs and claws.

Scientific progress has produced a painful division between our instinctual appetite for self-preservation and our intellectual desire for a life that has value. Oddly enough, in that conflict we find medical science in league, not with our more highly evolved rational faculties, but with our primitive biological nature. Each time I place myself in the hands of my well-intentioned doctors, nothing is more chilling than the possibility that the powers of modern medicine are out of touch with our highest human values.

Can science, which has created this dilemma, also find a solution? Can it perhaps live up to Bacon's promise that death will be eliminated? The human genome project promises the possibility of deleting all hereditary diseases and many constitutional weaknesses out of our DNA — or at the very least offering the chance to abort any pregnancy that might produce a less than long-lived specimen. Though the doctors may work Frankensteinian marvels, at some point the physical limitations of the body make themselves known, if not at 100 then at 200. And then we are face to face with the same existential dilemma our ancestors might have confronted.

Or perhaps there is another solution. It is offered not by medical science, but by high tech.

A Race of Silicon Immortals

Francis Bacon anticipated the possibility of life extension by spare-parts surgery. But why bother to preserve the perishing carcass at all? Why not simply extract the mind by copying it into a computer? As a disembodied electronic intelligence, the person might be sustained indefinitely. This fantasy of computerized mentality haunts the field of artificial intelligence.

Robert Jastrow of NASA looks forward to the time when, thanks to high tech, we shall become "a race of immortals." One day, he tells us,

> a bold scientist will be able to tap the contents of his mind and transfer them into the metallic lattices of a computer. Because mind is the essence of being, it can be said that this scientist has entered the computer and that he now dwells in it. At last the human brain, ensconced in a computer has been liberated from the weakness of the mortal flesh. . . . It is in control of its own destiny. The machine is its body; it is the machine's mind. . . . It seems to me that this must be the mature form of intelligent life in the universe. Housed in indestructible lattices of silicon and no longer constrained in the span of its years by the life and death cycle of a biological organism, such a kind of life could live forever.[5]

Jastrow's prediction is a high-tech variation on Manichaean themes that have long sounded through modern science: the hope of liberating pure reason from the physical facts of life — and incidentally from the messy bodily intimacies of sex. Note the assumption: "mind is the essence of being." Delete the body and identity remains intact.

At the birth of modern Western philosophy, Pythagoras and Plato seized upon mathematics as the purest expression of deathless being. Two thousand years later, at the beginning of the modern era, Descartes echoed that same desire to rise above the flesh when he separated calculating mind from corruptible matter and made mathematics the official language of science. As an essentially computational machine, the computer has inherited the flight from mortality as a subliminal goal that continues to cast its spell. In Jastrow's formulation, we have the Cartesian dictum *Cogito, ergo sum* pressed to its literal and logical extreme — "I" become nothing other or more than my cogitating brain. If, therefore, that brain can be simulated in silicon, "I" survive.

The astrophysicist Frank Tipler has pressed these possibilities even further. In his book *The Physics of Immortality*, he sets out to reinvent the scientific equivalent of the Christian resurrection. "The dead," he tells us, "will be resurrected when the computer capacity of the universe is so large that the amount of capacity required to store all possible human speculations is an insignificant fraction of the entire capacity." Following the Catholic evolutionary philosopher Pierre Teilhard de Chardin, Tipler refers to this as "the Omega Point," the grand climax of cosmic history. Humanity would then dominate the entire universe; we would have progressed "from Earth-womb into the cosmos at large."[6]

Long before that far horizon is reached, Tipler is certain that we will be able to simulate the body in all its most refined details — and improve upon it. It would then be unnecessary to preserve the carnal original; it might be cast aside in favor of its robotic equivalent. Such an "emulated person," Tipler argues, "would observe herself to be as real, and as having a body as solid as the body we currently observe ourselves to have." The simulated body would, however, have one very special quality: it would be deathless. Tipler sees the same great dividend in this that Jastrow finds in putting his brain in a box. In that form, disembodied minds of the future might be loaded aboard a spacecraft and fired off into the universe to explore the galaxies far, far away — needing no air, food, water, or exercise for the journey. Even boredom need not be a problem; a disincarnate intelligence could be placed in a comatose state for the thousands of years it might take to arrive at a destination light-years away.

Platonic mysticism continues to intrigue the world of high tech. Plato was convinced that it was the corruption of the flesh that separates us from the highest forms of knowledge. So he recommended the study of geometry as a sort of purgation of the senses; such study would elevate the mind above the body's mortality. Mark Slouka has this same strange alliance of the ascetic and the mathematical in view when he characterizes high tech as "an attack on reality as human beings have always known it." Cyberspace, he reports, is getting crowded with scenarios uploading consciousness into electronic networks. Behind these high-tech fantasies he sees "a fear and loathing of the natural world, of physical experience in its entirety."[7]

In the pages of *Wired* magazine, silicon immortality is among the constant themes of the rising cyberpunk intelligentsia. This may in fact be the emotional subtext for the advanced claims of artificial intelligence. Interviewed in *Wired*, Chris Langton, one of the founders of artificial life research, puts it this way: "There are these other forms of life, artificial ones, that want to come into existence. And they are using me as a vehicle for reproduction and for implementation." Vernor Vinge, looking further into the future, tells us that, "if we ever succeed in making machines as smart as humans, then it's only a small leap to imagine that we would soon thereafter make — or cause to be made — machines that are even smarter than any human. And that's it. That's the end of the human race within the animal kingdom."[8]

Jaron Lanier, creator of virtual reality and a maverick member of the computer community, believes these fantasies are among the major attractions of cyberspace. Many hackers "nurture hopes of being able to live forever by backing themselves up onto a computer tape."

> Nanotechnology might be used to create a supercomputer that will quickly figure out how to make nanomachines that can repair the human body and make old age an anachronism. . . . Or, perhaps most tellingly, the contents of our brains will be read into durable computers, so that our minds will continue after our bodies cease to function.[9]

This, Lanier believes, is what accounts for that curious new psychological category we call "nerdiness." Intellectually, the nerd is one who searches for ways to digitalize away all distinctions of quality, feeling, and affect. Emotionally, the nerd is given over to a defensive blandness that wants to shelter from human intimacy and physicality. Why should anyone have such an insistent desire to erase the barrier between the human and the mechanical, even in one's own personality? Because once we believe we are beyond that barrier, we are beyond death. Machines do not die.

The idea that identity is mentality has received some skeptical attention from science fiction. In Curt Siodmak's classic tale "Donovan's Brain," the image of life as a lump of bodiless gray matter is made to seem even more horrific than Mary Shelley's patchwork corpse. In the story, the merciless and predatory Donovan gleefully finds his scope for villainy expanded and relishes his new status as a single-minded, domineering intelligence. Free of the flesh, he is also free of all moral responsibility. He envisions living forever as a parasitic brain taking over whatever organism he may need.

Similarly, HAL, the computer in *2001*, is all the more monstrous precisely because he has no body. Knowing no community of the flesh with human beings, he has become all the more alien for lacking an organic dimension. He can murder with clinical dispassion. When he wipes out the crew members of the Jupiter Mission, their vital signs become so many flat lines on a computer terminal: for an entity without a body, the difference between life and death is a mathematical squiggle on a graph. HAL can only "die" when the modules of his electronic brain are disassembled one by one — at which point his last memory is of the tune "Daisy, Daisy," a love song about relations of the flesh that artificial intelligence can never know except as a data point.

In all these cases, science fiction remains true to Mary Shelley's dire warning. Life without this perishing body is as monstrous as ever the Frankensteinian original was. Or perhaps more so. The monster's carcass, though an unnatural creation, preserved at least some tenuous connection with humanity. In my sequel *The Memoirs of Elizabeth Frankenstein*, I imagine the monster's greatest suffering comes of pitying the unwilling many who have become his body. Elizabeth, in her encounter with the monster, records his words in her memoirs:

> Impatiently he all but growls, "Will you not understand? There are times when all the flesh and sinew of my body cries out to me with the voices of other beings, the dead that live again in me. This hand, this shoulder, this finger . . . this brain. As if I walked through a graveyard and from every grave I could hear the muffled voices speaking their names. Can you imagine what it was like to learn what I am? A thing? An artifact?

Monsters that lack even so much as a cadaverous body, though less hideous in appearance, are a far more alien breed. They remind us that the body, this supreme organic puzzle, remains the basis of our human identity. In it spirit and matter mingle in a marriage that admits of no divorce except at the price of our humanity. Walt Whitman, poet laureate of the body electric, had a greater wisdom to offer us in celebrating death as evenhandedly as ever he celebrated life. For "to die," he believed, "is different from what any one supposed, . . . and luckier."

In the Hour of Our Death . . . Who Decides?

It might seem that the solution to the problem of enforced living is obvious. *Just let people die when their time comes.* But neither living nor dying is simple any longer. Having so many skills and resources at hand to keep people alive has made a complex legal, financial, and technical affair of letting people die. There are tubes and wires to be removed from the body, monitors to be switched off, plugs to be pulled, papers to be filled out, reports to be filed, bills to be paid, accounts to be added up. None of this *just happens.* The patient's quality of life may be minimal; the patient may be comatose. Nevertheless, somebody must make the decision to end the heroic intervention that is making survival possible. But who should this be? The answer that leaps to mind is the patient, provided the patient is conscious and competent enough to give informed consent. But who decides that the patient is competent? Who decides if the patient is or is not "legally dead"? Who provides the information the patient needs for informed consent?

Obviously, physicians are bound to play some central part in these judgments. They already are, but in surreptitious ways that cloud the moral issues. There are, for example, "slow codes" that physicians invoke to back off from aggressive treatment of patients deemed beyond saving. The medical staff goes through all the necessary legal motions to save the patient, but with no real effort to achieve resuscitation. When the charade is done, everyone breathes a sigh of relief. Also called "show codes," "Hollywood codes," and "light blue codes," the practice has been condemned as unethical dissimulation.[10] That is where a new ethical question arises. *Can physicians be trusted?*

This is more than asking if doctors are professionally skilled enough to offer advice. Let us grant that they are. But giving advice has become a matter of *business* because death has been assimilated to cost-benefit analysis. More and more doctors now work for HMOs or within health care corporations that have their institutional eyes on the bottom line. Keeping patients alive costs money, often a great deal of money. Can doctors who are company personnel working to the standards of their employer be trusted to ignore the costs and act in the patient's best interests?

In the fall of 1997, the *Journal of the American Medical Association* published a study of "medical care at the end of life." The survey compared the ways in which critically ill patients were treated under two modes of compensation: fee for service, under which there is every incentive to provide aggressive treatment to keep the patient alive, and managed care, which provides no such incentive. Under managed care, doctors earned no more by keeping the patient alive and giving more care. Indeed, doctors and hospitals could only lose money by wasting their resources on "hopeless" cases. The results of the study were clear. Critically ill HMO patients were likely to die sooner.

That sounds shocking. But some physicians believe it is a positive feature of managed care. HMOs do not waste time on hopeless cases; they withhold treatment and cut the suffering short. HMO patients avoid what the editors of *JAMA* call "ineffective, painful, expensive, and unwanted medical interventions that deprive them of their dignity, personal interactions, and family savings." Even advance directives like living wills frequently fail to spare the patient prolonged pain and financial loss. As one doctor put it, "If you don't want to die with a lot of tubes in you, then HMO care may be the place to be." To which a consumer spokesperson replied caustically, "HMOs are wonderful for people who want to embrace euthanasia."[11]

The difficulty with the choice this study presents is that money is the decisive factor *on both sides* of the question. One doctor may be acting to make money for himself; another doctor — or the supervisor who reviews the doctor's decision — may act to save money for the HMO. In either case, money distorts the morality of the choice. And money is no sensible measure of life. It might make some sense for critically ill patients themselves to choose fee-for-service treatment or managed care *after* they have decided either to prolong their lives or to accept a quick death. But to be committed one way or the other *before* the crisis arrives is ethically absurd.

Here, then, is where we stand. If people cling to life desperately, irrationally, out of fear or panic, who has the right to tear that life away from them? If people wish to cast their lives away, again irrationally, out of despair or fear or unbearable pain, who has the right to force that life upon them?

In a 1995 television discussion on National Public Radio, former Health, Education, and Welfare Secretary Joseph Califano raised a tough question. He observed that the largest single Medicare expenditure is for the strenuous measures undertaken to save the lives of hopelessly ill elderly patients, many of whom have only a few more weeks to live. In 1992 the intensive care units of the United States consumed $62 billion; a Stanford University study has concluded that a disproportionate amount of that money was spent on the terminally ill for "potentially ineffective care." Califano argued that this was the most obvious place to start saving money on Medicare.

One wonders what he had in mind. Perhaps he envisions a formula that combines medical cost, the age of the patient, the likely number of years the patient might survive following the procedure, with possibly some coefficient worked in to measure the quality of life. The calculation might be programmed in the same way that major investment decisions are now computer-controlled on the stock exchange. The patient would then be allowed to live or die depending on how the numbers came out.

To which the response might be, "Easy for you to say." In the abstract, we can work out tidy formulations relating age to chances for recovery to cost. But medicine, as every hospital soap opera tells us, is hardly a matter of dispassionate cash choices. Suppose you had to inform a loved one that you were stopping treatment because of the expense. Can you imagine telling your wife or mother, your husband or father, that it just costs too much to try another bypass at this late stage? Can you imagine doing the numbers for them to prove their lives are not worth saving? No matter how serious our budgetary troubles become, the answer to such questions is never likely to be a cost-benefit assessment — at least not openly.

Rationing health care in life-and-death situations is like belling the cat: a solution that may look good in the talking stage, but turns out to be utterly impractical because nobody is going to step forward to do what the solution requires. Even if the medical ethics of the matter could be worked out by way of a seemingly fair and dispassionate formula, there is another major obstacle. Medicine these days has as much to do with lawyers as doctors. Can anyone doubt that, in this era of obsessive litigation, there are malpractice attorneys who are already preparing to bring suit against the first doctor, hospital, or insurance company that announces it will withhold life-saving care to sick, old patients for financial reasons? Does anyone doubt how juries selected to include a representation of seniors would decide such cases?

Some entitlements critics have raised the same point about the rising cost of Medicare. They believe we must stand prepared to invoke the "r word" — rationing. But suppose we suggest an even more courageous option: the "z word," meaning zero charge. Suppose, when medical costs rise beyond a certain point, treatment is offered without charge by physicians, hospitals, insurance companies, and pharmaceutical companies as an act of human kindness. One can predict the response. *Offer medical care for free? Unthinkable!* What does that leave us to conclude but that it is morally acceptable to sacrifice life for money, but not money for life?

The Duty to Die

Is there a "duty to die"? The question was first raised, and with jarring aggressiveness, in 1984 by the then-governor of Colorado, Richard Lamm. Lamm went on record strongly suggesting that the elderly should, as a matter of ethical cost containment, consider making room in the world for the young by simply doing with less medical care and letting themselves die.[12] The idea was taken up more comprehensively in 1987 by the medical ethicist Daniel Callahan in a study of "medical goals in an aging society." Callahan's concern was essentially that of the generational accountants: the nation faced a "new social threat . . . a demographic, economic, and medical avalanche." But unlike the economists who tactfully restricted themselves to the fiscal implications of the issue, Callahan was prepared to take the next, fatal step toward philosophical consistency. Life-extending health care, he argued, should be denied to all those who have "lived out a natural life span."[13] How long was that? About seventy or eighty years.

John Hardwig has pursued the same question, writing in the *Hastings Center Report,* a leading journal of medical ethics. His answer is yes, health care should be withheld from the elderly, even for "those who want to live." The conclusion sounds harsh, but in fairness one must note that Hardwig raises the question as a matter of personal morality, not as a matter of public policy. In what situation would he impose the duty on himself? Rather too analytically, he maps out a set of criteria that he hopes would lead him to answer yes. Foremost among the criteria is cost and emotional strain. If prolonging one's life should become a burden to one's family, and all the more so if one has reached an advanced age (he suggests seventy-five years) and had the benefit of a "full, rich life," then one is duty-bound to die.[14]

Hardwig's query may be legitimate enough as a matter of personal ethics. But issues of financial cost and emotional strain take us beyond the personal. His assumption is that health care costs are becoming too great for government programs to pay and so will soon have to be transferred to families. For Hardwig, money becomes a major ethical consideration. This, he believes, will "dramatically increase the number of Americans who will have a duty to die." Of course, by this criterion it would be a small step to concluding that the disabled bear the same duty, and perhaps even the children a family cannot afford. In the eyes of some, welfare policy might include such a criterion: the useless poor may as well be told they have a duty to vacate life and save the rest of us money.

Hardwig's argument is most persuasive when it is narrowly restricted to the family. For those lying hopelessly near to death, it does indeed tear at the heart to know that they are imposing an ordeal on those they love. Framed in that way, who would not feel shamed into considering suicide? But by introducing the burdens of family cost and care as if these were insurmountable problems, Hardwig distorts the issue. There are, after all, other societies, no richer than the United States, where the community has assumed a major responsibility for paying the costs and providing the care that the very sick need. In the Scandinavian countries, medical care and home care for the chronically ill and the aged are simply taken for granted under state programs. Of course, this governmental responsibility makes for high taxes; compassion costs. But to concede that the United States, of all countries, is at the end of its fiscal tether while the shopping malls are thriving makes a mockery of social ethics. It accepts a wasteful and extravagant standard of living as so absolute and immutable that some must pay for it with their lives.

There is a cultural dimension to the issue that Hardwig overlooks. Every chronically ill patient being kept alive by strenuous measures is the result of a centuries-long historical development. In a real sense, these people are the living criterion of progress in modern life. What sense does it then make to say that the grand consequence of that progress is the duty to die? There may, of course, be a *desire* to die. In despair and with no future worth living for, an individual may elect suicide. That choice, if it must ever be faced, is hard enough to make on personal grounds without overlaying it with cost-benefit considerations.

What we have in the concept of a duty to die is an agonizing example of what generational accounting has brought us to in the discussion of medical ethics. By obscuring the fiscal truth about entitlements, it has created the false impression that we cannot afford one penny more for Medicare. The main service the generational accountants are doing for "our children" is to offer them a way to guilt-trip sick parents into taking their own lives.

On the other hand, suppose we were to reformulate the question and adjust the financial burden. *How much more are you willing to pay in order to free your loved ones — and yourself — of ever feeling a duty to die?* Rather than asking the sick to choose death, suppose we ask ourselves to choose taxes? After all, death is a universal fact of human life. Only the very young can be excused for not being aware of their mortality. The rest of us know full well that illness, age, and death await us. If we elect to leave these matters on the shoulders of families, then we are behaving like irresponsible children. But if the New People can see their way clear to revisioning our criterion of wealth — reconfiguring it into something like the "national life expectancy" we touched upon in chapter 3 — we would regard the kindness we show to the sick and dying as a far more human gauge of our affluence. That kindness would no longer be a burden, but a measure of our social maturity.

Once we remove money from this most delicate and authentically tragic of human situations, we can begin to devise humanistic alternatives to rationing medical care or shaming the sick into suicide. In a study of medicine and death, Marilyn Wells speaks of a new medical-philosophical skill that we are bound to see the New People exploring. She has called for "midwives to the dying," the sort of counseling that can be found in hospices and has been vastly expanded as part of the AIDS crisis.[15] The day may not be far off when the words of Socrates, the works of Lao Tzu, Spinoza, and Montaigne, and the teachings of all the great spiritual masters will be as much a part of modern medicine as the latest piece of diagnostic technology.

12

Powers of the Mind

A SPECTER IS HAUNTING the senior community — and all those who wait on its borders. Its name is Alzheimer.

In the course of writing this book, every older person I interviewed from age fifty up admitted to fearing this dreaded disease more than death. Those who work with the elderly as doctors, caregivers, or teachers describe concern over Alzheimer's as an obsession. Medical authorities who write on aging tell of patients as young as sixty asking anxiously if their minds are going. What occasioned the fear? A minor lapse of memory . . . a name forgotten, a phone number misremembered, an appointment overlooked. But the lapse is immediately identified as a symptom of Alzheimer's. Ironically, for all the progress we have made in extending life expectancy, there may now be a greater anxiety about aging than ever before. The one fate all seniors fear the most — senility — has returned under a new name and with an even more ominous aspect. We have never had a more pressing reason to learn about the powers of the mind than now when longevity can sentence us to so long a term in the prison of dementia.

I had occasion to visit an Alzheimer's ward in a senior life care center. I was told that only a brave few of the several hundred older residents who lived there volunteered to help in the ward. The rest found it too disturbing. That part of the center was treated like the haunted wing of a Gothic castle. What I found there was understandably unsettling. There were fifteen people the day I visited, all of them frail, dozing in wheelchairs or staring vacantly into space. A few had suffered stroke; most were Alzheimer's sufferers. One or two were in minimal and episodic touch with the world around them; most were wholly withdrawn. Some mumbled to themselves, some sang, some wept. Walter, the only man in the ward, sometimes danced for the others. He had been an engineer but once taught for an Arthur Murray studio. He was still ambulatory. I was introduced to him. He had no time for me. He was leaving.

"Where are you going?" one of the caregivers asked.

"Home," he answered.

"Tell me about home," the caregiver answered.

Walter had no time for that. He wandered off around the room, then sat down again and fell silent.

The two nurses who supervised the ward had refined their methods for dealing with their charges. "Never correct a mistake," they told me. "Don't expect them to learn. Pick up on whatever they say and ask them to tell you more. They like your company."

"What do they talk about?" I asked. "Can you tell what's on their mind?"

"Like Walter, they talk about home, the home they lived in as a kid. They ask about their mothers. They say they're waiting for their mothers to take them home. They go back in time. It's like everything from now back to their childhood is being erased. In their minds, they're growing younger. At night, when you help them into bed, they usually curl into a fetal posture."

"Would they be better off in the care of their families?" I wondered.

The caregivers were adamant. "No, absolutely not. They're a great burden. Their children have a hard time handling them well, unless they can hire round-the-clock help. Even then, it's heartbreaking. They remember how their parents once were. They try to bring them back. They can't."

"Do you get attached to them?" I asked.

"We try not to. They are all so close to death. We just wait with them and let them go as gently as we can."

That day the residents of the Alzheimer's ward had had a party with games and balloons and cake and prizes. Everybody won prizes. Everybody wore party hats. The scene looked like kindergarten. It might have seemed demeaning. But these people were beyond that. They were also beyond the fear that must have been there once as the specter approached. That was the one mercy this disease granted. It allowed them peace.

But those of us who remain observing from outside their world have no peace. We are left to wonder at nature's cruelty in allowing the body to outlive the mind. Some fear that Alzheimer's is only the swift and extreme form of the fate that awaits us all.

"But That's Not Me!"

Senility is the besetting stereotype of old age. What the scatterbrained bimbo once was to women, what the Stepin Fetchit bootblack once was to African Americans, the doddering old codger is to seniors. Like all stereotypes, it is a blight upon one's life. Knowing that others are watching for the telltale traits to emerge — a moment of confusion or forgetfulness, a bad move behind the steering wheel — one spends each day seeking to prove "that's not me!" But in the case of the elderly, the stereotype has always had some modicum of truth. There are disabilities and diseases of the brain that account for what was once called senility. We now know these disabilities are not a matter of fate, nor are they exclusive to age. Most of the disabilities of age are a matter of challenging the odds. Like the soldier whose luck declines the longer he stays under fire, the longer one lives, the greater the chance that one or another mental weakness will have its chance to show up. If nobody had ever made it to the age of seventy, we might never know Alzheimer's disease existed. When Dr. Alois Alzheimer diagnosed his first patient in 1906, he described the condition he documented as "a peculiar, little-known disease process." He did not identify the process as a disease of age. Why should he? His first patient was in her forties and died at fifty-one. Now we know that this is one of the hazards that lies waiting along the distant reaches of the mortality slope.

How great is the risk? The best studies available suggest that, as of the mid-1990s, about 10 percent of those who reach the age of eighty-five may suffer some form of "dementia" — the word that has replaced "senility" as an acceptable designation. For those who reach their nineties, that figure rises close to one-quarter. About half the cases of dementia are due to Alzheimer's; most of the rest are due to stroke or Parkinson's disease. The most worrisome aspect of Alzheimer's is the fact that many of those afflicted with the disease can lose as much as one-third of their brain cells without displaying any symptoms of the disease before it kills them.[1] This makes early detection and treatment almost impossible.

The statistics for Alzheimer's disease are both consoling and worrying. The percentage of those who have fallen victim to dementia is high enough to cause legitimate concern. But at least we can now recognize that the worst cases are the result, not of inevitable degeneration, but of disease — a genetically determined disease that is being closely studied.

The mutated gene that seems to produce the disease has been identified and its action tracked. Like the assumed idiocy of the child who is born deaf and simply cannot hear, senility can now be seen as a birth defect, a corrupted gene visited unpredictably upon an unfortunate minority. By the time the New People have entered the Alzheimer's zone of life, the twisted logic of the gene may have been corrected; they may be able to enjoy their long life expectancy free of the specter.

Everything we once thought we knew about the aging mind is in need of radical revision, revisions that may help us understand minds both young and old. Previous studies of elderly populations were too often based on people who were, for the most part, poor, in bad health, and demoralized. Worst of all, they were frequently studied under institutionalized conditions. Samples were often drawn from a poorly educated population that had been treated as burdensome and dispensable. We now have significant longitudinal studies — the best known from the National Institute on Aging in the United States and from the University of Gothenberg in Sweden — that undercut all previous testing. These studies are unambiguous in their findings. Aging brings with it no automatic or genetically programmed decline in the powers of the mind, and often not in physical functioning either.[2]

Mind, Memory, and Meaning

The aging brain is now a subject of intense scrutiny. But we need to be clear about what laboratory studies of the brain can and cannot tell us. Can they, for example, tell us anything about the "mind" as distinct from the "brain"? It is a matter of great philosophical dispute where one draws the line between the two. One commonsense distinction holds that the "mind" is what thinks; the "brain" is what the mind thinks *with*. The brain is the physical basis for a process that may be no more physical than the various forms of energy that hold the atom together. If it makes any sense to put the matter that way, then scientific studies of the brain can, at most, be credited with helping us understand where and how the mind can fail. They tell us how well the brain is serving the mind's full capacity. If the brain is damaged by injury or aging, the mind may be encumbered and fall short of its total potentiality. But no scientific study is sufficient to define the upper limit of that potentiality, especially when the mind is working against physical resistance. Nor can studies of the brain help us understand powers of the mind, such as educability and aptitude, that are essentially social. Intelligence is often a matter of the company we keep.

Studies using new imaging techniques report that, thanks to the brain's massive interconnective redundancy, most seniors retain excellent cognitive capacity into their nineties. The overall brain shrinkage to which elders were once thought to be doomed is mainly a distortion introduced by the extraordinary effects of Alzheimer's disease.[3] Research along other lines, however, verifies the fact that older brains do tend to suffer from AAMI (age-associated memory impairment), or as one researcher calls it, the onset of the "Swiss-cheese memory."[4] The problem is age-related, but not *aging*-related. That is, it shows up more prominently in older people but has not been connected with some inevitable form of physical deterioration. Variation among the elderly in this respect is therefore very great; many remain able to outperform their juniors on memory tests.

The causes for AAMI are complex, and some are totally unrelated to age. For example many seniors use medications, especially sedatives and painkillers, with the side effect of impaired mental functioning. Others, who are no more forgetful than younger people, experience a low-level panic whenever their memory fails — as it might fail for anybody. But when older people forget, they become fearful that they are growing senile, or that others will think they are. In a social situation where such a lapse produces winks and nods from others, the problem is aggravated and the anxiety mounts. These are the private battles older people fight in a society that demands quick, unerring responsiveness — a quality, incidentally, that I have found as lacking among the smiling young people in shops and offices as among older people on the job. It is primarily for these younger workers, after all, that cash registers with pictures rather than numbers were invented, lest they need to memorize prices.

But in the old, as in the young, memory deficiency can be treated. With training, AAMI can be reversed; teaching people how to do that is the subject of programs, some federally funded, that are bound to grow in the years ahead. Among the most ambitious of these efforts are the Aging and Dementia Research Center at New York University Medical Center and the Memory Assessment Clinics headquartered in Bethesda, Maryland.[5] Seniors trained in these techniques often outperform much younger people. Efforts of this kind are a godsend to the elderly, but they are also something more. They have political implications. With the inhibiting fear of AAMI brought under control, the next older population is apt to gain the confidence and competence it needs to assert itself in much the same way that consciousness-raising studies once strengthened the civil rights and women's movements by breaking down disempowering stereotypes.

There is a curious feature about the mental anxiety of the old. A psychologist I know teaches courses for men and women over seventy to improve memory and problem-solving. She knows she achieves impressive results; her students tell her so, and she sees it in their conduct. But when she seeks to administer a test so she can collect some numbers, most of her students refuse to cooperate. They have no interest in scores. They dislike grading and avoid competition. So she cannot give the tests that will prove the efficacy of her methods. But that in itself is a "finding" of value. With maturity, scoring points, proving oneself, and competition lose meaning. They are seen for what they are: ego games that belong in the schoolroom. She tells me the greatest problem she has in drawing out the latent or long-repressed mental capacities of her students is their dismal self-image. They have been convinced that they are no longer capable of learning or even thinking. So she must begin by boosting their self-esteem, after which they go on to learn all she has to teach them about problem-solving, memory, and planning. I asked whether she thought the next generation of the old would present the same problem. She was convinced that would not be so. The seniors coming along — she had the New People in mind — are more confident and assertive and better educated. They are gifted with a greater sense of security and purpose.

When it comes to mental impairment, many retired people may actually be suffering from their way of life rather than from physical decline. Consider the mental state of people in their eighties or nineties who have survived their friends and relatives and live in great isolation — the situation for elderly people in any community that has no senior center or services. So the old seem out of touch because they *are* out of touch. We easily overlook the social aspect of memory and alertness. On the job we are paced by coworkers and a daily routine that helps us remember what needs to be remembered. Executives with a lot on their mind benefit from forms of collective memory that are made up of secretaries, administrative assistants, and computerized "to-do" reminders that keep them on track and on time. It might be the case that retaining as much minutiae as most of us do in the workplace is a highly unnatural stunt, a skill that flags when the pressure is off. As soon as one drops out of the workforce, one loses all this support . . . and may well grow "forgetful."

Retired seniors may then be too deeply intimidated by the senility stereotype to ask questions or assert themselves. Still others, impeded by poor eyesight or hearing, make mistakes, fail to respond rapidly, and grow withdrawn. Finally — and most interestingly — some elders may simply have other, greater issues on their mind than younger people around them can understand: questions about life, death, meaning, sin, salvation. They have stopped caring about the 10:00 A.M. sales meeting or the 2:00 P.M. district manager's report because all this has become boring. If their thoughts wander, they may be wandering into more philosophically meaningful territory where they need education or a spiritual discipline to keep their minds focused.

I sometimes suspect the reason elderly people are marked out for scamming has to do with the fact that they have come to care less about money in the bank. They trust too easily, not worrying all that much about what may become of their worldly goods, especially if they have outlived family and friends. That leaves them vulnerable to exploitation by those who have their minds on lesser values or unworthy pursuits. It is easy to write off what they suffer at the hands of con artists as the result of senility, but here again we are at a juncture of the mental and the social. It is not incompetence that the scammers play upon; it is the same vulnerability they look for in all their victims — something, *anything* that creates enough momentary trust to allow them to grab the money and run.

In the case of the elderly, it is loneliness and fear they target, and the tendency of those who are alone and afraid to weaken in response to any gesture of kindness. Telemarketers have become especially adept at conning isolated seniors. They scout them out the way a hawk scouts for mice. In one newspaper report, a seventy-seven-year-old widow confessed that she had sent thousands of dollars to a telemarketer because she became "addicted" to the attention she was being offered. "They were nice on the phone. They became my friends," she explained. Telephone fraud like this takes in an estimated $40 billion a year, the bulk of it from the elderly who will pay to make real the sad, fond hope that somebody cares about them. They trust because a friendly gesture matters more to them than money.

In the years ahead, the behavior that has for generations been identified as senility will be sorted into new medical and social categories, many of them treatable and reversible. Once again, we must realize that gerontology is a frontier field, long neglected on the assumption that people must not expect much in their senior years beyond an easy death. Just as techniques for toning and conditioning the muscles are giving seniors better physical ability, so too forms of mental exercise are lengthening the mental life span. New medications are being used to slow the brain's aging. Antioxidants called "nitrones" are proving to be of promise in not only preventing but reversing certain forms of AAMI.[6] More ambitious still is research on "cognitive enhancers," medications like ampakine drugs that boost the signals emitted by the neurotransmitters involved in memory and learning.[7]

No doubt there will be a succession of breakthroughs in the chemistry of cognition, but research of this kind can be misleading. At some point we must take another factor into account, something rather like the cultural bias that is now commonly recognized as a distortion of IQ and aptitude testing. Just as racial and ethnic factors may bias performance on standardized tests, so too age brings its peculiar influence to bear on the powers of the mind. Most academic and professional work emphasizes details — facts, figures, skills — that can be quantified and tested for competitively. Even younger people of divergent intellectual ability may be quite poor at that kind of performance and yet have fine minds. Elders may bring to the task a different orientation, an instinct to go for the big picture, the controversial issue, the questions that require thought and tough judgment. What we mistake for poor memory may be a different focus, a shift of emphasis, possibly a more mature grasp of issues. Seeing the forest as well as the trees is not a weakening of the mind, but an advance toward wisdom.

The Dynamic Brain

There are many molecular changes in the aging brain that have been identified. Some result from the same destructive impact of free radicals that we have noted throughout the organism. Since the brain is one of the few organs that does not (except in some minor respects) replace its cells, losing neurons might seem more serious than the loss of other body cells. In a few parts of the brain, a sizable percentage of neurons do vanish with age. The brain may even shrink in size, but recent research shows that in those centers most relevant to the higher functions there is no significant neuronal loss in dementia-free elders. And where there is some loss, other healthy neurons take over the function of those that have died. This is because the brain is designed as a network with all the redundant circuitry of a telephone exchange. "The brain," Dennis Selkoe, a neurologist and Alzheimer's expert, tells us, "is capable of dynamic remodeling of its neuronal connections, even in later years. As is true of other organs, the brain appears to have considerable physiological reserve and to tolerate small losses of neuronal function."[8] Perhaps for this reason age-linked changes in the brain produce only modest alterations in performance.

Richard Restak reaches the same optimistic conclusion in his summary of findings in brain research. "The mature brain," he tells us, "performs as well as the younger one in tasks requiring planning, organization, and the manipulation of information. Thus, the mature brain is not a defective version of a younger one." Statistically speaking, older people may tend to be at a slight disadvantage when they are competing with younger people in tests of simple mental rapidity. There is a slowing down of the transfer speed in moving short-term memories between what Restak calls the brain's "storage compartment" and its "permanent store." But "with advancing years, the brain redesigns itself to compensate for decreases in reaction time and general slowing."[9]

Thanks to research on aging, we are learning a great deal about the amazing plasticity and dynamism of the brain at all age levels — and perhaps coming to a greater appreciation of its many modes. Restak reports a revealing study conducted by Richard Shimamura at the University of California, Berkeley, in which senior faculty members displayed a distinct slowing of raw reaction time to stimuli projected on a screen — the sort of skill that might be essential for an air traffic controller. They were also slower in processing certain kinds of data, especially arbitrary associations, such as connecting a name with a face or a name with a phone number.[10] But this is the kind of data we can now delegate to computers, which are far faster in working through a database than the quickest human brain.

That finding raises an intriguing possibility. In chapter 8, we discussed the invariable depiction of high tech as a youthful development, one that belongs to the young and leaves the old behind. But in a very real sense it is older people who might be most empowered by the computer. What older workers lack is exactly what we have computers to do. For at least as long as we remain a data-intensive economy, computers can come to the aid of working memory in ways that make AAMI less detrimental.

If there were nothing more to be said about the powers of the aging mind beyond what gets lost along the way and how to compensate for it, we might be left with a dismal conclusion. But that is far from the whole story. The power of the aging mind in areas of interpretation, judgment, creativity, and imagination is undiminished and continues to benefit from educational stimulation. Even when Alzheimer's disease locks into the brain, there is some indication that mental exercise can diminish the damage. At least that is the conclusion of the nun study, a much-publicized experiment that charted the cognitive powers of the seven hundred School Sisters of Notre Dame over several years. The sisters ranged from seventy-five to over one hundred years old. It was discovered, when their brains were subjected to autopsy, that those who were the better educated and maintained the highest intellectual activity were able to remain self-reliantly independent to an older age, despite any physical decline. Even more striking was the finding that one of the oldest nuns — she had lived to 102 — remained independent and intellectually active despite having advanced Alzheimer's disease. The researchers concluded that she had built up sufficient "brain reserves" to remain symptom-free.[11]

The Trouble with Wisdom

This book is based on an assumption about the powers of the human mind that some will find controversial. I believe that as people grow older, they grow wiser — and indeed *want* to grow wiser, as if to make good use of life's final years. We obscure that fact when we insist that wisdom is a rare and exalted quality that few can achieve. In fact, it is everywhere around us. *Wisdom happens.* It happens as simply and naturally as learning happens in children. Just as children cannot help but learn with every breath they take, so adults, as they age, cannot help but become wise. Wisdom is that same act of learning as we go forward in life, with one difference. It is sufficient for children to greet the world with wonder; elders must add reflection — and do, quite spontaneously, because they have a broadening base of experience to draw upon for comparison and questioning.

Wisdom is examined experience, examined in the same way Socrates examined all that his pupils said, helping them find their way through

their thoughts, offering a word of criticism here, a word of encouragement there, bringing them to view the values and presuppositions that
underlay their beliefs with discriminating distance. Wisdom grows from
any ordinary life provided that life is taken seriously and brought under
reflection. That is all wisdom is, yet it is infinitely precious and wholly
indispensable to growing up. In our language, we speak of being "wised
up." Learning in the sense of being wised up does not make us smart in
ways that lead to writing books or winning awards, but it makes us
competent. Unless we are in a coma, every day we live wises us up by
bringing us how-to learning, hard-knocks learning, depression learning,
pleasure learning, boredom learning, anxious learning.

Far from being rare, wisdom is what life gives us with every passing
moment. If people need any help with wisdom, it is mainly to wake
them up to the fact that wisdom is happening here and now, and that we
need only learn to take our own experience seriously. If we are acting in
the world, we are learning by that action. And if we are not acting, we
are most likely thinking life over — or worrying it over, or regretting it,
or laughing at it, or crying over it. That is when wisdom happens most
importantly — in moments of reflection, when we go back over things,
replaying what happened, coming up with all we might have said or
done, wondering where we go from there. That is what I imagine people
are doing as they go through the day, driving to and from work, walking
the streets, loitering over lunch, lying awake at night. With a little
self-awareness, with companions to share the experience, and above all
with the courage to speak and act on the basis of what they have learned,
everybody becomes a practical philosopher. We all know this. We experience it every time we sit down with another person — friend, relative,
workmate — and talk about the dilemmas and decisions that punctuate
our lives. What we give and take in that simple encounter is the hard-
won smarts of everyday life.

Wisdom is — at least potentially — the most common and plentiful
human resource in the world. It is not in short supply. Why then do we
think it is so rare?

Because there are forces that make wisdom unwelcome. They shame
it into silence and so neutralize the role it has to play. In an industrial
world dominated by scientific precision and technological know-how,
by specialists and technicians, by experts in every walk of life, wisdom is
crowded out. It does not seem to know the right words, the formulas,
the facts. It is not up on the latest. The trouble with wisdom is that we

have, in a sense, become too smart for our own good in the modern world — smart in ways that seem to eliminate our need for the old Socratic project of self-examination. In the absence of self-examination, we lose touch with our true motivations and become rigid about values. We quite literally do not know what we are doing. And so we grow heedless and arrogant.

I have worked among academics and intellectuals all my life, some of them men and women of genius. Their minds are brilliant but too often carry a built-in resistance to wisdom. In their view, wisdom is an irritatingly fuzzy quality of mind, rather like judgment, interpretation, or taste. It is nothing that can be tested or objectively measured. There is no section on wisdom in the SAT exam; the Nobel committee makes no awards to the wise. Those who earn their living by using their brains feel more comfortable with performance that can be gauged by results, by clear logic, by numbers, by peer review. Professionals like qualities that can be identified by a title: M.D., Ph.D., M.S.W., R.N. But wisdom is among those virtues that need no license or degree. It is a quality of the person that cannot be taught. Proverbially, it can be an attribute of the unlettered, even of certain "wise fools."

To tough-minded intellectuals, talents that require no book-learning or special training smack of obfuscation and fraudulence. Up to a point, they are right. No society has been without its share of charlatans, fakers, and frauds. That was certainly true of our society in the past. Even today quacks and cults abound in the midst of our scientific civilization. I confess that when I find myself among the questionable gurus that gather along the New Age fringe, I grow as skeptical as any. I have been to anything-goes presentations on "spirituality" — some of them by franchised teachers — that finish by promising financial success, good looks, cosmic bliss, and weight loss. Caught between the hard edge of skepticism and the slough of gullibility, wisdom has no good choice in either direction.

In the contemporary world, the discussion of wisdom runs into a special barrier. It is among those powers of the mind that cannot be imitated by a computer. There are no programs for making wise choices. Ours is called the Information Age, but wisdom has little to do with information. After all, the people who are most widely credited with possessing wisdom — Confucius, Jesus, the Buddha — predated the Internet. Socrates openly declared that he knew nothing; he would be the last person to ask for information. That simple fact, that our culture was created by people working with nothing more than their naked wits, has become a heresy in our time. It is actively ignored in ways that can be comic. In 1997 the Apple Computer Company ran an ambitious series of advertisements that featured the faces of eminent intellectuals and artists — Edison, Picasso, Einstein, Frank Lloyd Wright, Martha Graham, Gandhi. The ad was out to sell computers by associating them with people who were "mavericks." It might also have added that all these mavericks shared one trait. None of them had ever used a computer.

If there is one quality elders should be able to claim as peculiarly theirs, it is wisdom. Yet what is the real value of wisdom if specialized knowledge monopolizes the culture and the alternative to specialized knowledge is so often regarded as holy fakery? When an industrial population needs solutions for its problems, it turns to experts. Experts have their role to play. But just as one could draw up an endless catalog of mindless follies committed by the untutored and anti-intellectual, one could also assemble a sizable collection of stupidities perpetrated by the experts and technicians whom we trust so implicitly and reward so highly. Much of the Promethean recklessness that has animated our technology in the modern world stems from an expertise that has lost touch with ordinary prudence, a know-how that does not know why.

What wisdom needs is to be liberated so that it can flood the mind and freely flow between us. That is the true task of elders; it is what the elder mind seems especially empowered to do.

An Education for Elders

As recently as the 1960s, medical science was dominated by a piece of scientific folklore about the aging brain. It was a matter of professional dogma that the brain actually shrank with age, losing cells at an accelerating rate with the passage of years. The loss was held to be most critical in the cerebral cortex, where the "higher functions" are quartered. Experts contended that aging people lost up to one-third of their cortical neurons, and that was taken to be the cause of senility.

Later research has shown this assumption to be quite wrong. What was mistaken for neuronal loss was another phenomenon, namely, the thinning out of the dendrites. The dendrites are connectors; they receive the impulses of surrounding neurons. We might regard them as the physical basis for the rich interplay of ideas and images that makes for a lively mind. Richard Restak uses a striking figure of speech to explain the role of the dendrites. "Picture in your mind a tree in its full summer bloom, when it has the greatest number of small branches and leaves. Now imagine that same tree in winter, when the branches are denuded and starkly outlined against a slate sky. That transition looks very much like what's seen when neurons from the young are compared to neurons taken from older brains."[12]

But this thinning is not a permanent loss; it is a symptom of disuse. It can be restored by putting the mind to work. Education is the tonic that restores dynamic neuronal connectivity. The active mind replenishes the brain with an expanding network of dendrites. That is good news for the individual, but it carries social and economic implications. If the most burdensome and costly disease among the elderly is dementia — including Alzheimer's disease — then the best prescription we have is *thinking*. The more subtle and complex, the better. And quite spontaneously, that is what is happening as a form of cultural self-medication.

Older students — now more and more understood to include students over sixty-five, not just over forty — are returning to school in numbers sufficient to shift the economic basis of higher education in the United States.[13] That is hardly surprising. Education is one of the major activities people take up in their retirement. As of the late 1990s, there were nearly four million elders over sixty-five enrolled in university courses, or 13 percent of the total in the age group. Everybody in higher education expects that number to rise steadily. One educator describes the rising enrollment of reentry baby boomers as a "windfall" for the universities alert to the opportunity at hand. The elder hostel movement has burgeoned into a worldwide community camped at many universities. Similarly, continuing education has developed a growing stake in senior enrollments. But older students are also enrolling in standard courses, sitting in among the young to take degrees and with each passing year taking up more space in the classroom. A local campus can be an ideal place to spend retirement time. It comprises art galleries, libraries, theaters, and physical education facilities. Older students, especially those resuming their higher education, may create a new teaching ambience; they can function as aides and assistants for instructors, offering better judgment and more long-term continuity.[14]

In my teaching experience, I became aware of the growing prominence of older students as long ago as the late 1970s. The students were mainly women in their fifties and sixties, some newly divorced, some widowed, all of them beyond their child-rearing years. Many found their way to school through a local counseling facility called the Center for Displaced Homemakers. I learned that women who found themselves "displaced" thought first of all of returning to school. Their main reservation was that they were not sure they "belonged" there, and so might not be welcome. Some of my colleagues, trained to teach the standard eighteen-to-twenty-four-year-old "prime-time" audience, did resent having older students in the class. They wondered what the point was. Most of these women had no career plans; they often did not care about finding jobs and found no meaning in grades and credits. They were notoriously noncompetitive when it came to grade point averages. All they seemed to want to do was learn.

They were, in short, ideal students. They came for the love of learning. I soon came to value having them in my classes and went out of my way to draw them in. In their presence, the demands on me as a teacher became more challenging and mature. The older students were not brilliant; they were simply more experienced. They had a sense of significance about things. They asked big questions about life, death, love, purpose. They took to great literature and philosophy because they saw its value. Teaching *King Lear* or *Madame Bovary* to older and then to younger students was like teaching in two different universes. That also created pedagogical problems. As senior students grew more assertive and outspoken — mainly with my encouragement — they tended to take over the class. The younger students felt at a disadvantage in the presence of mature minds. Some withdrew into silent resentment. The trick was to keep both groups in touch and learning from one another — a skill I was never offered in my training as a university teacher.

As the years have gone by, the number of older students has increased rapidly at my university, as it has at all schools. There are now more older men, many of them retired or downsized out of their jobs. Older students have begun to entertain career plans, so they come to learn employable skills as well as arts and letters. But whatever they study, they retain their maturity. That makes teaching them a joy. It is also a groundbreaking adventure. Just as students of the baby boom decades transformed higher education by bringing an air of dissent and experimentation to the campuses, the New People — who are, after all, those same boomers — may well initiate a similarly innovative spirit at the universities. We are approaching a time when the universities will have to make a generous place for the mature and the elderly. That will be where the numbers and the money can be found to rejuvenate the schools. At some schools, the older students may outnumber the undergraduates on campus, and so the campuses will have to grow up. They will become, at least in large measure, senior academies, in some respects resembling the famous Danish folk-schools of the nineteenth century.

There may be another front in elder education waiting to be opened: the Internet. Over 100 web sites are maintained by SeniorNet Learning Centers in nearly every state. For shut-in elders, this may present a valued opportunity. Nicholas Negroponte of the MIT Media Lab sees online communications as a chance for the old to give as well as receive. He reminds us that "the 20 million members of the AARP constitute a collective experience that is currently untapped. Making just that enormous body of knowledge and wisdom accessible to young minds could close the generation gap with a few keystrokes."[15] He might also have mentioned that the Internet could use a strong infusion of maturity to save it from sinking further into commercial inanity.

As the New People return to the college campuses, many may come to learn job skills, fully intending to remain in the job market. Others — the middle and senior old — may come to sign up for course work that alleviates age-associated memory impairment. But it is also likely that the traditional *studium generale,* the heart of the humanities, will have a special value for mature students. The classics, the hundred great books, the art treasures of the world — all these are still the most effective way to stimulate the dendrites that keep the gray matter alive. It will be an appropriate marriage of minds. Plato and Dante, Montaigne and Spinoza, after all, never wrote to be read by sophomores. I doubt there is a teacher alive who has not more than once wondered whether it makes any sense for us to be struggling to force the "greats" — as the English call the classics — upon students whose mental energy is so tied up with thoughts about grades, careers, success, sex, marriage — all the distracting preliminaries of adulthood. The effort is well intentioned, but it betrays the work. For what does the finest undergraduate curriculum produce in young minds but, too often, the kind of brittle facility one needs to pass exams or make smart conversation?

Great minds, whatever the field — the humanities or the sciences — demand mature minds to be fully appreciated. Yet in times past those few undergraduate years between eighteen and twenty-one were the last chance educators had to teach the high culture to the next generation. So we did the best we could. But now we have another, better chance. Students are coming back to us on the other side of youthful distraction, bringing a lifetime of experience into the classroom. What a grand opportunity! It is our chance as educators to salvage the wisdom of elders.

13

Rites of Passage

L EO TOLSTOY's *Death of Ivan Illich* may be the greatest short story ever written. It has certainly proved to be the most powerful reading experience I have known, a work of literature that captures the pulse-beat of life more convincingly than one would believe possible for words on a page. Whenever I assign it to my students, I give them careful instructions. They are to read the story at one sitting, with no interruptions. They are to read every word, slowly, skipping nothing, pausing along the way to let each section of the tale sink in. And when they are finished, they are to sit quietly, imagining that Ivan's story is their story. Certainly nobody who ever lived to tell about it has done a more persuasive job of presenting the experience of death than Tolstoy achieved in this work. The final moments of Ivan's life leave you convinced that Tolstoy has been through the ordeal and come back to tell about it.

While the assignment is frequently lost upon younger students, who tell me they find the story demanding or morbid, its impact upon more mature students has invariably been enormous. They have no trouble seeing themselves as Ivan and learning from his experience.

If I could, I would at this point make that same assignment to those of you who are beginning this chapter. Find the story. Read it. Instead, I will offer a brief and, of course, inadequate summary.

Tolstoy's Ivan is a minor government functionary in czarist Russia, one of thousands of the "superfluous men" in that regime. As remote as that era in Russian history may seem in every other respect, Tolstoy brilliantly develops Ivan as a modern Everyman, one who has spent his life building a tidy career of little more than personal importance, seeking to make himself moderately successful in one of his society's many bureaucratic niches. He is the essence of ordinary, a man who has never taken life to be more than routine, one who has carefully isolated himself from strong experience. One day, while hanging drapes in his home, he injures himself. The injury grows worse. A doctor is called. The doctor discovers that there is a serious condition, which is never clearly defined in the story. It is, in fact, death approaching. That is all that matters. The doctors cannot heal what ails Ivan; he becomes sicker and finally realizes he is doomed. The story traces his last days, hours, minutes of bewilderment, anger, self-pity, and finally resignation. The moment of his death becomes the only moment he has truly *lived*. The story builds until we reach that terrifying moment; it leaps from the page and takes you by the shoulders and shakes you. "Wake up!" it says. *"This man is you."*

The Far Side of the Ordeal

As a teacher, I have valued Tolstoy's story over the years because it uses death so powerfully to teach the magnificence of life. Yet as universal as Ivan's experience is, the very fact that his plight deals with illness and doctors and patients now limits it to a certain historical period. A century later, the tale may need to be rewritten to capture the defining life-and-death experience of the New People. What we need in order to make the story relevant to our time is a "death" that does not happen — not yet. We need the story of an Ivan who comes just that close to dying — but then *survives*. Death pauses; it waits, longer for us than for any previous generation. That is becoming more and more the special experience of our time. By the thousands people now undergo medical miracles that rescue them from diseases and disabilities that would have killed them a generation ago. They pass through the shadow — and are then sent back into the world to start their lives again. As one member of a cardiac support group described his experience, "It was as if the angel of death drove by my house and waved. 'I'm busy now,' he said, 'but I have your address. I'll be back.'" That experience is becoming as commonplace as marriage or divorce, a routine part of the modern world.

Today Ivan Illich would be likely to confront a greater trial. *Life*. He would return to take up his career, his family life, his ambitions. But how would life look to someone who has been on such close terms with death? What would it then mean to "wake up"? Tolstoy would have to deal with an Ivan who might not be willing to continue being a bureaucratic zombie, but who insisted on making his life *mean* something.

We have learned to recognize these great revelatory landmarks over the course of a life as rites of passage, moments that shake people out of their accustomed routine and elevate them to a new level of existence. In traditional societies, these rites are usually highly structured occasions that usher people into a new phase of existence: from childhood into adolescence, from adolescence into maturity, from maturity into old age, and finally from old age into death. In this respect more than any other, primary people have proven themselves wiser than us: they take the course of life seriously, seeing it as an educational progression. It may very well be that the absence of rites of passage makes it harder for us to grow into a true elder status.

In many rites of passage, episodes of great fear are designed to capture the full sense of crisis that faces us at the main turning points in life. Sometimes death is mimicked, as if one were dying to one's old self and being reborn into new life. Young boys in some tribal societies are put through the moment of their own death and taken into the terrors of the underworld — and then ushered back. Outside of religious communities, we have few rites of passage that retain the dignity and depth of these traditional practices. To that degree, we have cheapened the quality of life. Perhaps that has something to do with the cult of youth. We cling to youthfulness with no desire to move on, even though the effort to hold back is futile.

But now a new kind of rite of passage is upon us. It is highly structured and involves the threat of death, even to the point of literally, physically endangering our lives. It is not make-believe. Like the rites of the past, this one too calls upon expert practitioners, high priests of a sort, to guide us through to the far side of the ordeal. And when we emerge, we are in a different stage of life. The rite is medical crisis. It usually happens in a hospital, perhaps an emergency room, at the hands of doctors. What happens all around in this strange ambience — the blood tests, the X-rays, the CAT scans, the medications — can be almost ceremonial in its solemnity and precision. Often the procedures hurt: one is jabbed, cut, shaved, scrubbed, made nauseated. They can certainly frighten. Being inside a CAT scan is a nerve-wracking experience of mystification. Episodes like this can jar, rend, batter . . . but they may have no spiritual meaning, at least not yet. It is simply a close call.

That is how I recall thinking about the medical crisis I once passed through. When, after emergency surgery that came close to costing me my life, I returned to my senses, I woke feeling as if I had hit rock-bottom: feeble, dazed, unable to eat or drink or move. I learned I had lain in the intensive care unit hallucinating for hours at a stretch. My body felt shattered to pieces — as I have heard shamanic apprentices feel after they have been through one of their vision quests. But for them the experience is one of transcendence. For me it was nothing but numbness and confusion. I wanted desperately to take hold of a friendly hand as if that would keep me in one piece. Slowly, I came to realize I had been through a close call. A phrase came to mind: I had *dodged a bullet*. But I knew I had been through far more than that. Or at least I felt I *should* make something more of it than a lucky break. I *wanted* this to count for more. But it was up to me to supply everything the hospital and doctor could not. I almost felt cheated. After suffering all this, I should have become wiser. My life should have been turned around and renewed. But I saw no way that was going to happen. The doctors came to check me out; nurses came to take my vital signs. I was in the hands of caring experts; I was grateful. But nobody came to minister to my soul.

With the best intentions, medical professionals often take it to be their duty to return those they have saved to their "normal" life — that is, to the routine they had before. In their view, medical crisis is a bad patch in the road; the sooner you get over it and put it behind you, the better. Their goal is to make us "good as new." If patients can resume their job and their family responsibilities, that is ideal. It is as if the upshot of the exercise is to gloss over the terror and anguish of the crisis. Nothing could be further from the purpose of a rite of passage: to punctuate life memorably, to stand as a landmark along the way. In some tribal societies, the body is marked during the rite; blood is taken, a scar is left, a part cut away, to serve as a reminder. Our medical rites of passage often seek to eliminate any reminder of that kind. If possible, the body is left whole and unmarked, or perhaps repaired by cosmetic surgery later on. In my case, it was not. The scar, an ugly one, remains as a chapter in my life etched upon my flesh.

Yet seen from another angle, the medical crisis has features that could be of the highest therapeutic value if used in the right way. It is above all a deviation from all normal routines, sanctioned by an air of emergency. Work and family responsibilities are postponed; bills wait to be paid; appointments are canceled. Bedridden and largely incapacitated, patients are left with a great deal of time on their hands to think. If they are given nothing better to do, they while the time away watching television. But that need not be the way the occasion is used. It is, after all, a situation where social conventions are put on hold, as if to clear a space. One's food is prescribed, like it or not; everybody under care dons the same ridiculously awkward and revealing gowns; nurses, who will take no nonsense, appear with bedpans, esoteric equipment, and medications at all hours of the day and night. They expect their patients to do as they are told, to eat what they are served, to undress and be washed with no great show of modesty. Of course it is an ordeal; one comes to deplore it. And the healthier one becomes, the more agonizing it all is. But this is exactly what many rites of passage are designed to be: a suspension of the ordinary, a time of tribulation when one's fate is entrusted to the judgment of others who know what is best.

In the years ahead, more and more of us are going to be leaving hospitals after a brush with death that subjects us to a crisis like this. We will have a story to tell; but if all it comes down to is the excitement of a hair's-breadth escape, the story will soon wear thin. My experience led to an odd result. Though I am a writer and teacher somewhat skilled in words, I discovered with some embarrassment that there was not much I had to say — at least nothing that sounded earthshaking. One cannot expect others to make much of phrases like "glad to be alive"; they do no justice to the event. Yet that was what I felt. That was all I felt. For me, it was a discovery that yearned for expression. Perhaps this is what religious people find at church testimonials: the chance to stand up and say what everybody has heard a hundred times. "Praise the Lord! I am saved." The words are a formula; one utters them knowing that everybody present will be able to fill in the full feeling behind them.

The modern world provides some techniques for articulating ineffable moments in life. Support groups were created for that purpose. As a self-help, therapeutic invention, the support group dates back to the 1930s and the creation of Alcoholics Anonymous, a movement based on local associations of people who share the suffering of a common condition. Those who gather at AA meetings do not come expecting to hear eloquent declarations. They listen for the emotional subtext, from which they judge the authenticity of what is said. A perceptive therapist might see the possibility of using the medical crisis in somewhat the same way, as an occasion for building the kind of camaraderie that keeps the experience alive.

In the longevous society, we will need therapists who know the value of deepening the medical rite of passage. They will want to work with that moment, not as a trauma to be talked away but as the beginning of a quest. Very little current therapy has that skill or intention. Most therapists, after all, take their degrees in "marriage, family, and childhood," relationships that belong to early and midlife. Death transcends those relationships; it reaches out for the solitude that lies beyond society. What may be more appropriate than therapy is a heavy application of philosophy. The medical rite of passage cries out for the sort of "support" that only great minds and great hearts can offer.

Near Death . . . Or Near Enough

The publication in 1970 of Elisabeth Kübler-Ross's *On Death and Dying* struck an important new note in medical science. The book opened for frank discussion what had been among the most unmentionable of subjects. Initially, Kübler-Ross's interest was limited to the medical care of the dying. What she had to say on this score was of great importance. She was able to document the fact that medical people and hospitals were seriously insensitive to the special needs of the dying. Doctors in particular posed a problem. They rarely got around to the task of comforting those they could no longer help; they knew no way to prepare their patients for death. So they tended to write off the terminally ill as a black mark on their record.

Kübler-Ross, who had worked among the casualties of the Nazi death camps, suggested a simple but brilliant idea: treat death as you would any well-defined stage of life — the final stage. Examine how people face their mortality and work with that. She was able to identify a pattern in the emotional life of the dying with distinct phases: denial, anger, bargaining, depression, and acceptance. Each requires special handling and above all patience. If dying people are allowed, or better still helped, to move through these phases, their death becomes more bearable, even welcome. Along the way, they might require painkillers like morphine, perhaps in heavy doses. Give them, Kübler-Ross recommended. Because their needs are special, it might even be a good idea to move the dying to a hospice, where people skilled in their treatment can give them the attention they need.

The seminars Kübler-Ross offers on these techniques have helped transform our thinking about death. There was always a subtext to her work. She believes our treatment of the terminally ill is of great benefit to the live and healthy who are nowhere near dying. Simply knowing that such care exists can make everybody's life more secure. Soon after the publication of her book, workshops on "The Art of Dying" were offered as adult education courses. A new field of inquiry opened at universities: thanatology. At a certain point, however, Kübler-Ross's work began to take on mystical and occult overtones that caused it to lose professional respectability. Some of her patients described what they had been through on the brink of dying as an out-of-the-body sensation. Strange beings might appear to them, or colored lights. On the basis of her research with the terminally ill, Kübler-Ross portrayed the experience of dying as an altered state of consciousness. In later writing, she endorsed these more sensational ideas about death, even claiming to have had out-of-the-body experiences of her own and contact with a spirit guide. On the basis of her patients' experience, she professed to have proven the reality of life after death and the validity of reincarnation. When she began working with California channelers in the late 1970s, she lost a great deal of her credibility among doctors — who did not, it should be noted, even try to find a professionally acceptable equivalent for her techniques.

But by then death had gone from the status of a distasteful subject to a sort of craze, especially along the New Age fringe. The counter culture of the 1960s is often thought of as a youth movement, and it very largely was. But oddly enough, the discussion of death and dying became one of the great topics of that period, and especially among the young. Writing in the English journal *Encounter* in 1970, Melvin Maddocks mordantly asked, "Has death become the supreme authenticator for a generation that craves more than anything to be authentical?" In a period when young people were hunting for exotic forms of experience, anything that sounded even remotely psychedelic was sought out. The field of inquiry rapidly grew into a sensational fad. Movies on the subject, from *Resurrection* to *Ghost*, have invariably proved to be good box office.

Later still in her career, after she had suffered a debilitating stroke and was sadly incapacitated, Kübler-Ross repudiated many of these extreme claims and indeed became quite bitter. She felt convinced that medical science was falling far short of her expectations for dealing with death. Her own hospital experience had been miserable.

If some of her more aberrant beliefs have discredited her in the medical establishment, that is an overreaction. Her research and her methods for dealing with the dying have much to offer. Frankness on the subject is to be welcomed. But in one respect, her fascination with dying cheapened the experience she set out to reclaim. Whatever her intention, the more mystical turn her thinking took in the 1970s was a move in the wrong direction. Not all near-death experiences are accompanied by exotic visions, dazzling lights, and communications from beyond. It is wrong to arouse such expectations. Being near death may bring pain and insecurity and finally the sense of a life that has been left unraveled. For many what remains of their medical crisis is a vivid sense of mortality. That is all there is. One awakens thinking, *I nearly died . . . I might not have come back . . . this moment might never have occurred.*

Devaluing that insight — just that and nothing more — leads to an unfortunate result. It discourages people from making all they can of the near-death experience that most of us are apt to go through. Every heart patient who has been put on a heart-lung machine during surgery has been closer to death than any shaman ever was. There may be no psychedelic light show, but there is much to ponder when one returns from the anesthetic depths. One has brushed against one's own mortality. This is not an extravagant or euphoric high; it is simply what one knows as a fact. Yet that fact can be the occasion for philosophical reflection.

Ars Moriendi: The Art of Dying

In the ancient world, every religious tradition offered a body of wisdom whose purpose, if time and circumstance allowed, was to encourage the contemplation of mortality before death was suddenly at hand. The advice was collected into "books of the dead" that summoned up courage, counseled serenity, and often graphically described what the dead would experience beyond the grave. Modern nonbelievers like to think that religion is an emotional crutch for the weak and fearful. But the books of the dead are not always comforting; there might be terrors and testings in the afterlife as well as consolations. In the Western world, most books of the dead date from the time of the Black Plague in the later Middle Ages, when death was an object of constant fear. In that age of the *danse macabre,* entire villages were wiped out. With death waiting in ambush around every corner, tracts were written to meet the needs of the time. They were called *ars moriendi* — studies in the art of dying. Their central teaching was that "in the midst of life we are in death."

Much of this literature was morbid in the extreme. Its strategy was to prepare people, young and old, rich and poor, beautiful and ugly, for death by teaching disgust and contempt for the corruptible flesh and the pursuits of this world. Many came to believe life was not worth living. Once again, the strategy was not always meant to subdue fear with false hope. Most *ars moriendi* tracts, as was only realistic at the time, held out no promise of recovery or of easy salvation beyond death. Downplaying the threat of death is a distinctly modern deception, using the scientific mystique of the doctor to mislead. As one student of the subject observes,

> The approach to the dying . . . was thus diametrically opposed to the practices that until recently dominated modern western medicine. In hospitals, it used to be a common practice for the attending physicians and other medical personnel to use all possible means to conceal from the patients the diagnosis and prognosis of serious diseases and to join with the relatives in elaborate games to obscure the reality of the situation.[1]

In the classic books of the dead, supernatural figures identified as psychopomps, leaders of dead souls, mercifully waited for the dying individual like guides at the border of a new land. The god Hermes was among these, the deity of twilight, of wind, and of travelers. The attributes are all spiritual symbols: wind for the spirit, twilight for death, travel for the road of life. In another of his attributes, as the god of thought, Hermes represented the transcendent quality of mind, that which outlives the perishing body. In traditional cultures, there were also human guides who claimed the powers of the psychopomp. These were the shamans, advisers whose authority was derived from the experience of having symbolically died and returned to the body. The shaman was one who had wandered in other worlds, above the Earth or below, scouting out the perils and pitfalls. When the shaman sought to heal the sick, it was with the intense awareness that a cure might not be found; then it was his or her job to escort the soul forward.

The healing part of the shaman's calling has been taken over by physicians, who, as specialists, may know little about their patients' whole anatomy. As for the soul . . . that is for psychologists to deal with. But few therapists have studied the art of dying. Most confine themselves to childhood traumas and troubled marriages, sexual dysfunction and career pressures. Those who hire them for their services are still in the midst of life, struggling and scuffling, taking their jobs and marriages very seriously. They would not gladly pay to be told there are matters of greater concern even than love or money. I suspect they come to therapy to have their worries validated. Therapy continues, but the calling of the psychopomp has been forgotten. Yet that is the figure our new medical rites of passage call out for, one who is ready to guide toward death, but also back into life, one who knows the spiritual value of crisis.

The Politics of Healing

Healing has not always been practiced as a form of science. For that matter, it has not always had that much to do with medicine understood as mending the body or dispensing pharmaceutical concoctions. The legendary medicine man of tribal lore was more a priest than a doctor. "Medicine," as Native Americans understood the word, was a global capacity that might include making rain, exerting personal power, hexing one's enemies, invoking the fertility gods, having great visions, as well as healing the sick and consoling the dying.

When it comes to counseling the dying, it is enough of a problem that modern medicine restricts itself to the limits of science. It is even more of a problem that the science of medicine has been overtaken by the *business* of medicine. Science makes knowledge important; business makes money important. Where, in this mix, does the task of the psychopomp fit in? It is not a service one can sensibly bill for by the quarter-hour. What HMO would be willing to pay for a service called *ars moriendi?* All this may have to change in the years ahead as doctors and medical counselors find themselves meeting a new public, one that has outlived (though not necessarily solved) the dilemmas of youth and midlife.

Imagine a different paradigm borrowed from an earlier era. Once the most learned physicians in the Western world were monks. The monasteries were the best hospitals one could find. Often all the monks could do was comfort rather than cure, though comfort is hardly to be underestimated as a healing quality. Healing was then practiced by men — and sometimes by nuns too — who were spiritually trained, people who could prescribe for the soul as well as the body. They were contemplatives rather than men of a worldly calling. Can we imagine something like this reemerging in our time: medicine practiced as a spiritual discipline within the setting of an intentional community of men and women who see their work as a vocation?

That possibility may seem outlandish if the vision we have of modern medicine is that of television dramas like *ER* or *Chicago Hope*. But medicine was once so pursued; the monks even carried on a kind of research, exploring the medicinal powers of herbs. If something of that spirit could be reinvented in our time, many of the financial issues surrounding medicine would be far less urgent. Physicians would not need to evaluate themselves by the money they make. And from such a stance, they might be better positioned to challenge the obscene profiteering of the health care industry. Vocational healers could be fully trained in their science; they surely would not need to be ascetics or mendicants, but neither would they be entrepreneurs. The honor due them would not depend upon their earnings, but upon their role as true therapeuts, healers of the body and soul.

As strange as this must sound, I can imagine medical practice attracting a new kind of caregiving talent, the same sort of talent that volunteers for the Peace Corps or rescue work in troubled places around the world. There are those highly motivated to provide service like this; many are already toiling in clinics and emergency rooms, under the pressures of marketplace medicine. Others are on the job now as medical missionaries and relief workers where famine, plague, or war have struck. These are the people whom television reporters seek out when they cover great disasters in distant places. They may be interviewed anonymously; we have no idea who they are or how they came to be where they are. As often as not, they are Americans. We can be sure of only one thing. They are not taking these risks and making these sacrifices for money. They are skilled and caring people, and they do more to hold our world together than politicians or financiers.

What if we provided people like this with the support and opportunity they need to band together into medical orders, keeping a common house, maintaining a nursing home and hospice, offering the medicine appropriate to the living and dying needs of the New People? Would we not be creating a new cultural category: compassionate heroism?

The training of vocational healers would be rich in the *ars moriendi*. It would include the ability to stand by the terminally ill as a psychopomp, or to draw upon those who have that special sensitivity, whether they are medically trained or not. In Tolstoy's story, Ivan Illich's psychopomp turns out to be an unlikely choice: it is the peasant lad Gerasim who waits patiently at the bedside to do what little he can to comfort the dying man. "We must all die," the lad replies when Ivan apologizes for putting him to so much trouble. Gerasim's simple compassion and candor are Ivan's first glimpse of the truth he must accept. There are centers and communities that have formed already around the needs of the dying where the talents of a Gerasim could be of great value. What we still lack are ways to deal with the near-death crisis that does not kill but leaves us shaken to our foundations and in search of a new beginning that may stretch out across the years.

There are at least a few people exploring that frontier. One of them, Rachel Remen, both a medical doctor and a therapist, works from the premise that the negative aspects of crisis — the pain, the anxiety — can be precisely the most effective means of deep transformation. She is the friend and healer who helped bring me through the medical crisis that was my rite of passage. "In avoiding all pain and seeking comfort at all costs," she writes, "we may be left without mercy and compassion. In rejecting change and risk, we often cheat ourselves of the quest. In denying suffering, we may never know our strength and our greatness."[2]

Currently, Remen is teaching "The Healer's Art" at the University of California Medical Center in San Francisco. She describes the course as "an experiential and didactic curriculum in relationship-centered care which presents the human and sacred dimensions of both the physician and the patient." "What we tell the students," she says, "is that who they are is as important as what they know, and that what they are bringing with them to medicine is as central to their physicianhood as anything they will learn in med school." The course has led to a new Center for Integrative Medicine on the campus that will add wholistic and humanistic values to the standard curriculum. That is a welcome sign of maturity in health care, though not one that will easily be assimilated into the prevailing system of managed care, where the economic bottom line is rapidly becoming the top line, cruelly restricting the time physicians can spend with their patients as well as the trust that patients can place in their doctors.

This study holds that longevity leads to wisdom. But even so, wisdom needs to be midwifed and given the courage to speak what it knows. For many, the decisive point in getting beyond the follies of senior life may lie in making skillful use of the medical crisis. But if that crisis is to

function as an authentic rite of passage, it requires structure and guid-
ance, a good professional ear for the telling nuance, an ability to work
with and through fear. Counseling of this kind should not be a casual
aspect of medicine left to some informal, catch-as-catch-can procedure.
It should be respected as an integral aspect of medicine, not only as part
of geriatric care or the management of terminal illness, but as a way to
bring people back from the brink of death with a sense of life-enhancing
insight.

In one of the few contemporary efforts to re-create the *ars moriendi*,
the pastoral counselor Robert Neale devised a number of exercises for
dealing directly with the anxieties that surround death, especially for the
old. Writing in the early 1970s, Neale felt that death had become almost
"pornographic" with respect to the secrecy and shame that surround it.
His conclusion was that "death is an ultimate mystery. Such a mystery
makes an excellent screen on which to project all our concerns about life.
The fear of death is a projection of our most basic fear. Our fear of death
is really our fear of life."[3]

In effect, Neale discovered that death, the silent presence, elicits the
ultimate transference. Skillfully presented, it is the ideal blank screen
that every therapist seeks to become for the client. Before this dark
witness, one's entire life comes under examination. The anxieties that
Neale found to be most dominant in many of his clients are instructive.
There was, for example, the fear of "incompleteness and failure." People
feared they had not measured up to the demands of life and saw death as
"a forced retirement." If we are tied to values like that until the end of
our days, we will always see age and death as evils.

It may seem odd to put it this way, but the compassionate use of
medical crisis as a rite of passage might be a politically significant act of
the highest order. Searched to its full philosophical depth, the near-
death experience has enormous transformative power. Unless people are
aggressively encouraged to forget what they have been through, it is
difficult to imagine that many would return from that existential ordeal
without caring more about the simple pleasures of life and about one
another. As folklore teaches us, "death levels all ranks." It "lays the
shepherd's crook beside the scepter."

Only the very young are apt to emerge unchanged from a scrape with
death, simply because life, with its insistent demands for performance
and achievement, closes in so rapidly after the crisis. But where that
does not happen, there is the possibility of wisdom, that deeper dimen-

sion of knowledge born of suffering and self-examination. My conviction is that those to whom this rite of passage does bring wisdom will find it impossible to take acquisitive habits and egotistical values as seriously as they might once have done. Competition and selfish interest will mean less, and money will be seen for the sad illusion it is.

I cannot say exactly what sort of politics might follow from the careful instructional use of the medical crisis; it would very likely be a politics that transcends the categories of conservative or liberal or radical, none of which were created to delve into the eternal questions. Ideology is ephemeral, a matter of issues and arguments. Underlying all the issues is the tone in which we address life and one another. To know that we are all mortal as powerfully as Ivan Illich came to know it, to understand that all have experienced heartbreaking loss, is to know ourselves as Everyman. "Winning" matters most when contenders have little time to take stock before the game is over. So politics has always been a matter of choosing sides in the fury of the passing moment. But with a bit more time on their hands, the New People have the chance to find the common humanity that all sides share.

14

The Survival of the Gentlest

RECENTLY, out of curiosity, I visited a local video arcade. What I saw as I walked through brought many of the themes of this book into sharp focus.

The arcade was filled exclusively with boys in their early and mid-teens, all of them fiercely concentrated on the games before them. I stopped at the machine that had drawn the largest gathering. Its title, "Killer Instinct," flashed above the screen in crimson lights. While one boy played, the others, intent as a young war party, looked on, totally absorbed in the animated mayhem before their eyes. Along with a complete martial arts repertory (jump, jab, kick, duck, punch), the game featured an armory of gruesome weaponry: sabers, grenade guns, rockets. Video games give no quarter. With a flick of the trigger, a player can slice off a head, knock down a building, blow up a city. The results register on the screen with maximum gore and screeching explosions.

Philosophy gets taught in many ways, and never more effectively than when it comes disguised as mere entertainment. The boys, so earnestly at play, were surely not aware of the cultural genealogy behind the games that held them mesmerized. "Killer Instinct" might just as well be called "Survival of the Fittest." That was the theme behind the electronic violence in this arcade; all the games were adolescent exercises in social Darwinism, that harsh philosophy of life that dominated our society through the early centuries of industrialization. Here was the heritage of Darwinian natural selection being played out among the young as shoot-outs, street-fights, hand-to-hand combat. A battle to the death with no holds barred, and may the best man win. One must say "man," because this is exclusively masculine terrain, no women in sight. Some games include a female martial artist, but she — a bosomy, bikini-clad caricature — is hardly there to enlist female interest.

As I watched this garish contemporary pastime, I wondered: do these games not reveal how childish this philosophy has always been? *Little boy* childish. How good it would be if these electronic simulations were the last, sad remnant of social Darwinism in our culture, a marginal adolescent amusement that the boys would soon outgrow.

But that is not what has happened. Social Darwinism has seen a recrudescence. At the 1984 Democratic convention, then-governor of New York Mario Cuomo used his keynote address to warn the nation about this unexpected twist of fate. The survival of the fittest was back in force in our national policy. The Reagan administration, so Cuomo contended, believed that "the wagon train will not make it to the frontier unless some of our old, some of our young, some of our weak are left behind by the side of the trail. The strong will inherit the land!"

The reasons for the reemergence of social Darwinism are many, not least of which is the timidity of an American liberalism that continues to stray from its rich historical roots in populist and progressive tradition. This failure of the liberal center has allowed conservative opportunists to target all the most humane social programs of the past century for destruction. The New People bear a heavy responsibility for this turn of events. The major thrust behind the contemporary conservative backlash is distrust of government. And in a painfully ironic sense, the protest movement of the 1960s is the source of that backlash. It taught America how easily power corrupts a nation's leaders. Accusations of high crimes on the part of ruling elites that once had to be screamed in the streets to an incredulous public finally proved to be true — and continue to be documented as the CIA and FBI release more secret documents each passing year. But by a devilishly clever editing of that lesson, conservative elements have focused the public's wrath exclusively on "Washington," leaving the expanding corporate establishment all but invisible to criticism. In the 1960s and 1970s, when protesters attacked the "power structure," it was hardly welfare mothers, the post office, or the National Park Service they had in mind, less still the efforts of the Justice Department and the federal courts to defend civil rights.

This opportunistic attack on the institutions of our national community often advertises itself as "populism." But it is a populism that has nothing to do with the great battle cries of its namesake: "soak the rich" and "share the wealth." Historical populism, the protest of brave, impoverished farmers, was clear about the great issue: "the people versus the interests." And no interest was more virulent than "the money power." Today the anger is there, but not the political acumen that once gave that anger a sensible moral target. Instead, the animosity is deflected away from the global corporate heights and *downward* — against the disempowered. It becomes scapegoating, and at last that scapegoating has reached the nation's seniors, now seen as a parasitic dependency load that will be our fiscal ruin.

Not since the 1920s has Darwinian competitive toughness run so rampant in the land or commanded so much public admiration. In a 1997 PBS documentary dealing with the stock market, the central figure was a mutual fund manager, a celebrity financier who had at the time run up a moneymaking record of astounding proportions. His every word and appearance were being carefully tracked by thousands of admiring investors. Watching him on the job, I was struck by how much he resembled the boys playing "Killer Instinct." He too was computer-obsessed. Like a lion in a cage, he paced the floor between desks crowded with video terminals. He wore a telephone headset that put him in touch with New York, London, Tokyo. As calls came in, he flashed a look at the screens and snapped decisions. "Buy, sell, buy, sell! Five thousand, a hundred thousand, sell at fifty, buy at one hundred," he barked, peppering his words with aggressive invectives. "Wipe 'em out! Ka-bam! Nuke that! Rat-a-tat-tat!" He too was jabbing and ducking and punching. He had become a financial street-fighter, a Dow Jones warrior, one of the fit who had earned his survival. And what was the proof of his fitness? Money. Nothing but money.

Darwin, Farewell

The survival of the fittest has a curious history. It is linked to the population theories of Thomas Malthus, which have long since been open to serious question. The longevity revolution carries us into a demographic phase neither Malthus nor Darwin could have anticipated, surrounded as they were by a savage industrial world that valued neither wisdom nor compassion, nor even mature judgment. In that world the survival of the fittest was a hoodlum idea that managed to stow away on an intellectual luxury liner disguised as reputable science. Many still assume the phrase was coined by Charles Darwin to explain his theory of evolution. Darwin used the words, but he did not invent them. In a late edition of his *On the Origin of Species,* he reached outside the field of

biology to borrow the phrase from the then-prominent social philosopher Herbert Spencer. Spencer, who had politics on his mind, not
biology, patterned his ideal of fitness on the dog-eat-dog competition of
the industrial marketplace. He saw the world as a jungle where the
strong devour the weak.

In fact, no real jungle was ever as brutish as the early industrial cities
of the modern world. No beast of prey was ever so voracious as the early
industrial entrepreneurs were for money and power. But that made no
difference to Spencer. In his view, it was the law of nature that the strong
should prevail and the weak sink into poverty. He went further. The
poor, being unfit, had to be eliminated. *Literally* eliminated. "The whole
effort of nature," Spencer believed, "is to get rid of such, to clear the
world of them, and make room for better." On these grounds, Spencer
opposed not only charity but public sanitation, public education, public housing, pure food and drug regulation. If his society had offered
entitlements, he would have advocated ending them, the better to sweep
away the useless old. Were he still with us today, Spencer would surely
be taking sides with those who are laboring to end Medicare and in-
sisting that it is the duty of the old to die if they cannot pay their own
bills.

By associating his theory with Herbert Spencer's politics, Darwin
attracted a public he might not otherwise have reached. The business
community at once latched onto his theory and turned it into the
ideology called social Darwinism. The great captains of industry fancied
themselves to be the "fittest" — and thus deserving of all the money
they could lay their hands on. Darwin had given them a way to justify
their brutality and avarice. Nineteenth-century America, Richard Hofstadter comments, "was like a vast human caricature of the Darwinian
struggle for existence and survival of the fittest. Successful business
entrepreneurs apparently accepted almost by instinct the Darwinian
terminology which seemed to portray the conditions of their existence."[1]

With the advent of the welfare state and other more humane forms of
social policy in the twentieth century, social Darwinism might have
passed swiftly from the scene as the self-serving social ethic of the
wealthy few. The Great Depression and two world wars made such
fierce bravado ring hollow; its association with Nazi racism was especially damning. But with the collapse of Soviet power in Europe in the
1980s, those who speak for market economics, especially in the United

States, have been quick to claim victory in the cold war. And to the victor belong the spoils, including the philosophical spoils. From eastern Europe to China, national economies, including those that were committed to socialism only a decade before, are turning to ruthless corporate and political elites to achieve rapid development. As they do so, they are adopting the competitive values of the free market.

The global economy, so filled with the opportunity for quick riches, has given social Darwinism a temporary new lease on life. It has placed a premium on toughness, avarice, and rapacity. Around the world, "development" has come to mean sweatshops and wage slavery. Sometimes we are told bluntly by corporate leaders that profiteering and selfishness are good, that only hard-charging entrepreneurs deserve to prosper and the rest must hustle or suffer. Welfare "as we know it" must end; entitlements must be terminated; security is a thing of the past. More often we hear euphemistic appeals to "self-reliance," "competitiveness," and "personal responsibility." It all comes down to the same remorseless creed: the world and its wealth belong to the strong, and the devil take the hindmost. Ironically, just as the world industrial economy has grown affluent enough to provide a decent standard of life for all, we are hearing the war cry of rugged individualism again.

It is not easy to speak out against money and power, even in the name of human kindness. Nevertheless, the industrial societies of the world will be forced to leave the Darwinian jungle, not as a matter of abstract philosophical preference, but as a matter of objective demographic necessity. In a maturing world, the Darwinian struggle for existence simply has no place. It is as defunct as the antics of robber barons in the Gilded Age. An aging society cannot be a society of entrepreneurial zealots. The need for mutual aid and cooperation is built into the very bones and sinews of a senior population. As societies mature, hard competition ceases to be a viable choice in life. To some that will seem a loss, but many of us have been waiting for the day — including the wisest economists, for whom the central issue has been not the production but the use and distribution of wealth.

A generation before the New People arrived on the scene, in the depths of the Great Depression, John Maynard Keynes, the premier economist of the twentieth century, allowed himself to envision some highly utopian vistas on the far side of the economic crisis. His words lead us to that critical line where the abstractions of the marketplace end and the life of the soul begins.

> When the accumulation of wealth is no longer of high social importance, there will be great changes in the code of morals. We shall be able to rid ourselves of many of the pseudo-moral principles which have hag-ridden us for two hundred years, by which we have exalted some of the most distasteful of human qualities into the position of the highest values. . . . All kinds of social customs and economic practices affecting the distribution of wealth and its rewards and penalties which we now maintain at all costs, however distasteful and unjust they may be in themselves . . . we shall then be free, at last, to discard.[2]

The great changes that Keynes presaged now lie before us. All we need do is awaken to the true magnitude of our industrial affluence in order to make those changes real. A "new code of morals" is already in the making among us as we explore the deeper ethical dimensions of longevity. The old need help. They must be free to say they need help. Ethically speaking, it is hitting below the belt to make that appeal seem weak or unworthy, and it is a lie to say it is unaffordable. What neither we nor the living planet can afford is the fiercely rapacious vision of life that has for so long driven industrial civilization. Demographics and the logic of progress are against it. Our marvelously productive industrial economy has for far too long been entrusted to the control of men who are still no more than tall children — overly rich, overly pampered, twelve-year-old boys playing with the lives of whole societies and the resources of the Earth as if they were counters in a great global video game. They have long outlived whatever entrepreneurial value they may once have had. It is time for our fate to be taken into the hands of adults. In the era of the longevity revolution, the "fittest" are the gentlest, those who touch the lives of others with kindness and strive to strengthen our sense of community. The New People who survive long enough to join the next senior generation are voting with every breath they take for a compassionate social order.

Grandparent Power

Like all ideas, scientific theories ripen with human experience, taking on ever greater complexity and subtlety. Atomistic physics, for example, flourished in an age obsessed with clockwork mechanics and mathematical simplification, crude images that contemporary physics has long since outgrown. That same maturing process is even more marked in biology and anthropology. With the passage of time, our insights into human nature and culture deepen, granting a greater role to symbiosis and mutual aid. The "grandmother hypothesis" is a recent example of such a shift in values, an idea that could only arise at a time when age and gender are undergoing serious reappraisal. The hypothesis is an effort to redress the balance in our understanding of evolution, moving the idea away from compulsively masculine competition toward more nurturing and convivial virtues. We are beginning to see how many people social Darwinism edited out of the human story — among them the old.

The grandmother hypothesis focuses on one of the peculiarities of our species: midlife menopause. Human females are the only members of the primate family to live so long after their final pregnancy. They survive and, as we are learning by the day, can be quite robust. But why should this be? Evolutionary selection supposedly favors traits that make a difference in reproduction. But what advantage is there in women's capacity to outlive their reproductive powers by so many years? As early as 1957 the evolutionary biologist George C. Williams specu- lated that the midlife cessation of childbearing in humans gave mothers the chance to offer more attention to bringing up their young, thus giving their characteristics a better chance to survive. Baby boomers might think of this as "quality time" for parenting. Providing more care for the young may have helped evolve the longer infancy during which human babies grow a larger brain, learn to speak, and master a complex culture.

But if it is an advantage to have an attentive mother, how much more so to have a caring grandmother who has lived long enough to help feed and protect her daughter's young. In turn, the mother who outlives her childbearing years becomes a grandmother herself, and in that ca- pacity she enhances the parenting that the next generation of young can expect to receive. The anthropologist Kristin Hawkes believes there may even be a Darwinian justification for grandmotherly kindness. "Natural selection," she suggests, "favored menopause because only grandmoth- ers who are not busy feeding their own children have time to provision grandchildren." Hawkes has shown that in at least one well-studied hunting-and-gathering society, the Hadzas of Tanzania, postmenopaus- al women contribute significantly to the care of the young, offering help when it is needed most by pregnant and lactating mothers. Her research leads to a daring departure from standard evolutionary theory. Rather than viewing males as the family's principal breadwinner, she believes grandmothers empowered the human species to become the planet's dominant animal.

> The extension of life past menopause was a watershed event in human prehistory. With a labor force of elder females available to help provision the young, adults were then free to colonize new territories unavailable to those primates that did not provision their weaned young. . . . Suddenly humans could migrate to places where it required full adult strength and cunning to extract food. They could go wherever they pleased. After all, there were older women around to help.[3]

But why exclude the possibility that grandfathers may also have been on hand to help? In his pioneering studies of tribal elders, David Gutmann concludes that elders both male and female have been an enormous but largely unrecognized advantage to our species. He too focuses on the key role of grandparents, whom he calls "the wardens of our precious human heritage." They provided for the extended parenting that enriches the lives of the young. In hunting and early agricultural societies, where young men provided the agility to chase big game or the muscle needed to guide the heavy plow, older men may have been of little use in the primary economy. What are we to imagine they were doing after injury, age, or illness forced them to give up hard physical labor and risky exploits? Was there perhaps a kind of prehistoric retirement that left them home to join with the older women in gathering food, telling tales, and passing on the lore of the group? We may never know for sure, but grandparents, male as well as female, may have been the providers that gave evolution the opportunity it needed to make us fully human.

When the first Neanderthal burial sites were explored, paleontologists were surprised to find that they included the bones of old, often incapacitated men and women. These were people who had lived comparatively long lives — perhaps reaching fifty — and had been respectfully buried. Why had such supposedly "primitive" — indeed, pre–homo sapiens — humans troubled to spend the resources necessary to care for members of the group who could not pull their own weight? The authors of an otherwise quite unsentimental study of prehistoric societies conclude that such burials reflect "a degree of humanity not always displayed towards one another by members of civilized societies." They take this to be clear evidence of the "love and compassion . . . that in the last resort made possible the future achievements of man even in the field of material endeavor."[4] Elders, in short, made our higher evolution possible.

Attributing so important a role to grandparent power is highly speculative, but no more so than all the scenarios anthropologists dream up to account for human origins. There is no good evidence for believing that prehistoric humanity comprised wily brutes formed in the image of J. P. Morgan or Attila the Hun. That is only what one generation of anxious and ambitious men decided to find in our ancestral past. The theories we devise to explain who we are and how we got that way may never be fully proven, but they reveal a great deal about who we are here and now. Social Darwinism, based as it was on an image of the state of nature where each made war against all, was a savage reflection of early industrialism. The grandmother hypothesis embodies the values of our postindustrial future, a world where, as a matter of political necessity, kindness will have to count for more than predatory cunning. If paleolithic grandparents did make themselves useful — whether as repositories of the tribal memory or as caring child-minders — then we may be at the point of seeing their generosity and gentleness regain its primordial place in society.

This much is certain: human society has always been a blending of energy and wisdom — alas! more often too much of the first, too little of the latter. The young provide the energy to get things done, but it takes the wisdom of more experienced heads to know how best to use that energy. Industrialism has vastly expanded the energy of the youthful Western world, but it has contributed nothing to our wisdom. Machines have no souls. One need only look around to see where the power of that soulless technology has led us — into a global economy that heedlessly strips the planet of its riches and its dignity as if there were no tomorrow. That leaves us with the paradox that the New People will have to resolve. For the whole of the modern period, we have thought of the future as the cultural property of youth. But when it comes to the deep future — the enduring health and beauty of the planet — it may be the old, precisely because they have fewer years ahead of them, whose wisdom has the most to offer. In thinking about the future evolution of our species, we could do worse than to restore caring and sharing to their proper place in the human story.

NOTES

INDEX

Notes

1. Discovering a New People

1. Theodore Roszak, *The Making of a Counter Culture* (New York: Doubleday, 1969; Berkeley: University of California Press, 1996).
2. Sidney Blumenthal, *Our Long National Daydream* (New York: HarperCollins, 1998).
3. Richard Suzman et al., eds., *The Oldest Old* (New York: Oxford University Press, 1992).
4. Robert Binstock, "The Oldest Old and 'Intergenerational Equity,'" in ibid., p. 399.
5. Walter Bortz (former president of the American Geriatrics Society), *DARE to Be 100* (New York: Simon & Schuster, 1997); DARE stands for Diet-Attitude-Renewal-Exercise, Bortz's long-life formula. He has also written *We Die Too Long and Live Too Short* (New York: Bantam Books, 1991). Jean Carper, *Stop Aging Now!* (New York: Harper Perennial, 1996); Rebecca Latimer, *You're Not Old Until You're 90* (Nevada City, Calif.: Blue Dolphin, 1997); David Mahoney, *The Longevity Strategy: How to Live to 100 Using the Brain-Body Connection* (New York: John Wiley & Sons, 1998). There is also *Reversing Human Aging* (New York: William Morrow, 1996) by Michael Fossel.
6. Mike Males (*Scapegoat Generation: America's War on Adolescents* [Monroe, Maine: Common Courage Press, 1996]) is particularly bitter in his indictment of the senior population, including the baby boomers.
7. William Frey quoted in Jonathan Tilove, "Generation Gap Becoming Racial Gap," *San Francisco Examiner*, November 23, 1997, p. A17. Also see Peter Brimelow, *Alien Nation* (New York: Random House, 1995), and Frederick Lynch, *The Diversity Machine: The Drive to Change the White Male Workplace* (New York: Free Press, 1997).
8. See Mireya Navarro, "The Silver Haired Legislature: A Political Powerhouse in the Making," *New York Times*, October 19, 1997, sect. 1, p. 10.
9. Robert Binstock, "The Oldest Old and 'Intergenerational Equity,'" in Suzman et al., *The Oldest Old*, p. 404. Also see Laurie Rhodebeck, "The Politics of Greed? Political Preferences Among the Elderly," *Journal of Politics* (May 1993): 342–64.

10. Janet Novack, "Strength from Its Gray Roots," *Forbes,* November 25, 1991, pp. 89–92.
11. Gerald Larue, *Geroethics: A New Vision of Growing Old in America* (Buffalo, N.Y.: Prometheus Books, 1992), pp. 265–66.
12. See, for example, Paula Brown, Doress-Worters, and Diana L. Siegal, *The New Ourselves, Growing Older* (New York: Simon & Schuster, 1994), ch. 30 ("Changing Society and Ourselves").
13. Maggie Kuhn, *No Stone Unturned* (New York: Ballantine Books, 1991), pp. 132, 138.

2. The Third Millennium Blues

1. Sidney Gulick, *The American Japanese Problem* (New York: Scribner's, 1914), p. 68.
2. Richard Leone, "Stick with Public Pensions," *Foreign Affairs* (July/August 1997): 39.
3. On the lobbying efforts of the Concord Coalition, see Trudy Lieberman, "Social Insecurity: The Campaign to Take the System Private," *The Nation,* January 27, 1997. Also see E. J. Myers, *Let's Get Rid of Social Security* (Amherst, N.Y.: Prometheus Books, 1996) for a compendium of anti-entitlements arguments all based on the standard conservative assumption that increasing taxes to continue Social Security is out of the question.
4. Lester Thurow, "The Birth of a Revolutionary Class," *New York Times Magazine,* May 19, 1996, pp. 46–47. Also see Lester Thurow, *The Future of Capitalism* (New York: William Morrow, 1996).
5. Robert Ball, "A Secure System," *American Prospect* (November/December 1996): 34. In the same issue, see Jerry Mashaw and Theodore Marmor, "The Great Social Security Scare."
6. Peterson quoted in John Cassidy, "Spooking the Boomers," *New Yorker,* January 13, 1997, p. 31.
7. James P. Smith, quoted in *San Francisco Chronicle,* November 21, 1995, p. C6.
8. Rob Norton, "Cheating Tomorrow's Children," *Fortune,* July 10, 1995.
9. Larry J. Kotlikoff, *Generational Accounting: Knowing Who Pays, and When, for What We Spend* (New York: Free Press, 1993).
10. Dean Baker, *Robbing the Cradle?* (Washington, D.C.: Economic Policy Institute, 1995).
11. Quoted in *San Francisco Chronicle,* December 22, 1995, p. B2.
12. The figure for the United States would be 43 percent, for Germany 160 percent, and for Japan 200 percent. Pushed to these limits, the tax burden for entitlements would absorb very nearly all the lifetime income of the working population.

   Among European nations, the former Soviet Union may be doing the worst job of dealing with its seniors as it fitfully makes the transition to a market economy. The previous socialist entitlements have been stripped to the bone before anything has emerged to take their place. It is reportedly a commonplace sight to find elderly Russians on the streets hawking the last of their personal possessions to buy food or peddling bootleg vodka.

Prospectively the worst-case scenario for seniors in the years ahead will be in China, where the government is fiercely determined to develop the economy. Senior care has taken on a particularly menacing aspect, if only because of the magnitude of the problem. When the over-sixty population doubles by 2025, that will amount to 400 million people. By then China, which has mandated single-child families, may have halved its birth rate, but its fiscal problem will be more demanding than ever. Why? Because the portion of the population then on the increase, the elderly, will be far more expensive to maintain, while the younger generation will fall below replacement level. The Chinese government is already resorting to warehousing its seniors in substandard, urban "collection centers" that have a bad reputation for abusing their inmates. Judging by reports on the problem, one might almost conclude that the Chinese government wishes it could have edited medical science out of Western technology.

13. Government estimates cited in Andrew Rosenbaum, "The Medicare Brawl," *New York Times,* October 1, 1995, p. 14.

14. Richard Leone, "Stick with Public Pensions," *Foreign Affairs* (July/August 1997): 40–41.

15. "Health Care System Denounced," *San Francisco Chronicle,* December 3, 1997, p. D1.

16. Malcolm Sparrow, *License to Steal: Why Fraud Plagues America's Health-Care System* (New York: Westview Press/HarperCollins, 1996). See the interview with Sparrow in the *National Retired Teachers Associates Bulletin* (October 1997): 14–16. Sparrow's estimate is higher than the government's estimate of $23 billion. He recommends a number of reforms in the Health Care Financing Administration, which governs Medicare, among them a schedule of rewards for reporting fraud.

17. In July 1997, a report by the Inspector General of the Department of Health and Human Services detailed the loss of $23.2 billion from Medicare in 1996 alone due to waste and fraud. At the time, the Congress was debating the need to raise Medicare deductibles for seniors to keep the system solvent. The higher deductibles would recover some $4 billion, far less than a crackdown on the cheating that goes on in the system.

18. Third Millennium's *Declaration* is available from Box 20866, New York, N.Y. 10023. Its web site at www.thirdmil.org features a clock that totals up the national debt by the minute.

19. See Jean Davies Okimoto and Phyllis Stegal, *Boomerang Kids* (Boston: Little, Brown, 1987). The 1993 national census reported that eighteen million adult children between the ages of eighteen and thirty-four were living with their parents, up from thirteen million in 1970. As of the mid-1990s, 53 percent of the eighteen-to-twenty-four population was living with their parents; that number was 47 percent in 1970.

20. G. Pascal Zachary, "Parents' Gifts to Adult Children Studied," *Wall Street Journal,* February 9, 1995.

21. Frances and Calvin Goldscheider, *Leaving and Returning Home in Twentieth-Century America* (Washington, D.C.: Population Reference Bureau, 1994).

22. Lori Simon-Rusinowitz et al., "Grandparenting at Century's End: Grandparents in the Workplace," *Generations* (Spring 1996): 41–45. This paper was researched for the American Society on Aging in 1996. Also see Robert Butler, "Living Longer, Contributing More," *Journal of the American Medical Association*, October 22, 1997, p. 1372.

23. As of 1993, only 12 percent of the elderly were estimated to be below the poverty level: about $7,000 for a person living alone, $8,700 for a couple. In contrast, before Medicare was adopted in 1965, those above sixty-five made up more of the poor than any other group in the United States.

24. Christina Duff, "Profiling the Aged: Fat Cats or Hungry Victims?" *Wall Street Journal*, September 28, 1995.

25. Editorial, *Wall Street Journal*, January 8, 1997, p. A18.

26. Charles Morris, *The AARP* (New York: Times Books, 1997), pp. 165–69.

3. Entitlements and the Ethics of Affordability

1. Roy Lubove, *The Struggle for Social Security 1900–1935* (Cambridge, Mass.: Harvard University Press, 1968), p. 39.

2. John Blum et al., *The National Experience*, 6th ed. (New York: Harcourt Brace Jovanovich, 1985), II:685.

3. William Graebner, *A History of Retirement* (New Haven, Conn.: Yale University Press, 1980), pp. 10–17.

4. Michael Harrington, *The Other America: Poverty in the United States* (New York: Penguin Books, 1963). Ch. 6 ("The Golden Years") covers the plight of the aged.

5. Quoted in Sharon Curtin, *Nobody Ever Died of Old Age: In Praise of Old People, In Outrage at Their Loneliness* (Boston: Little, Brown/Atlantic Monthly Press, 1972), p. 33.

6. Richard Calhoun, *In Search of the New Old: Redefining Old Age in America, 1945–1970* (New York: Elsevier, 1978), covers senior politics through the Great Society period.

7. David Hackett Fischer, *Growing Old in America* (New York: Oxford University Press, 1977), p. 192.

8. Robert Butler, *Why Survive? Being Old in America* (New York: Harper & Row, 1975), pp. xi–xii.

9. Curtin, *Nobody Ever Died of Old Age*, p. 35.

10. See the report by Miles Benson, *San Francisco Examiner*, August 18, 1997.

11. Rachel Filinson and Stanley Ingman, eds., *Elder Abuse: Practice and Policy* (New York: Human Sciences Press, 1989).

12. In 1995, twenty-four thousand Americans above the age of sixty-five attempted suicide; six thousand succeeded — a 32 percent increase over 1980. Eighty percent of the suicides were white males. The AARP makes literature available on the subject. For the pamphlet "Suicide of Older Men and Women," write to AARP Fulfillment, EE01180, 601 E Street, NW, Washington, D.C. 20049. Also see Caryl Stern, "Why Depression Is a Silent Killer," *Parade*, September 28, 1997, pp. 4–5.

13. Townsend's political autobiography can be found in *New Horizons: An Autobiography* (Chicago: J. L. Stewart Publishing Co., 1943).

14. Diana Walsh, "The Fear Merchants," *San Francisco Examiner*, February 8, 1998, p. A1.

15. James Riley, *Sickness, Recovery, and Death: A History and Forecast of Ill Health* (London: Macmillan, 1989).

16. Anthony Smith, *The Body* (New York: Viking, 1985).

17. Quoted in David Perlman, "Research on Genes and Disease of Aging," *San Francisco Chronicle*, November 7, 1995, p. A3.

18. Gina Kolata, "New Era of Robust Elderly Belies the Fears of Scientists," *New York Times*, February 27, 1996, p. 1.

19. Jack Rosenthal, "The Age Boom," *New York Times Magazine*, March 9, 1997, pp. 40–42.

20. Leonard Hayflick, *How and Why We Age* (New York: Ballantine Books, 1994), p. 335.

21. See the analysis by William Mundell and Jack Friedman, "A Low Price for Better Health Care," *New York Times*, June 22, 1997, p. F13. They claim that the main correctable cause for the high cost of American health care is "chronic underinvestment in basic medical research over the last 25 years."

22. Bernard Starr, "This Longevity Is Killing Us: Healthy Choices for Sick Health Care," *Barron's*, January 15, 1996.

4. The Ecology of Wisdom

1. The poll in question was commissioned by the AARP and several insurance and mutual fund companies. It was reported by the Associated Press on October 17, 1997.

2. Anne and Paul Ehrlich, "Growing Beyond Our Limits," in *Triumph of Discovery* (New York: Scientific American, 1995), p. 182.

3. Zalman Schachter-Shalomi and Ronald Miller, *From Age-ing to Sage-ing* (New York: Warner Books, 1995), p. 47.

4. See the analysis by Stephanie Strom, "Japan Growth Plan Delayed; Doubts Abound," *New York Times*, December 17, 1997, pp. 1, 7.

5. Kotlikoff quoted in *San Francisco Chronicle*, December 22, 1995, p. B2.

6. Stephen Kinzer, "$650 a Baby: Germany to Pay to Stem Decline in Births," *New York Times*, November 25, 1994.

7. Lucy Scott and Meredith Angwin, *Time out for Motherhood* (Los Angeles: Jeremy Tarcher, 1986), is an authoritative survey of late-mothering in the United States.

8. Joel Cohen, *How Many People Can the Earth Support?* (New York: Norton, 1995). One of these groups is Childless By Choice (P.O. Box 695, Leavenworth, Wash. 98826; e-mail: 76206.3216@compuserve.com). It works to "dispel the negative stereotypes surrounding childless couples so that there can be greater acceptance of our choice by others." It issues a newsletter and distributes literature.

9. Lester Brown et al., *State of the World* (New York: Norton, 1984), p. 2.
10. Judith Stacey, *Brave New Families* (Boston: Beacon Press, 1991), and *In the Name of the Family: Rethinking Family Values in the Postmodern Age* (Boston: Beacon Press, 1996).
11. See, for example, Lawrence Wright, "Silent Sperm," *New Yorker,* January 15, 1996.
12. Gail Vines, "Some of Our Sperm Are Missing," *New Scientist,* August 26, 1995, pp. 22–25.
13. Theo Colborn, *Our Stolen Future* (New York: Dutton/Signet Books, 1996).
14. Michael Rose quoted in Malcolm Gladwell, "The New Age of Man," *New Yorker,* September 30, 1996, p. 67.

5. The Compassionate Economy

1. Marc Freedman, "The Aging Opportunity," *American Prospect* (November–December 1996). Also see Simon-Rusinowitz et al., "Grandparenting at Century's End."
2. Robert Butler, "Living Longer, Contributing More," *Journal of the American Medical Association* 278, no. 16 (October 22, 1997): 1372–74.
3. Gene Koretz, "Wiggle Room in the Workforce," *Business Week,* October 27, 1997, p. 34.
4. Arlie Russell Hochschild, *The Unexpected Community* (Englewood Cliffs, N.J.: Prentice-Hall, 1973), p. 19.
5. Milton Friedman, "The Case for the Negative Income Tax," *National Review,* March 7, 1967.
6. See the report "Guaranteed Annual Income: A Hope and a Question Mark," *America,* December 11, 1971, p. 263.
7. U.S. Chamber of Commerce, *The National Symposium on Guaranteed Income,* Washington, D.C., 1966. For a survey of the debate, see J. Philip Wogaman, *Guaranteed Annual Income: The Moral Issues* (New York: Abingdon Press, 1968), and Robert Perrucci and Marc Pilisuk, *The Triple Revolution: Social Problems in Depth* (Boston: Little, Brown, 1968).
8. Jane Holtz Kay, *Asphalt Nation* (New York: Crown Books, 1997), estimates the cost of road repairs at $200,000 to $400,000 per mile. But the figure can soar well beyond that in some urban areas. In my vicinity, a recent freeway construction job occasioned by an earthquake in 1989 has reported a cost of $400 per inch. Kay's book is a persuasive plea for devehicularization.
9. Bill McMillon, *Volunteer Vacations* (Chicago: Chicago Review Press, 1993).
10. A 1997 survey by the National Alliance for Caregiving estimates that between the late 1980s and late 1990s, the number of households in which an elderly relative, usually a parent or grandparent, had become a dependent rose from 7 million to 22.4 million. See Beth McLeod, "Caregiving Challenge," *San Francisco Examiner,* June 2, 1997, p. B5.
11. H. M. Zal, *Sandwich Generation: Caught Between Growing Children and Aging Parents* (New York: Plenum Insight, 1992); James Atlas, "The Sandwich Generation," *New Yorker,* October 13, 1997.

12. Harriet Sarnoff Schiff, *How Did I Become My Parent's Parent?* (New York: Penguin Books, 1997), Kenneth Scileppi, *Caring for the Parents Who Cared for You* (New York: Birch Lane, 1995), Sheelagh McGurn, *Under One Roof: Caring for an Aging Parent* (New York: Parkside Publishing, 1992), Claude Amarnick, *"Don't Put Me in a Nursing Home!"* (New York: Garrett Publishing, 1996). Also see Rosalynn Carter, *Helping Yourself Help Others: A Book for Caregivers* (New York: Times Books, 1994), and Thomas Cassidy, *Elder Care: What to Look For, What to Look Out For!* (New York: New Horizon Press, 1997). *Parent Care Advisor,* a helpful newsletter, is available from LRP Publications, P.O. Box 980, Horsham, Penn. 19044. Web sites include Eldercare Web and Eldercare Web/Aging, Dying, and Death at http://ice.net/~kstevens/ELDERWEB.HTM, and Geropsychology at http://www.premier.net/~gero/geropsyc.html.

13. Ken Dychtwald, *Age Wave: The Challenges and Opportunities of an Aging America* (Los Angeles: Jeremy Tarcher, 1989), p. 243.

14. See Rodger McFarlane, *The Complete Bedside Companion: No-Nonsense Advice on Caring for the Seriously Ill* (New York: Simon & Schuster, 1997); Cappy Capossela and Sheila Warnock, *Share the Care: How to Organize a Group to Care for Someone Who Is Seriously Ill* (New York: Fireside Books, 1995).

15. David Tilson, ed., *Aging in Place: Supporting the Frail Elderly in Residential Environments* (Glenview, Ill.: Scott, Foresman & Company, 1990), is a survey of the many forms that on-site aging takes. The book was published through the American Association of Homes for the Aging.

16. On NORCs and other forms of caregiving, see David France, "The New Compassion," *Modern Maturity* (May–June 1997): 33–41.

17. As of 1997, RSVP was funded under the Corporation for National Service at $35 million and was running 460 local groups. Call (800) 424-8867 for information. The National Senior Service Corps has a web site: www.cns.gov/senior-a.html. The Foster Grandparent Program also has a website: www.cns.gov/fgp-a.html.

18. Freedman, "The Aging Opportunity."

19. Ronald Reagan quoted in *Time,* October 19, 1981, p. 47. Neither Reagan, who took Calvin Coolidge as his presidential ideal, nor George Bush, whose model was Herbert Hoover, ever inquired into how well volunteerism during the Coolidge-Hoover era of the 1920s dealt with poverty on the farms and in the slums of a prospering economy.

20. Figures from Jeremy Rifkin, *The End of Work: The Decline of the Global Labor Force and the Dawn of the Post-Market Era* (New York: G. P. Putnam's Sons, 1995), p. 241. Rifkin's study is a thought-provoking defense of Third Sector economics. Also see Jon Van Til, *Mapping the Third Sector: Volunteerism in a Changing Social Economy* (Washington D.C.: Foundation Center, 1988).

21. Horace Deets quoted in Maggie Kuhn, *No Stone Unturned* (New York: Ballantine, 1991), p. 208.

6. The Senior Follies

1. Butler, *Why Survive?*, p. 417. Also see Robert Butler and Herbert Gleason, eds., *Productive Aging* (New York: Springer-Verlag), 1985.
2. Lucy Scott with Kerstin Joslyn Schremp, Betty Soldz, and Barbara Weiss, *Wise Choices Beyond Midlife: Women Mapping the Journey Ahead* (Watsonville, Calif.: Papier-Mache Press, 1997), p. 6.
3. Betty Friedan, *The Fountain of Age* (New York: Simon & Schuster, 1993), pp. 29, 199.
4. Carl Jung, *Memories, Dreams, and Reflections* (New York: Vintage Books, 1961), reviews Jung's discovery of the Child archetype. Also see Joyce Mills and Richard Crowley, *Therapeutic Metaphors for Children and the Child Within* (New York: Brunner/Mazel, 1986), pp. 32–36, and W. Hugh Missildine, *Your Inner Child of the Past* (New York: Pocket Books, 1963).
5. James Hillman and Michael Ventura, *We've Had a Hundred Years of Psychotherapy and the World's Getting Worse* (San Francisco: HarperSanFrancisco, 1992), p. 6.
6. Thomas Harris, *I'm OK — You're OK* (New York: Avon, 1967), p. 17.
7. Robert Bly, *The Sibling Society* (New York: Vintage Books, 1997).
8. Thomas Gordon, *Parent Effectiveness Training: The No-Lose Program for Raising Responsible Children* (New York: P. H. Wyden, 1970).
9. David Gutmann, *Reclaimed Powers: Toward a New Psychology of Men and Women in Later Life* (New York: Basic Books, 1987), pp. 4, 5, 7. See especially ch. 10 ("Deculturation and the Passing of the Elders").
10. Daniel Levinson, *The Seasons of a Man's Life* (New York: Alfred A. Knopf, 1978), p. 46.

7. Maturity and the Media

1. Freedman, "The Aging Opportunity," p. 40.
2. Thomas Frank, *The Conquest of Cool: Business Culture, Counter Culture, and the Rise of Hip Consumerism* (Chicago: University of Chicago Press, 1997), pp. 5, 26.
3. These figures come from a report on the senior market carried by National Public Radio's *Marketplace* (produced by KUSC in Los Angeles), June 27, 1996.
4. Dychtwald, *Age Wave*, pp. 69–74. Also see Virginia Munger Kahn, "How to Make Money from Those Aging Baby Boomers," *New York Times*, June 16, 1996, p. F3.
5. Cheryl Russel quoted in Dychtwald, *Age Wave*, pp. 276–77.
6. Jerry Della Femina, "When Will Madison Avenue Get It?" *New York Times Magazine*, March 9, 1997, p. 74.
7. Susan Champlin Taylor, "Primetime's Big Sleep" (*Modern Maturity* [November–December 1995]: 38–43), sets out to investigate why the still-popular program *Murder She Wrote* was canceled by CBS. The answer had little to do with demographics or money. Advertisers and media consultants simply felt embar-

rassed to be connected with a program that appealed to an over-fifty audience. This is called ageism.

8. Marilyn Zeitlin, "The Hollywood Greylist: Too Old to Be Hired, Too Young to Be Retired," *DGA NEWS* (September–October 1991): 15–19.

9. Malcolm Caldwell, "The Coolhunt," *New Yorker*, March 17, 1996.

10. Jon Herskovitz, "High School Girls Fashioning Japan's Pop Culture," *San Francisco Chronicle*, November 29, 1997, p. 1.

11. Some enterprising people in advertising and the media are already in touch with the demographic facts of life. See David B. Wolfe, *Serving the Ageless Market* (New York: McGraw-Hill, 1994). Also see Peter Weaver, "Opportunity Knocks as America Ages," *Nation's Business* (August 1996): 30–32. For statistics on population and income, a good source is Age Wave Inc. (1900 Powell St., Suite 800, Emeryville, Calif. 94608), a public relations firm that consults with media and advertisers about the senior generation.

12. Frank, *The Conquest of Cool*, p. 235.

8. The Planned Obsolescence of Elders

1. Paul Goodman, *Growing Up Absurd* (New York: Random House, 1960).

2. Don Tapscott, *Growing Up Digital: The Rise of the Net Generation* (New York: McGraw-Hill, 1998).

3. For my purposes here, I have used a sample from several newsgroups. They include alt.society.generation-x, alt.punk, alt.slack, alt.drugs, alt.drugs.culture, alt.cyberpunk, alt.cyberspace.rebels, alt.rave, alt-destroy.the.world, alt.life. sucks, alt.bitterness, and alt.angst.

4. Some computer-friendly social commentators celebrate these seemingly neurotic features of online communications. Sherry Terkel (*Life on the Screen: Identity in the Age of the Internet* [New York: Simon & Schuster, 1995]) sees many grand postmodern possibilities in the multiple personalities people create at the keyboard. I leave it to the therapists to decide whether lying about yourself to strangers who are lying to you about themselves is the best way for adolescents to work out a sane and stable identity. Some might say that our many opportunities for role-playing — on the Internet, over CB radio, on talk-show call-ins, or in singles bars — offer a troubling measure of urban alienation. In contrast, how many ways do we have for people to know themselves and others for who they really are?

5. Sheldon Turner, letter to the editor, *San Francisco Chronicle*, August 13, 1996.

6. "Generation War a Myth: Seniors and Gen-X, It's Time to Unite!" *Solidarity* [United Auto Workers] (September 1996): 7.

7. Carolyn Lochhead, "The Issue Clinton, Dole Won't Touch," *San Francisco Chronicle*, October 21, 1996, p. 1.

8. The phrases are Stewart Brand's and Nicholas Negroponte's. See Brand's *Media Lab: Inventing the Future at MIT* (New York: Viking Books, 1987).

9. William Wolman and Anne Colamosca, *The Judas Economy: The Triumph of Capital and the Betrayal of Work* (Reading, Mass.: Addison-Wesley, 1997),

predicts that high-tech workers will eventually suffer the same job insecurity and degradation of wages that blue-collar labor has.

10. Elaine Aron, *The Highly Sensitive Person: How to Thrive When the World Overwhelms You* (New York: Carol Publishing Group, 1996).

11. Lewis Mumford, *The Pentagon of Power* (New York: Harcourt Brace Jovanovich, 1970), p. 435.

9. Longevity and Gender

1. Among the groundbreaking studies of senior sexuality are Alex Comfort, *A Good Age* (New York: Simon & Schuster, 1978), and Robert Butler and Myra Lewis, *Love and Sex After Sixty* (New York: Harper & Row, 1988). More recently, there is David Gutmann, *Reclaimed Powers: Men and Women in Later Life* (Evanston, Ill.: Northwestern University Press, 1994), and Doress-Worters and Siegal, *The New Ourselves, Growing Older.* For more philosophically oriented discussions, see Susan Griffin, *The Eros of Everyday Life* (New York: Doubleday, 1995), George Leonard, *The End of Sex: Erotic Love After the Sexual Revolution* (New York: Bantam Books, 1984), and Morris Berman, *Coming to Our Senses: Body and Spirit in the Hidden History of the West* (New York: Bantam Books, 1990). Also see Joan Elizabeth Lloyd, *Now and Forever Let's Make Love* (New York: Warner Books, 1997). Betty Friedan's *Fountain of Age* is a thorough critical survey of love among the elders.

2. Royda Crose, *Why Women Live Longer Than Men, and What Men Can Learn from Them* (San Francisco: Jossey-Bass Publishers, 1997), pp. 20–21.

3. Friedan, *The Fountain of Age*, p. 165.

4. Guttman, *Reclaimed Powers*, p. 236.

5. Paul Shepard, *Nature and Madness* (San Francisco: Sierra Club Books, 1982).

6. Catherine Keller, *From a Broken Web: Separation, Sexism, and Self* (Boston: Beacon Press, 1986), p. 122.

7. Jean Baker Miller, *Women's Growth in Connection* (New York: Guilford Press, 1991), pp. 25, 26,

8. Fione Hobbs and Bonnie Damon, *Sixty-Five-Plus in the United States* (Washington, D.C.: U.S. Department of Health and Human Services, 1997). Also see Silvia Sara Canetto, "Gender and Suicide in the Elderly," *Suicide and Life-Threatening Behavior* 22, no. 1 (1992).

9. Crose, *Why Women Live Longer Than Men*, p. 74.

10. Erik Erikson, "Identity and the Life Cycle," *Psychological Issues* 1, no. 1 (New York: International Universities Press, 1959).

11. Levinson, *The Seasons of a Man's Life*, pp. 98–99.

12. James Hillman, *The Soul's Code* (New York: Random House, 1996), p. 121.

13. Bly, *The Sibling Society*, pp. 44–45, 180.

14. Levinson, *The Seasons of a Man's Life*, p. 328.

15. Jed Diamond, *Male Menopause* (Naperville, Ill.: Sourcebooks, 1997), though from an out-of-the-way press, is among the few works that provide an honest and illuminating survey of male aging from both the medical and psychological perspectives. There is also a fine work of fiction, Isaac Bashevis Singer's *Old*

Love (1979). Women, in contrast, have many wise works to draw upon, among them Simone de Beauvoir, *The Coming of Age* (New York: Norton, 1973), Charlotte Painter, *Gifts of Age* (San Francisco: Chronicle Books, 1985), Paula Brown Doress, *Ourselves Growing Older: Women Aging with Knowledge and Power* (New York: Simon & Schuster, 1987), Janet Ford and Ruth Sinclair, *Sixty Years On: Women Talk About Old Age* (London: Women's Press, 1987), Doress-Worters and Siegal, *The New Ourselves, Growing Older,* Caroline Bird, *Lives of Our Own: Secrets of Salty Old Women* (Boston: Houghton Mifflin, 1995), Letty Cottin Pogrebin, *Getting over Getting Older* (Boston: Little, Brown, 1996), and Carolyn Heilbroner, *The Last Gift of Time: Life Beyond Sixty* (New York: Dial Press, 1997).

16. Sam Keen, *Fire in the Belly: On Being a Man* (New York: Bantam Books, 1991).

10. The Disease Called Aging, the Mistake Called Death

1. Gerald Gruman, *A History of Ideas About the Prolongation of Life* (Philadelphia: American Philosophical Society, 1966), pp. 70–71.
2. While I was working on this manuscript, the oldest known human being died in August 1997. She was Mme. Jeanne Calment of Arles, France. Mme. Calment was known to be 122 years, 146 days old at her death.
3. For example, see Thomas Perls, "The Oldest Old," *Scientific American* (January 1995): 70–75.
4. See the report on Roth's work in the "Forever Young" cover story, *Time,* November 25, 1996, p. 93.
5. Richard Weindruch, "Caloric Restriction and Aging," *Scientific American* (January 1996): 46–52.
6. Quoted in "Simple Question: Why Do We Die?" *San Francisco Examiner,* November 24, 1991, p. B7.
7. Steven Lamm, *Younger at Last: The New World of Vitality Medicine* (New York: Simon & Schuster, 1997).
8. "Estrogen Stakes Claim to Cognition," *Science,* May 2, 1997, pp. 675–78.
9. Daniel Rudman at the Medical College of Wisconsin in Madison was able to achieve a remarkable result with HGH. He reversed the aging effects of sixty-year-olds, bringing them the physical condition of forty-year-olds. When the HGH was withdrawn, the gain was lost. But further tests were then unable to duplicate that result. See Richard Restak, *Older and Wiser* (New York: Simon & Schuster, 1997), pp. 41–43.
10. See the preface to Leonard Hayflick, *How and Why We Age* (New York: Ballantine Books, 1996), for a brief description of the research on telomeres. Also see the summary in *Time,* November 25, 1996.
11. David Concar, "Death of Old Age," *New Scientist,* June 22, 1996.
12. Quoted in Ronald Klatz, *Grow Young with HGH* (New York: HarperCollins, 1997), p. 53.
13. Malcolm Gladwell, "The New Age of Man," *New Yorker,* September 30, 1996, pp. 56–70. As is so often the case in biology, however, research suggests that

telomeres are more devilishly complex than the original model indicated. As of 1997, research had called into question the function of telomerase both in the production of tumors and in the immortalization of cells, at least in experimental mice. Peter M. Lansdorp, "Lessons from Mice Without Telomerase," *Journal of Cell Biology* 139, no. 2 (October 20, 1997): 309–12.

14. Editorial, *New Scientist*, January 24, 1998, p. 3.

15. Dwayne Banks and Michael Fossel, "Telomeres, Cancer, and Aging," *Journal of the American Medical Association* (October 22–29, 1997): 1345.

16. Leonard Hayflick, *How and Why We Age*, p. 335.

17. Caleb Finch and Rudolph Tanzi, "Genetics of Aging," *Science* 278 (October 17, 1997): 411.

18. Quoted in Alvin Toffler, *Future Shock* (New York: Bantam Books, 1970), p. 208.

19. *Time,* November 25, 1996, p. 92.

20. *New Scientist,* October 7, 1997.

21. Martin Raff, "Death Wish," *The Sciences* (July–August 1996).

22. Kate Douglas, "Making Friends with Death-Wish Genes," *New Scientist,* July 30, 1994, pp. 31–33. Also see Richard Duke, David Ojcius, and John Ding-E Young, "Cell Suicide in Health and Disease," *Scientific American* (December 1996): 80–87.

23. Roger Lewin, "Shock of the Past for Modern Medicine," *New Scientist,* October 23, 1993, pp. 28–32.

24. Klatz, *Grow Young with HGH,* p. 58.

11. The Future of Death

1. Condorcet quoted in Jacques Choron, *Modern Man and Mortality* (New York: Macmillan, 1964), p. 135.

2. For a survey of public opinion on the right to die, see "Love and Let Die," *Time,* March 19, 1990.

3. Sheldon Nuland, *How We Die: Reflections on Life's Final Chapter* (New York: Alfred A. Knopf, 1994), p. 259.

4. Theodore Roszak, *The Memoirs of Elizabeth Frankenstein* (New York: Bantam Books, 1996).

5. Robert Jastrow, *The Enchanted Loom: Mind in the Universe* (New York: Simon & Schuster, 1984), pp. 166–67.

6. Frank Tipler, *The Physics of Immortality: Modern Cosmology and the Resurrection of the Dead* (New York: Doubleday, 1994).

7. Mark Slouka, *War of the Worlds: Cyberspace and the High-Tech Assault on Reality* (New York: Basic Books, 1995).

8. Vinge, author of *True Names,* quoted in *Wired* (June 1995): 161.

9. Jaron Lanier, "Agents of Alienation," *Journal of Consciousness Studies* 2, no. 1 (1995): 76–81.

10. For a full discussion of slow codes and a survey of the literature, see the *New England Journal of Medicine* web site at www.nejm.org/public/1998.

11. Daniel Cher et al., "Method of Medicare Reimbursement and the Rate of Potentially Ineffective Care of Critically Ill Patients," *Journal of the American*

Medical Association (September 24, 1997): 1001–7. See the report in *San Francisco Chronicle*, September 24, 1997.

12. Lamm quoted in "Saving a Few, Sacrificing Many — At Great Cost," *New York Times*, August 8, 1989, p. 23.

13. Daniel Callahan, *Setting Limits: Medical Goals in an Aging Society* (New York: Simon & Schuster, 1987). Also see his *What Kind of Life? The Limits of Medical Progress* (New York: Simon & Schuster, 1990).

14. John Hardwig, "Is There a Duty to Die?" *Hastings Center Report* 27, no. 2 (1997): 34–42.

15. Marilyn Wells, *The Good Death* (New York: Bantam Books, 1997).

12. Powers of the Mind

1. See the report by Richard Knox, *Boston Globe*, December 18, 1997.

2. The results of the latest research on both the mental and physical aspects of aging are summarized in Friedan, *The Fountain of Age*, pp. 71–103. Also see Butler and Gleason, *Productive Aging*.

3. Daniel Goleman, "Studies Suggest Older Minds Are Stronger Than Expected," *New York Times*, February 26, 1996, p. 1.

4. Dharma Singh Khalsa, *Brain Longevity: The Breakthrough Medical Program That Improves Your Mind and Memory* (New York: Warner Books, 1997), p. 151.

5. The Memory Assessment Clinics can be contacted at 8311 Wisconsin Ave., Bethesda, Md. 20814. The clinic makes pamphlets and teaching aids available. Also see Danielle Lapp, *Don't Forget: Easy Exercises for a Better Memory at Any Age* (Reading, Mass.: Addison-Wesley, 1995). Dr. Lapp runs a memory research program at the Stanford Medical School. Mind Works, "the Mental Fitness Connection," teaches courses at senior centers in California using remarkably effective cognitive techniques. Contact Connie Lynch, Mind Works, 228 Cambridge Ave., Kensington, Calif. 94708, for advice and materials.

6. "Novel Antioxidants May Slow Brain's Aging," *Science News*, January 25, 1997, p. 53.

7. David Concar, "Brain Boosters," *New Scientist*, February 8, 1997, pp. 32–35.

8. Dennis Selkoe, "Aging Brain, Aging Mind," *Scientific American* (September 1992): 135–42. Also see Khalsa, *Brain Longevity*, p. 151.

9. This research is summarized in Richard Restak, *Older and Wiser*, ch. 2.

10. The research by Richard Shimamura is summarized at length in ibid., pp. 70–73.

11. D. A. Snowden, "Linguistic Ability in Early Life and Cognitive Function and Alzheimer's Disease in Late Life," *Journal of the American Medical Association* 275, no. 7 (1996): 528–32.

12. Restak, *Older and Wiser*, p. 106. The research he quotes on dendrites is by Guy McKhann of Zanvyl Krieger Mind/Brain Institute at Johns Hopkins.

13. The Institute for Higher Education Policy of Washington and the Boston-based Education Resource Institute report that, between 1970 and 1993, the number of Americans above the age of forty in our universities rose from 5.5 to

11.2 percent. The number of over-forties in adult education courses tripled during the same period.

14. Stephen Joel Trachtenberg, "Preparing for the 'Baby Boomers': Older Students Will Bring New Opportunities to Colleges," *Chronicle of Higher Education,* March 21, 1997, p. B7.

15. Nicholas Negroponte, *Being Digital* (New York: Vintage Books, 1996), p. 203.

13. Rites of Passage

1. Stanislav Grof, *Books of the Dead: Manuals for Living and Dying* (London: Thames & Hudson, 1994), p. 26.

2. Rachel Naomi Remen, *Kitchen Table Wisdom: Stories That Heal* (New York: Riverhead, 1996), p. 75.

3. Robert Neale, *The Art of Dying* (New York: Harper & Row, 1972), p. 37.

14. The Survival of the Gentlest

1. Richard Hofstadter, *Social Darwinism in American Thought* (Boston: Little, Brown, 1955), p. 74.

2. John Maynard Keynes, *Essays in Persuasion* (New York: Harcourt Brace, 1932), pp. 369–70.

3. Natalie Angier, "Theorists See Survival Value in Menopause," *New York Times,* September 16, 1997. The grandmother hypothesis is also reported in the *Proceedings of the National Academy of Sciences,* February 1998.

4. Grahame Clark and Stuart Piggott, *Prehistoric Societies* (New York: Alfred A. Knopf, 1965), p. 63.

Index